An Australian Indigenous Diaspora

An Australian Indigenous Diaspora

Warlpiri Matriarchs and the Refashioning of Tradition

Paul Burke

berghahn
NEW YORK • OXFORD
www.berghahnbooks.com

First published in 2018 by
Berghahn Books
www.berghahnbooks.com

© 2018, 2023 Paul Burke
First paperback edition published in 2023

All rights reserved. Except for the quotation of short passages for the purposes of criticism and review, no part of this book may be reproduced in any form or by any means, electronic or mechanical, including photocopying, recording, or any information storage and retrieval system now known or to be invented, without written permission of the publisher.

Library of Congress Cataloging-in-Publication Data

Names: Burke, Paul, 1956- author.
Title: An Australian Indigenous Diaspora : Warlpiri Matriarchs and the Refashioning of Tradition / Paul Burke.
Description: First edition. | New York : Berghahn, 2018. | Includes bibliographical references and index.
Identifiers: LCCN 2018001778 (print) | LCCN 2018024690 (ebook) | ISBN 9781785333897 (ebook) | ISBN 9781785333880 (hardback : alk. paper)
Subjects: LCSH: Warlpiri (Australian people)--Social life and customs. | Women, Aboriginal Australian--Social life and customs. | Aboriginal Australians--Migrations. | Migration, Internal--Australia.
Classification: LCC DU125.W37 (ebook) | LCC DU125.W37 B87 2018 (print) | DDC 305.899/159--dc23
LC record available at https://lccn.loc.gov/2018001778

British Library Cataloguing in Publication Data
A catalogue record for this book is available from the British Library

ISBN 978-1-78533-388-0 hardback
ISBN 978-1-80073-926-0 paperback
ISBN 978-1-78533-389-7 ebook

https://doi.org/10.3167/9781785333880

The title of this book could be translated into the Warlpiri language as follows:

Warntarlajarrija ngurrakarikirra

('Those who turned away to another home' –
the idea of Indigenous diaspora)

Contents

List of Illustrations, Maps and Figures	viii
Acknowledgements	ix
Introduction	1
Chapter 1. Origins of the Warlpiri Diaspora	9
Chapter 2. 'Getting Away': Reasons and Pathways	67
Chapter 3. Making Alice Springs a Warlpiri Place	97
Chapter 4. Warlpiri Women of Adelaide	129
Chapter 5. Ambivalent Homecomings and the Politics of Home and Away	154
Conclusion	186
References	209
Index	229

Illustrations, Maps and Figures

Illustrations

Illustrations 1.1 and 1.2 The march past at Yuendumu sports weekend and the Baptist congregation outside the first church circa 1960s 32

Illustration 3.1 The yard of the Christian *jilimi*, Alice Springs 108

Illustration 5.1 Royalty meeting at Yuendumu May 2010 172

Maps

Map 1.1 Location map of traditional Warlpiri country and contemporary Warlpiri settlements 13

Map 1.2 Major migration patterns of Warlpiri people, 1880–1960 18

Map 1.3 Location of Warlpiri 'wards', 1957 20

Map 1.4 Location of the Warlpiri in Australia 49

Map 1.5 Location of the Warlpiri in the Northern Territory 50

Map 3.1 Distribution of Warlpiri residents in Alice Springs, 2009–2013 101

Map 4.1 Distribution of Warlpiri people in Adelaide, 2009–2013 132

Figures

Figure 5. Partial genealogy of the 'prisoner' of Queensland 163

Acknowledgements

The credit for this book goes largely to a remarkable group of mature Warlpiri women who extended their networking and risk-taking to me and this project. Principal among these was the late Bertha Nakamarra Dickson (c.1958–2010). Her ex-husband at Kintore, the late Andrew Japaljarri Spencer (c.1958–2015), my friend and sponsor from my days as a legal aid and land council lawyer in the 1980s, continued his benevolent patronage of me notwithstanding his apprehension about the decline in my social standing since my days as a lawyer. The other Warlpiri matriarchs of the diaspora who became my main informants included Winki Napaljarri Spencer, Belle Nakamarra Dickson, the late Mary Napurrula Rockman, the late Charlotte Napanangka Langdon, Patsy Napaljarri Rose, the late Jeanie Nungarrayi Herbert, Esther Nungarrayi Fry, Norah Nangala Watson, Pamela Nangala Sampson, the late Rachael Napaljarri Jarrah, Berryl Brown, Daisy Foster and young matriarch Bess Nungarrayi Price. The other Warlpiri people who cooperated with the research are too numerous to name. I thank them nonetheless. At Yuendumu, Tess Napaljarri Ross had to peer at me (peer review?) for quite a while and reimagine my greying hair before exclaiming in recognition 'Japaljarri!' She became my chief confidant, research assistant and consultant about the project. Tess and her partner, Richie Jampijinpa Robertson, were my pioneering travelling companions to Adelaide, Katherine, Darwin, Kununurra, Halls Creek and Balgo. Like a number of my Warlpiri informants I have taken refuge at various times in the Baptist Church at Alice Springs, Yuendumu, Ali Curung, Katherine, Darwin and Adelaide. They treated me well and even if they had detected the whiff of a papist in their midst, they hid their alarm from me. My own family and friends have provided invaluable support and respite in numerous locations. My base in Alice Springs was the home of my sister, long-term Alice Springs resident and teacher, Christine Burke. Resident Alice Springs intellectual Dave Price and I raged and commiserated together over a few beers. Bob Durnan provided me with the deep history of the town camps of Alice Springs. My anthropological colleague and unlikely friend, Åse Ottosson, took an interest in the project and managed our differing perspectives. Neil MacAuslan, the manager of the Aboriginal Associations Management Centre, shared his experience of distributing mining royalties among the Warlpiri. Bi-cultural adepts Maxine Carlton and Kay Smith provided invaluable perspectives. In Adelaide Michele Cochran provided a restful base and supportive company. In Darwin I was helped by Mary Laughren and Robert Graham, Mark and Desiree Hathaway, and Penny Evans; and in Newcastle by Terry Price, Louise Campbell, and Paul and Kate Dunstan. Thanks to Frank Baarda and Wendy Baarda for practical support and arcane knowledge of Yuendumu. At the Australian National University, Nicholas Peterson, Francesca Merlan and Ian Keen have been my advisory committee and chief mentors. Nic Peterson was the first to encourage me to focus on Warlpiri migration when I pitched a number of ideas to him as he was sitting in his office like a movie mogul trying to pick a hit. He has provided constant practical support and encouragement over the course of the fieldwork, including the use of his own ANU research vehicle, an indispensable part of this project. Maggie Brady alerted me to the significance of Granovetter's work on weak social ties. Brendan Gibson encouraged me at a critical point. An acknowledgements section should not turn into a miserable litany of deaths as this one could be if I had comprehensively listed all my informants who died before the publication of this book. But that is the way it was and it unnerved me – anthropologist as the angel of death. The deaths of a few particular Warlpiri friends not only closed off some aspects of the project, they also revealed how much I had come to rely upon them for my own well-being during the difficulties of the fieldwork and more generally. I felt diminished by each one. I acknowledge the Australian Research Council which funded the project through a post-doctoral fellowship (DP0987357). As always, my wife and partner, Rosemary Budavari, helped keep the whole show on the road. I acknowledge the permission of the Australian National University Press and the University of Hawai'i Press to incorporate into this book some previously published material (Burke 2015, 2018).

Introduction

'Dulcie' Telephoned from Alice Springs

Disrupting the calm of my suburban home in Australia's 'bush capital', Canberra, in the 1990s, were occasional phone calls from my Aboriginal friend, 'Dulcie', a middle-aged Warlpiri woman who lived 2000 km away in Alice Springs in the centre of Australia.[1] With her news of her family, our friends in common and enquiries about my family, these phone calls were a fragile thread to my other life as a legal aid and land council lawyer in Alice Springs in the 1980s. That was a big, intense and varied experience, not least for the revelation of my identity as a 'whitefella' and a 'settler'. Having a job representing Aboriginal clients on criminal charges or in pursuing their land claims did not necessarily entail friendship with the clientele. But 'Dulcie' and, even more so, her Warlpiri husband of the time, specialised in befriending the new legal aid lawyers. I readily responded to these overtures and our families developed an ongoing relationship which included trips to their remote Aboriginal settlement of Yuendumu 350 km north-west of Alice Springs and to their outstation a further hundred kilometres from Yuendumu. When in Alice Springs they stayed at our house, usually camping in a line of makeshift bedding in the backyard (San Roque 2011 describes a similar situation of hosting remote settlement visitors). Such friendships were not unusual during that time of optimism about the possibilities of the new Aboriginal-controlled NGOs pursuing a new deal for Aboriginal people in the policy era of self-determination. Through 'Dulcie's' family I came to know many Warlpiri people, worked on their land claims and attended their funerals. After nearly a decade of intense work and the birth of my two children in Alice Springs, a scary misadventure being washed away in a Toyota in a flash flood and a particularly sad Warlpiri funeral, I retreated with my young family to a less intense existence in Canberra. There I set about turning myself into an anthropologist to explore all the interesting questions that the professional practice of law tends to foreclose. 'Dulcie's' telephone calls caught me in the middle of that transition and they usually ended with mutual invitations to visit, although I thought the difficulties of unfamiliar travel and the cost would make 'Dulcie's' appearance in Canberra unlikely. Then there was the global financial crisis of 2007. One aspect of the Australian Government's response was a financial stimulus which put a one-off lump sum in the bank accounts of welfare recipients, including 'Dulcie's', and thus she did appear in Canberra for the long-promised holiday. We became for a short time a distant Warlpiri outpost.

I did not realise it at the time, but 'Dulcie's' skill and conscientiousness in extending her personal networks and overcoming constraints to long-distance travel were years later to become some of the central themes of my Warlpiri diaspora research. My doctoral research had been a sedentary project about anthropologists as expert witnesses in native title claims (Burke 2011) and following that I was looking for an original project that would take me back to my Warlpiri friends and acquaintances. I had heard about a more permanent Warlpiri outpost in the 1990s at the unlikely site of the small South Australian town of Murray Bridge, over 1,500 kilometres from Alice Springs. I wondered how it came about, how it was sustained and how common such outposts were. The significance of these questions can only be understood fully if something is known about Aboriginal people in the cultural geography of Australia and where the Warlpiri fit in.

The Warlpiri in Aboriginal Australia

At the time of the first white settlement at Sydney Cove in 1788 the continent of Australia was entirely occupied by Aboriginal people. Although there were cultural differences among Aboriginal groups across the continent (see, for example, the seven case studies in Keen 2004), there were common features that tended to emphasise the relatively small-scale affiliation to a locale and to networks of kin. Large gatherings for ceremonies did take place and local groups were typically connected to neighbouring groups through shared mythology which in desert areas included segmented ownership of long-distance Dreaming tracks or song lines recounting the creative exploits of ancestral beings over vast distances. But their economy, principally hunting and gathering, was on a relatively small scale and social organisation was relatively loose, there being nothing on the scale of ongoing tribal organisation like the chiefdoms of Africa. There was no large-scale, standing Aboriginal army and nothing approaching the scale of the militaristic clubs of the Plains Native Americans or the Maori warriors of New Zealand. Among Aboriginal people punishment for the breach of laws was mostly a question of self-help and the mobilisation of kin for relatively small-scale raids or revenge expeditions. This meant that, for the most part, the dispossession of Aboriginal people happened in a piecemeal and localised fashion along an expanding frontier as white settlement spread from a few colonial towns on the eastern and southern coasts of Australia often preceded by alien diseases and brutal violence sometimes described by historians as frontier wars.[2] One comparative constitutional historian has found the origins of the peculiar absence of treaties in Australian colonial history in the relative absence of large-scale warfare in the colonisation of Australia (Russell 2005).

The combination of localised, small-scale Aboriginal economy and society with the vast distances in Australia meant that those Aboriginal people who lived on land that was remote from the main cities and towns were not dispossessed of their lands or did not have their traditional lives disrupted until much later in the colonising process. This was even more the case for those who occupied land that was difficult for the colonisers to exploit economically because of the relative harshness of the terrain. The end result has been a much shorter contact period for Aboriginal people of the interior of the continent and in the remote north. The Warlpiri, whose traditional country was in the Tanami Desert of central Australia, were one of these groups whose intermittent contact with white people only began in earnest in the early decades of the twentieth century.

This particular combination of localised culture and protracted, piecemeal colonisation had a number of profound consequences both on Australian society and on anthropology. The most obvious consequence is that the Indigenous people of Australia are now a small minority of the broader population, although in many remote places in northern Australia, including the Warlpiri settlements, they form a local majority. In 2011 the Aboriginal and Torres Strait Islander population of Australia was estimated to be 669, 881 which is 3 per cent of the total population of Australia.[3] Of this total, about 6 per cent identified as Torres Strait Islanders. About a third of Aboriginal and Torres Strait Islanders live in capital cities; one quarter live in remote or very remote regions (calculated on the basis of distance from service centres); and the remainder (around 44 per cent) live in regional towns and cities.

The Indigenous population is not only geographically dispersed, it is also culturally diverse. This is partly due to the distinctively undifferentiated Australian legal definition of who is an Aboriginal or Torres Strait Islander person. Up to the late 1960s official government policy and laws reflected a high degree of differentiation, usually in terms of the dilution of 'blood' (imagined degrees of racial dilution) and the terminology of 'full-blood' as opposed to 'half caste'. Then, in a more liberal policy era, official definitions eventually landed upon a threefold cumulative test: any degree of biological descent plus self-identification plus community acceptance. This definition encompassed Aboriginal and Torres Strait Islander people who suffered widely differing impacts over the course of colonisation; who looked very different, in the old terminology incorporating both 'full-blood' and 'half caste' and those who looked similar to European people; with widely differing degrees of continuity and attenuation of use of traditional languages and traditional high culture (rituals, song, dance, arts); and with differing degrees of social mobility within the broader society. This inclusive approach tends to bedevil national policy discourse, producing a continual tension between nationwide uniformity, at the level of policy principle, and local diversity of Indigenous lifeworlds (as to Indigenous heterogeneity, see Rowse 2014 and 2017: 334–401).

This inclusive definition, combined with the lack of recognition of indigenous self-government in Australia, means that some of the legal racial distinctions made in North America, for example, are not officially sanctioned in Australia. Thus, ideas of there being a legally recognised group of Metis, or of women losing their status as an indigenous person if they marry a non-indigenous person, or of native American Indians losing their rights as indigenous persons if they are disenfranchised by their tribe, are all foreign to current Australian circumstances. Challenges to Aboriginality tend to happen in other forums, in personal encounters and in private spheres such as corridor talk or sceptical private commentary on the European appearance of some Aboriginal people who appear on television. Sometimes this private commentary spills over into contentious rants by conservative shock jocks about 'light-skinned Aborigines', and the even more incendiary tag 'White Aborigines'. For a compelling dissection of the issue by an Indigenous intellectual, see Paradies (2006).

Aboriginal Internal Differentiation, its Preoccupations, its Reflection in Anthropology

It is the one quarter of Indigenous people who live in remote or very remote regions that were originally of interest to the newly professionalised social anthropology of the early twentieth century. The stage had already been set for this remote-area orientation by the worldwide enthusiastic reception of Spencer and Gillen's *The Native Tribes of Central Australia* (1899) which directly influenced Durkheim, Freud and others (Kuklick 2006). The richness of that account and the rapidly deteriorating circumstances of Aboriginal people helped to reinforce the orientation of anthropology towards remote areas 'before it was too late' to obtain ethnographic accounts of a living culture. This orientation led to an early scientific expedition to make contact with Warlpiri people, among other remote groups, and eventually to fully fledged, long-term participant observation among Warlpiri people commencing in the 1950s. Within worldwide anthropology the Warlpiri and other remote Aboriginal peoples became renowned for their hunter and gatherer economy, the complexity of their kinship systems and formal social organisation, their ritual life, and their distinctive cosmology encapsulated in the phrase 'the Dreaming'. In short, they were a people socially embedded in their kinship networks and spiritually emplaced in their traditional country.

The focus on the remote, traditional Aborigines did not go unchallenged. Some Aboriginal people in less remote 'settled' Australia came to the view that anthropology's valorising of the high culture of remote Aboriginal people was making their own struggles for political recognition and independence more difficult. From this perspective, remote-area ethnography can be seen as supplying material for the 'repressive authenticity' of the state.[4] Although such dichotomies between remote-area and 'settled' Australia tend to be overplayed, they continue to provide rhetorical resources for contemporary debates within Australianist anthropology (see, for example, Cowlishaw and Gibson 2012). Suffice it to say, I am committed to revising traditionalist ethnography by placing experience-near accounts of Aboriginal people within the broader context of intercultural history. This orientation arises out of historical anthropology and earlier internal critiques that insisted upon the relevance of economic and cultural interconnections with the nations and global systems that encapsulated tribal societies (Fabian 1983; Wolf 1982). In Australianist anthropology, Francesca Merlan has made significant ethnographic and theoretical contributions to exploring the idea of the intercultural (Merlan 1998, 2005, 2007). To be clear, I also see the intercultural as a critique of the continuation of radical domain separation (Aboriginal from non-Aboriginal) in anthropological accounts of contemporary Aboriginal people. This applies to the study of Aboriginal people in both 'settled' and 'remote' areas.

The Warlpiri in Aboriginal Australia

Outside anthropological circles I doubt whether the Warlpiri ever impinge upon the consciousness of the mass of non-Indigenous people in the cities of Australia. Although they are a relatively large language group, the Warlpiri, at about 3,500 strong, are a small minority within the small Indigenous minority of Australia. Most non-Indigenous Australians never have any direct experience of any Aboriginal people let alone Warlpiri people. Occasionally there is a Warlpiri football star in the national competition, or a famous Warlpiri artist who might break through in the national media, or a quirky news item about the Yuendumu sports weekend inevitably described as 'the Aboriginal Olympics'. But Indigenous issues more generally are always in the national media in what some see as the distinctively Australian high profile of Indigenous concerns. In media coverage of Indigenous issues the Warlpiri tend to get homogenised to the broader grouping of the remote, traditional Aboriginal people who retain their language and high culture traditions. Thus, when the search began for Aboriginal women who could perform traditional dances in the opening ceremony of the Olympic Games in Sydney in 2000, they eventually found hundreds of Aboriginal women from central Australia, some of whom were Warlpiri. The Warlpiri and remote Aboriginal people have also become the object of concern in relation to their deteriorating social conditions including widespread alcohol abuse, endemic cardiovascular disease and kidney failure, chronic unemployment, child sexual abuse and youth suicide, and government plans to ameliorate them. Most recently these plans have included a controversial, neo-liberal inspired intervention to quarantine a percentage of welfare income for wholesome purposes and other measures (explained in more detail in Chapter 1).

To actually go to one of the four Warlpiri settlements to meet them would be a major logistical undertaking from any capital city; for example, from Sydney it would involve a three-and-a-half-hour plane trip to Alice Springs in the parched centre of Australia (2000 km) and then a three-and-a-half-hour four-wheel-drive trip to Yuendumu (300 km). In recent years most of that road has been sealed, but to press on to Nyirrpi (another 150 km) or to Willowra (another 160 km) or to Lajamanu (another 600 km) definitely requires a four-wheel-drive vehicle to negotiate the corrugated dirt roads. In the scheme of things, these settlements are small (Yuendumu 800 people, Nyirrpi 200 people, Willowra 250 people, Lajamanu 700). As one would expect in the desert, they are dusty places. Their appearance reveals something of the context. The substantial and relatively well-maintained school, police station, health clinic, the grocery store and the number of vehicles (usually less well maintained) reveal that these settlements are not located in a third world country, despite the dilapidated appearance of some (but not all) of the housing stock. But it is still a place where hunters and gatherers have been settled and are, generally speaking, yet to internalise the bourgeois manners of the house proud, the fenced garden and concern for neatness and tidiness. Instead, there is a seeming unconcern about the dilapidation, the ramshackle additions to houses, the improvised beds placed outside to catch the breeze on stifling summer nights, the improvised pathways, the large amount of discarded rubbish and the roaming mangy dogs. But, perhaps the most shocking thing for the imagined metropolitan visitor who may never have encountered an Aboriginal person in their everyday suburban life, here the vast majority (80 to 90 per cent) are Aboriginal people who speak their own distinctive language and continue to perform their initiation ceremonies. White people are a minority, consisting of most of the service providers, the teachers, nurses, police, administrative staff and shopkeepers.

The Warlpiri people living on the fringes of their traditional country are, in anthropological theory, all tightly bound to each other in overlapping networks of kin and bound very tightly to their traditional country. So how is it that some of them make a life for themselves in distant towns and cities? This is the central question of this book. Part of the answer lies in the processes of stratification and differentiation within the Warlpiri population that have been set in train by various government projects over their relatively short contact period. Another part of the answer lies in the prized personal autonomy of individuals in hunter and gatherer societies and traditional life-cycle developments that see women gain authority and personal autonomy as they grow older. These 'internal' developments link up with particular projects and the changing valuation of tradition in the broader and encapsulating society to produce what I have called in this book the matriarchs of the Warlpiri diaspora. As I hope to demonstrate in this book, especially in Chapter 3, 'Dulcie' was exemplary of the bold networking that enabled her and the other Warlpiri matriarchs to take advantage of this unique juncture.

Notes

1. Since both pseudonyms and real personal names are used in this book, I indicate pseudonyms with single quotes. For convenience I sometimes use the word 'Aboriginal' when referring to the indigenous peoples of continental Australia rather than the more compendious 'Indigenous' which seems to be a shorthand word to refer to the Aboriginal and Torres Strait Islander peoples of Australia. The use of 'Aboriginal' instead of 'Indigenous' also reflects the usage of my older informants. The switch to 'Indigenous' in government nomenclature and also vernacular usage occurred in the 1990s. The rapidity of the switch and the elusive rationale for it were confounding at the time. It was not clear whether it was simply a pragmatic solution to the cumbersome repetition of the phrase 'Aboriginal and Torres Strait Islander' or whether there was some positive preferment of the term 'indigenous' that had gained prominence in international fora, particularly in the drafting of an international convention on the rights of indigenous peoples. For whatever reason, 'Indigenous' has now become firmly entrenched as correct usage in Australia. The capitalisation of Indigenous alerts the reader that it is a reference to the

particular indigenous people of Australia rather than the global category of indigenous peoples.
2. See, for example, Clements (2014), Connor (2002), Reynolds (2013) and Richards (2008). The degree of frontier violence was the subject of conflictual academic debate in the 1990s and this debate became more widely politicised as a struggle over what version of history was appropriate for contemporary expressions of national Australian identity. This struggle became known in Australia as 'the history wars' (see Macintyre and Clark 2003; Veracini 2006).
3. Australian Bureau of Statistics (ABS) Estimates of Aboriginal and Torres Strait Islander Australians, June 2011, via ABS website (www.abs.gov.au), accessed 22 March 2016.
4. The phrase 'repressive authenticity' is the rhetorical crescendo of Patrick Wolfe's structuralist history of Australia and critique of the role of anthropology in Indigenous–settler relations in his *Settler Colonialism and the Transformation of Anthropology* (1999). For a convincing dissection of Wolfe's approach, see Morton (1998).

Chapter 1

ORIGINS OF THE WARLPIRI DIASPORA

Of Bold Warlpiri Matriarchs, Cultural Entrepreneurs and Those 'Mad for Grog'

If one follows those Warlpiri people who have left their remote home settlements in central Australia to put down roots and make a life for themselves in distant towns and cities, one discovers, among a range of disparate individuals, remarkable women whose stories are yet to be told. Their stories could only have been partially anticipated by existing ethnography that continues to emphasise their still-accessible ancient language and culture, their spiritual emplacement in traditional country and their social embeddedness in networks of kin. At the core of several diverse locations of this Warlpiri diaspora are the middle-aged Warlpiri matriarchs. They are the survivors of their own disentangling from Warlpiri husbands, sometimes survivors of their own previous addictions. They are the bold women who have entered into relationships with white men not knowing exactly where it might take them.[1] They are the ones who have used their exceptional bravado or artistic skill or educational achievement to enlarge their personal social networks into unique configurations that help sustain them in the diaspora. In evading key traditional obligations to accept particular Warlpiri marriage partners, they were all set on a course of reconfiguration of what is salient about being a Warlpiri person; at the same time they were managing the sometimes conflicting demands of continuing involvement with kin[2] and projects close to their own hearts. These projects included raising and educating their children, pursuing their own education, running a functioning household that could support a wider group of kin, becoming a professional artist, or being an elder in a Christian church. It is in pursuing these projects, and in other more radical assertions of personal autonomy in the spirit of a Bacchanalian adventure, that the Warlpiri matriarchs, sometimes subtly and sometimes more confrontationally, reoriented themselves away from the traditionalism of the remote settlements.

In the course of this book I will introduce a number of such matriarchs. In an Alice Springs town camp we will meet 'Dulcie',[3] a grandmother separated from her Warlpiri husband, and for whom the move to Alice Springs enabled the flourishing of her exceptional adventurousness and networking ability among non-Aboriginal people. In another town camp in Alice Springs, we will find 'Sarah', the head of a household of middle-aged Christian Warlpiri women supporting each other in much the same way as in a settlement widow's camp (*jilimi*). In the Darwin town camp of Bagot, there are similar households and a small group of Warlpiri women ex-drinkers there who form the core of a Pentecostal church at the camp. In Adelaide, we will find a closely related group of Warlpiri women artists living in the same suburb and who share the same professional art wholesaler. In a different Adelaide suburb, we will meet 'Barbara', another long-term Warlpiri resident of Adelaide and the busy matriarch of a large family who occupy three separate houses in close proximity to each other and who co-operate daily in all domestic matters. In a separate Adelaide household, we will find 'Valmae' who, with her white husband and a retired principal from her old settlement school, established an extraordinary project of hosting children from the remote settlement of Ali Curung so that they could attend school in Adelaide. Finally, we will meet the exceptional figure of 'Natalie', who, more than any other Warlpiri matriarch I encountered in the diaspora, created a network of friends largely outside of her Warlpiri kinship networks and, through her strength of personality, completely inverted the typical gender order of the settlements.

While the Warlpiri matriarchs of the diaspora form the core of this study, the diversity of the circumstances of Warlpiri diaspora locations needs to be immediately acknowledged. A persistent feature of all such locations was Warlpiri people who had made a deliberate decision to leave their Warlpiri settlements and take up the drinking life in town. The home settlements, which had a history of prohibition of alcohol when they were Aboriginal Reserves, continued this prohibition under the new legislation which allowed individual settlements to declare themselves 'dry areas' (see Bourbon, Saggers and Gray 1999; d'Abbs 1987; Sessional Committee on Use and Abuse of Alcohol by the Community 1993). Although such legislative prohibitions were never totally effective, the relative ease of the availability of alcohol in towns meant that many in the Warlpiri diaspora were refugees from alcohol restrictions, taking up the drinking life in makeshift camps or in official town camps in Darwin, Katherine, Tennant Creek and Alice Springs, or in the parklands of distant cities like Adelaide. Even among this group there were a range of reasons and circumstances behind their move. For older women, the decision was frequently associated with them becoming widowed. For one Warlpiri man living in the notorious Hoppy's Camp in Alice Springs, approximately 200 metres from a major liquor outlet, it seemed to be about the exhaustion of all the possibilities at the major Warlpiri settlement of Yuendumu, a sort of early retirement option. He had previously worked in various jobs at Yuendumu, including in the Warlpiri literature production centre at the school, and he was well known among the other drinkers as an unusual person who liked to read magazines during his enforced sobriety on Sunday when it was difficult to obtain liquor.

In addition to those who were 'mad for grog', there were those, again mostly Warlpiri women, who had married non-Aboriginal people and eventually settled in the home town of the non-Aboriginal spouse. This partly explains the existence of Warlpiri outposts in Cairns, Darwin, Muswellbrook, Melbourne, Murray Bridge and Adelaide. One non-Aboriginal man, who had partnered with a Warlpiri woman at Yuendumu, returned to his home town of Newcastle with their young son while she remained at Yuendumu. Many Warlpiri people married into different language groups in various settlements throughout central Australia and at least one is in Arnhem Land. A number of Warlpiri professional Australian Rules ('Aussie Rules' or 'AFL', Australian Football League) football players from Yuendumu and Lajamanu lived on the Gold Coast of Queensland and one of the most famous Warlpiri sons, a first-grade AFL star, used to live in Melbourne (Mackinnon 2010). Other subgroupings within the broader Warlpiri diaspora included those who could be considered as the involuntary diaspora: the teenagers in secondary boarding schools in Darwin, Alice Springs and Melbourne; the many young Warlpiri men in jail and alcohol rehabilitation centres in Alice Springs and Darwin; and the dialysis patients in Alice Springs, Tennant Creek, Katherine and Darwin. The extent to which the diverse Warlpiri people in any one location interact with each other and form a group will be explored throughout this book.

If one follows the Warlpiri migrants into the towns and cities, one not only sees the remote settlements in a new light through the eyes of those who have left, but also sees the theoretical underpinnings of more sedentary community studies in a new light.[4] Therefore, the aim of this chapter is to initially provide a concise account of traditional Warlpiri culture and personhood and how these have been transformed over the contact period up to the present. I will then outline the theoretical agenda that is suggested by the adoption of the idea of diaspora as the overarching framework. This will be done by briefly outlining the literature on migration in Indigenous Australia and some North American counterparts. Although this literature does not adopt the terminology of 'Indigenous diaspora', it is in many ways a precursor to such theorising. I will then extract the relevant themes from the literature on transnationalism and global diaspora as they apply to indigenous diaspora. This will involve further specification of the term 'Warlpiri matriarchs' and the way in which personal social networks are expanded through non-traditional marriage, friendship and other kinds of relationships.

The Warlpiri in Global Anthropology

The intense academic interest in the Warlpiri was no doubt generated by their relatively late contact with European people, in the 1920s and 1930s. This late contact provided the possibility that even under conditions of early dispersal because of massacres and their post-war concentration into a few remote government/mission settlements, their previous life would still be vividly accessible through those who had grown up in the desert and who continued to practise their language and traditions in the new settings. This proved to be spectacularly true. It resulted in an extensive anthropological archive on the intricacies of Warlpiri traditional culture. The Warlpiri material was part of the development of an Australianist regional literature, with its own themes, debates, research agendas and possibilities for comparison and revision of earlier understandings. Contributions to this literature were also shaped by changes in metropolitan anthropological theorising.[5]

The most obvious counterpoint to diaspora is the emplacement of Warlpiri people in their own traditional country and the extent to which they are deeply embedded in networks of kin. The overarching and multifaceted concept of *Jukurrpa* (Dreaming) links all kinds of right behaviour (avoidance relationships, marriage rules, the care of sacred objects, the performance of rituals, sex roles, methods of hunting) to a localised foundational era in which the topography of the country was given its final shape and the rules of social life were instituted by ancestral beings. More intimately, the powerful traces of the foundational ancestors remain in the country as sometimes dangerous, sometimes benign generative spirit essences (*kuruwarri*) that animate the foetus in the form of a spirit child *(kurruwalpa)* and literally leave their mark on the baby's skin (cf. Glaskin 2012). In the right ritual circumstances, the power of these localised generative spirit essences could be summoned, for example by pressing their sacred designs (also *kuruwarri*) on the body of an initiate to transfer some of their power, or to increase particular species or to effect sorcery. In summary then, a central idea of Warlpiri traditional culture was the circulation of generative spirit essences between the local landscape and individuals (Meggitt 1962; Merlan 1986; Morton 1987; Munn 1970; Musharbash 2011; Peterson 1972).

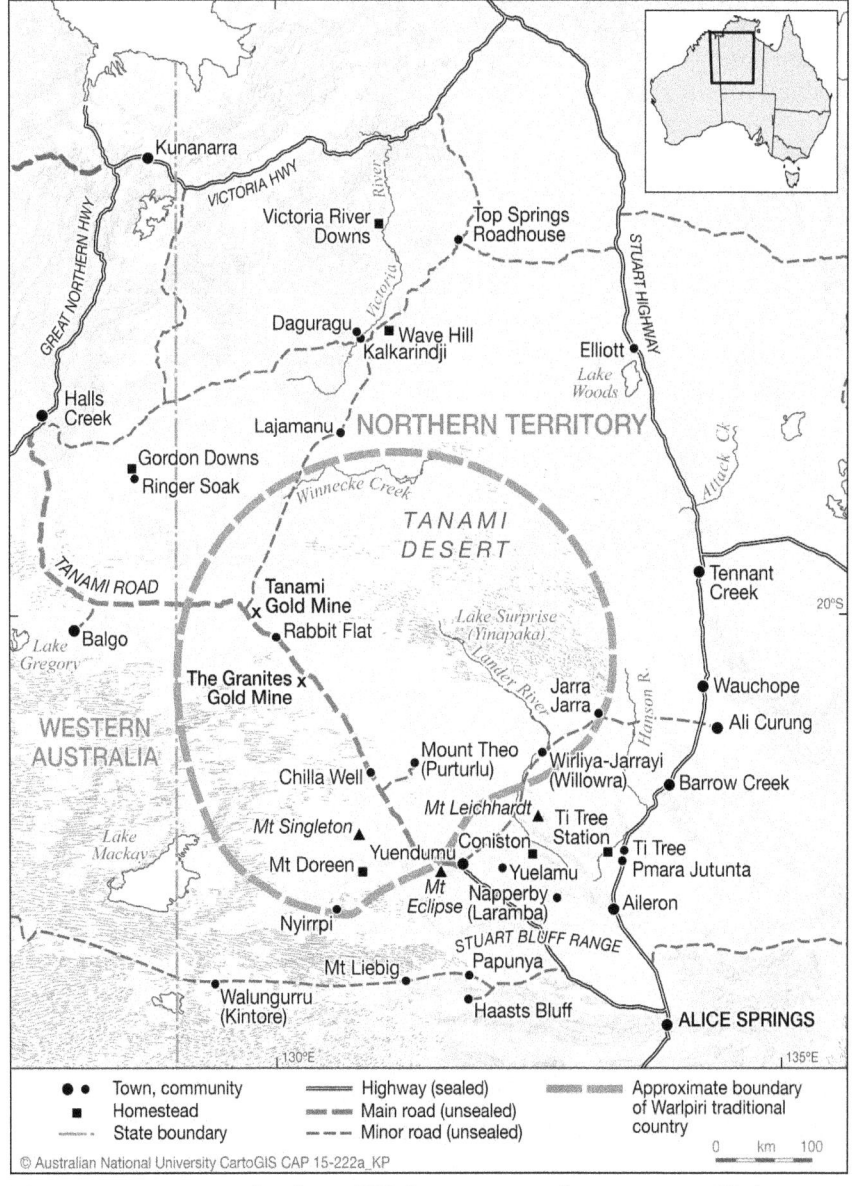

Map 1.1 Location map of traditional Warlpiri country and contemporary Warlpiri settlements

Associated with such ideas of circulation have been the parallel, and somewhat contradictory, folk theories of immutable personality traits and a life-cycle of gradual expanding knowledge of and constructive engagement with those generative spirit essences through gendered rites of passage and other rituals. The traditional songs narrating the travels and exploits of the Dreaming ancestors provided a complex, interconnected map of traditional country and cultural patrimony whose transmission was gendered and hierarchical. In the days of the hunting and gathering economy, Warlpiri people were even more existentially and ecologically bound to localised country. There were few permanent water sources. Hunting ranges expanded and contracted with the seasonal rains. There was an encyclopaedic accumulation of knowledge of the relatively localised sources of food and bush medicines. These accumulations of localised connections were also accompanied by emotional identifications with traditional country and the traditional designs representing localised Dreamings (the same word, *kuruwarri*, being used for both the spirit essence and the design), and a strict etiquette about not speaking for another person's traditional country, not using their sacred designs or performing their rituals.[6] Men sometimes cried when they saw the *kuruwarri* designs on sacred boards retrieved for local ceremonies since they were reminded of their deceased ancestors who owed their being and ritual identity to that *kuruwarri* (Peterson 1972: 25).

In some Australian Aboriginal cultures the emotional and spiritual/existential links between Aboriginal people and traditional country is elaborated in specific practices and discourses of facilitating the return of spiritual essences in the body to the place of their origin upon the death of individuals. This facilitation of the recycling of spirit essences is most clearly articulated in the early ethnography of Arnhem Land (for example Warner 1937: 412–42) and this ethnography has tended to be appropriated as an element in general portraits of traditional Aboriginal society as wanting to be buried in one's own country.[7] As we shall see in Chapter 5 (Ambivalent Homecomings), general ideas about the correctness of being buried in one's traditional country (sometimes broadly interpreted as any Warlpiri country or any of the Warlpiri settlements) represent one strand in the contemporary Warlpiri politics of the choice of burial site. But among the Warlpiri, the desire to be buried in one's own country does not appear to have the same degree of institutionalisation and normative force as in other Aboriginal groups, a point noted by Myers in relation to the neighbouring Pintupi (Myers 1986: 134). The early Arnhem Land accounts emphasised drawing the deceased's totemic designs on the corpse and the singing of the clan's totemic songs to facilitate the return of spirit essences. While there are some similar elements in Meggitt's account of his interviews about Warlpiri mortuary practice (the orientation of a man's corpse towards his lodge Dreaming, the painting of conception Dreaming designs on the bodies of mourners), most of the account relates to the expression of emotion and the adjustment of relationships between the surviving relations (Meggitt 1962: 317–29). It involved ritualised grieving, including self-inflicted injuries, 'sorry cuts' for men, and the cutting of hair of the wife and mother-in-law of the deceased. The hair of the corpse was removed and eventually recirculated as hair string. The personal possessions of the deceased were distributed to prescribed categories of relations. There commenced a complete taboo on speech for the widow and a taboo on everyone using the deceased's personal name. The corpse was placed on a tree platform safe from scavenging animals and an inquest was held. It is tempting to think that this muted elaboration (compared to Arnhem Land) arose out of the vastly different ecological imperatives of the desert living of the pre-contact Warlpiri. The deceased's shelter and its remaining contents would be burned and the band would then continue on in their nomadic circuit to the next water source, leaving their own shelters behind. As will be outlined below, the tradition of moving residence upon the death of a close relation became problematic in settlement conditions and even more so in the towns and cities of the diaspora. In the pre-contact era, the appropriate category of relation would return to the tree platform a year later to bury most of the bones in an unmarked grave, sometimes a hollow termite mound, and particular bones would circulate in ceremonial exchange among the relations.

While the summary account of traditional relations to land outlined above may give the impression of relatively strict and exclusive boundedness, much intensive research and theoretical revision has tended to soften those edges into heartland areas or clusters of sites and to recognise the complexity of crosscutting legitimate individual claims (for an overview, see Elias 2001: Chs 2, 5 and 6). It is not necessary for my purposes to recount the various positions taken in debates about Warlpiri traditional land tenure since it is commonly accepted that Warlpiri traditional country provides a peculiarly intimate sense of homeland. The Warlpiri understanding of 'Being' presupposes emplacement in country and this is what gives Warlpiri migration its heightened connotation of loss and is one justification for the use of the terminology of diaspora.

The social embeddedness of Warlpiri people in networks of kin attached to particular tracts of country would also seem to be the antithesis of the mobility of modernity that underpins migration within nation states and contemporary global transnationalism and diasporas. Traditional Warlpiri social embeddedness is founded on the small-scale, kin-based social solidarity in which one looks to close kin for everything: obtaining rights to land and its sustaining flora and fauna; sponsorship through rites of passage; the successful performance of such rituals; the acquisition of traditional knowledge; the acquisition of a spouse; personal security in the event of aggression;

and recruitment for retaliation. Marriage rules based on preferred categories of kin ensured a fairly tight regional endogamy and the processes of promised marriage bound different kin groups together in reciprocal obligations. Moreover, general social pressure to show generosity towards kin meant that a major element in Warlpiri sociality was the continual testing and re-enactment of kinship ties through requests for assistance, now summarised as 'demand sharing' (Peterson 1993, 2013; Peterson and Taylor 2003).

Earlier anthropological approaches sought to provide a comprehensive overview of Warlpiri society by describing how different subsystems (religious, kinship, political, economic) were integrated into a functioning whole. Consequently, rule-following and parochialism tended to be emphasised. The evocative, exemplary vignettes in Meggitt's ethnography, and general revisions inspired by Myers' more individually focused approach, allowed for other aspects of the pre-contact era to be more clearly imagined. Thus, although compliance with marriage rules was extremely high and initiation ceremonies were performed according to well understood roles and itineraries and the patchwork of traditional countries were more or less maintained, such results were the product of variable individual striving, skilful achievement and vigilance. This individual assertion occurred in a context of a high degree of interpersonal violence, the pervasiveness of sorcery and the possibility of execution by a raiding party. Coupled with the discipline of the daily search for food, one can imagine such a life would have been busy, physically arduous and socially demanding, even if one accepts the variable degrees of social intensity over a typical year. The intensity of social interaction would be at its peak in the relatively large congregations for regional ceremonies and would then diffuse with the dispersal into much smaller foraging groups when the rains came. I do not want to equate this intensity with unrelenting seriousness since I think there is plenty of evidence for a very indulgent attitude towards children and an ease to laughter, especially in sex segregated groups. What I am trying to set up, though, is an argument, explored in more detail in Chapter 2 ('Getting Away'), that much of the permanent migration from the settlements has the character of an escape from the intensity of settlement life as it developed through the second half of the twentieth century (see below), just as the outstations movement, peaking in 1980s, was, at least partly, similarly motivated (Kesteven 1978: 21–22).

There is another possible revision of what could be called Warlpiri parochial ethnocentrism, suggested by Myers' work and more general theorising about the nature of contemporary global diasporas and their relationship to cosmopolitanism. Such a revision would supplement the overwhelming evidence of localising tendencies in traditional culture. The first step of such a revision would be to query any assumption of the universal scope of traditional parochialism (contra Kolig 1981) and consider the implications of the inherent cultural necessity to extend one's social world, especially in sparsely populated areas.[8] The second step would be to examine the variety of regional interconnections (see, for example, Keen 1997). It seems likely that such regional extension resulted in a kind of tribal cosmopolitanism, as some local Aboriginal people came to know relatively distant unfamiliar languages, kinship systems and rituals. This limited cosmopolitanism may have predisposed at least some Warlpiri to engage with the very different settlers as they arrived in different guises and on different projects.

Long Dreaming tracks, with their associated songs and rituals and precisely specified handover points between different language groups, provide a clear model of the coexistence of localising tendencies with the possibilities of regional extension. For a well-documented example of a multi-language group Dreaming track involving the Warlpiri and their southern neighbours, see Mountford (1968). The preconditions for such extension were generally present: pervasive multilingualism; broad similarities in their economy; and certain cultural precepts and practices, including the ability to translate one system of social categorisation into another (with varying degrees of difficulty). These preconditions enabled trade, intermarriage at the margins, regional ceremonies, regional dispute resolution mechanisms and the trading of rituals between different groups. Significantly for the formation of a diaspora, regional interconnections gave those involved in serious transgressions, such as manslaughter or wife-stealing, the opportunity to attempt to avoid retribution by physically removing themselves from those most affected, and living with more distant groups (not complete strangers), who had no immediate kin obligation or emotional investment in punishing them.

Warlpiri Intercultural History and Patterns of Migration

From the 1880s there may have been a trickle of Warlpiri people leaving their traditional country for early pastoral stations established to the west, north and east of Warlpiri country.[9] There may have been a similar trickle to small settlements along the telegraph line which bisected the Northern Territory on a north-south axis.[10] However, the first significant disruption to traditional local organisation would appear to be the Tanami gold rush of 1909 which at its peak brought 500 miners directly into Warlpiri country (Meggitt 1962: 21). But it seems to have been the severe drought of 1924–1929 and the Coniston massacre of 1928 that precipitated a large-scale exodus of Warlpiri people from their traditional country in many different directions.[11] At various destinations they joined other Aboriginal people in tribally mixed camps. This long-distance outmigration was somewhat reversed following the 1933

18 • An Australian Indigenous Diaspora

establishment of Mount Doreen Station (a pastoral or ranching enterprise) in southern Warlpiri country and the congregation of many Warlpiri people there. When the new government and mission settlement of Yuendumu was established in 1946 most of the Warlpiri at Mount Doreen Station were relocated to it, along with other Warlpiri people who had gathered at the police

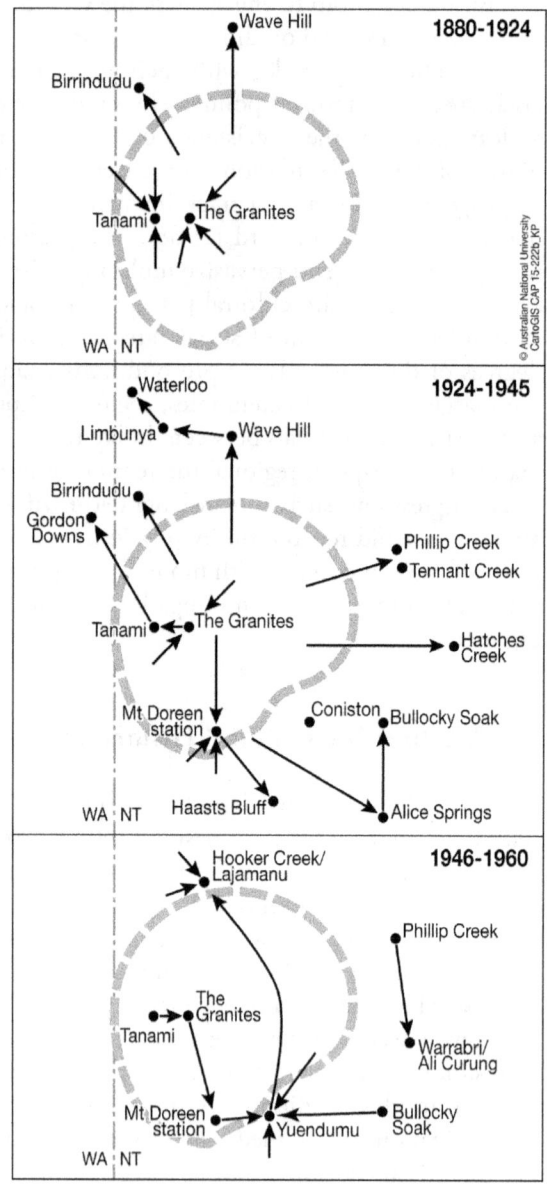

Map 1.2 Major migration patterns of Warlpiri people, 1880–1960

ration depot at Tanami, at the mining camp at The Granites and at Bullocky Soak on the Stuart Highway.

Prior to their re-congregation at Yuendumu some Warlpiri people had already moved to the west and the south, either via Mount Doreen Station or directly from their traditional country. A few became integrated into the predominantly Arrernte settlement of Hermannsburg and others into the predominantly Luritja/Pintupi settlement of Haasts Bluff and later Papunya. The experience of growing up in a predominantly non-Warlpiri settlement, using a non-Warlpiri lingua franca, seems to have had profound implications for the identity of the settlement-born generation in favouring the majority identity in any settlement.[12] At Balgo, Billiluna, Halls Creek and Kununurra in Western Australia I made contact with the descendants of some of the Warlpiri who had travelled west in the pre-Yuendumu era and I heard about others at Fitzroy Crossing and Broome. Their relative isolation is reflected in a genre of stories told by Yuendumu residents about the surprise discovery of Warlpiri speakers by contemporary Warlpiri travellers to Western Australia. There may in fact have been many outlying Warlpiri people who did not participate in the momentous post-war re-congregation of Warlpiri in joint government/mission settlements outside their former traditional country at Yuendumu, Lajamanu, Phillip Creek and Ali Curung and in their traditional country at Willowra. The 1957 Northern Territory Register of Wards provides a fascinating snapshot of Warlpiri demography around this time, demonstrating simultaneous congregation in the training settlements of the assimilation era alongside continuing widespread dispersal on pastoral stations tapering off to very distant locations.[13]

The map of the distribution of Warlpiri 'wards' (on page 20), together with the previous maps showing the approximate extent of Warlpiri traditional country and early migration patterns, demonstrate two fundamental truths about the founding of the Warlpiri settlement of Yuendumu: its scale was unprecedented for the Warlpiri; and, in relation to traditional country, it was still a diaspora location. The partial return to traditional country facilitated by later land claim research and the outstation movement was delayed for more than twenty-five years, although occasional visits were made to relatively accessible sites. Emblematic of this long delayed return was the failure of later efforts to find Kulpulurnu, a major water source and rain Dreaming site in the middle of the Tanami Desert (Elias 1998). One of my own Warlpiri research collaborators reinforced the idea of Yuendumu as a diaspora location by taking me to a rare Desert Walnut tree (*marranki*) in the West Camp of Yuendumu. For him the tree represented the true Warlpiri country of the Tanami Desert where that species of tree was plentiful.[14]

The unprecedented scale of Yuendumu brought together previously separate local bands and subgroupings who had spoken their own dialect of

Warlpiri and who had been orientated towards separate permanent water sources. This must have entailed the added social tension associated with large congregations of Warlpiri people and, in the case of the settlement, must have exacerbated those tensions because the residents could not disperse after the rains into smaller groups, foraging primarily over their own territories, as was previously the case. While stories of the early days of the

Map 1.3 Location of Warlpiri 'wards', 1957

settlement emphasise satisfaction and even pride in Warlpiri consolidation there and the early co-operative efforts, for example, to clear land for an airstrip, there are also accounts of relatively large-scale and lethal fights in the camp.[15] The frequency and seriousness of the fighting was one of the justifications for the establishment of Hooker Creek (Lajamanu) in 1949, namely to disperse the combatants (Meggitt 1962: 29; Hinkson 2014: 78).

The world of the Warlpiri settlements from the 1950s to the present was no doubt diverse and more complicated than is revealed in the ethnographies and the accounts of the further dramatic changes of statecraft towards Aboriginal people over the period (but see, for example, Campbell 2006; Coombs and Stanner 1974; Hinkson 2002, 2005; Jordan 2003; Maddock 1981; Michaels 1986; Rowse 1990; Steer 1996). From the perspective of the already completed research on the Warlpiri diaspora, however, it is possible to identify some transformations, both on the settlements and in broader society, which have enabled or undermined the establishment of a diaspora. One of the settlement transformations could be summarised as a gendered, social stratification resulting from an uneven engagement with various government and missionary projects, particularly with regard to education. These new means of social stratification held the potential to cut across traditional hierarchies based on age, sex and the possession of esoteric ritual knowledge. I have explored the issue of newly emerging social stratification elsewhere using the idea of different generations of intermediary figures over Warlpiri contact history (Burke 2013a).

In the pre-contact era, strict egalitarianism between mature men and the constant assertion of personal autonomy had a strong levelling effect and, among other things, made any authoritarian political structures impossible.[16] The early settlement period, however, provided opportunities that were previously unavailable for some Warlpiri men to pursue new forms of distinction and influence. These ambitious few returned from their service in the native corps in the Second World War with improved English and new work skills, including one in carpentry and another who was the first Warlpiri man to learn to drive a truck. The man with the carpentry skills helped to build the missionary's house and the first Warlpiri truck driver got prestigious jobs assisting in the administration of the settlement. Both became trusted intermediary figures, one being referred to by the missionaries as the 'headman' of the camp (Steer 1996: 36). Such designations typically underplayed the traditional levelling and fragmenting tendencies, but they also alert us to the probability that prestige and status gained in such colonial projects could be deployed in intra-Warlpiri competition in the camp and in augmenting their ritual prowess.[17]

The nature of the next generation of intermediary figures was intimately connected with the biggest and most consistent of state projects: education.

From the contemporary perspective of mass disengagement from formal education on the settlements, the greater than 90 per cent attendance rates of the 1960s at the height of the assimilationist training settlements seem remarkable, even if the greater regimentation of everyday life during that era is taken into account. As in broader society, education on the remote settlements created a new kind of social stratification as those who did well were encouraged into further education in boarding schools and post-secondary vocational training. It seems not to have been only individual talent alone, since there emerged particular families whose members had attained the most success in education. Those families tended to monopolise the few prized jobs on the settlements in the school, the health clinic, the council office, the Baptist Church and later as police aides. It was as if particular kin groups had made a joint strategic decision about engagement with the projects on offer.

In any event, it resulted in a small minority of relatively well educated, bi-cultural adepts, say 50 to 100 out of a population of 3500, whose knowledge of the broader world and ability to function in it became exceptional among the broader Warlpiri population. Their ranks include long-serving Warlpiri teachers, leaders in the Baptist Church, and leaders in broader political engagements with land councils and political parties.[18] They tend to dominate Warlpiri interaction with state agencies and are masters of 'two laws talk' and discussion of 'two-way education': in other words, they were able to articulate a Warlpiri way or a Warlpiri law in contradistinction to European ways and law.[19] Some of them became involved in new media (video, radio and later television broadcasting).[20] More recently, they became familiar with indigenous political rights discourse. As we shall see, a number of them are disproportionately represented in the Warlpiri diaspora, although many also remained on the settlements. A long-term white resident and teacher at Yuendumu also noticed how some of those who had been away to boarding schools adopted house cleaning routines that marked them out among the other Warlpiri as 'living clean' compared to the relaxed standards of the majority, a carry-over from the absence of such routines in humpies (makeshift huts) around the settlement and in their pre-contact past.[21] Merlan has also noted how the idea of housework had failed to take root as a kind of service that Aboriginal people could provide to their kin (1991: 278). Thus, even though the bi-cultural adepts may have been unable to convert their co-residents to their preferred standards, they would be aware of the likely standards of white people and would on occasion on the settlements and in the diaspora be heard apologising to white visitors for the state of their houses. Most of the Warlpiri, however, accepted the prevailing conditions and did not consider them as a problem needing explanation.

Christianity played a significant part in the lives of a number of the early Warlpiri pioneers of the diaspora, some of the matriarchs in the Warlpiri diaspora and many of the Warlpiri in the ranks of the bi-cultural adepts who remained on the settlements. Baptist missionisation is synonymous with the very beginning of Yuendumu and eventually all of the Warlpiri settlements where they were the sole Christian missionary denomination. In the 1960s and 1970s the Warlpiri were Baptist. The Baptist missionaries, in particular the long-serving Rev. Tom Fleming (1950–1975), were well integrated into settlement affairs from the beginning through their provision of education, medical services, film nights, a retail store and, significantly, their relatively benign attitude towards the continuation of initiation ceremonies. In the 1970s Nicolas Peterson (personal communication) noted that Warlpiri men who became very involved in the church were somewhat marginalised from the main ceremonial leaders in the camp. My observations in the 1980s were of a continuing compartmentalisation of traditional ritual and church domains but of a broader group of ceremonial leaders being willing to participate in church services and to attend, if not organise, the innovative Christian *purlapa*.[22] The Easter *purlapa*, for example, used traditional media (Warlpiri language, singing styles, body decorations, dancing and stagecraft) to retell the Easter story: a sort of Warlpiri Passion play that was well attended (also see Jordan 2003; Laughren 1981). Photographs from the 1960s and 1970s reveal that church attendance was high, as it continued to be in the 1980s. My personal observations in the 1980s and my attempted reconstruction of the earlier era of missionisation lead me to conclude that the Warlpiri became much more positively disposed towards Christianity than another desert group at Jigalong in Western Australia described by Tonkinson (1974). In the Jigalong case, the relatively unsuccessful missionisation by a small Pentecostal sect was described as a 'failed crusade'.[23] In the period of my research, however, the Baptist Church was also struggling and there was competition from a proliferation of Pentecostal churches. I attributed the staunchness of the remaining Baptist holdouts largely to the experience of the 'Fleming time', especially to Fleming's personalised approach. This approach was exemplified by the annual Christmas party at which every child was called out by name and presented with a small gift. I also think there was a cumulative effect due to Fleming's length of service. The Baptist Church has been there literally from the beginning, becoming familiar, helping people and being a steady point of reference through changing times. The present nostalgia tends to overlook some of the cultural challenges presented by the missionaries, who, for example, discouraged the licentious concluding aspects of some traditional rituals and discouraged card games involving gambling (a major Warlpiri pastime both then and now). The missionaries initially insisted on the use of English in Sunday services and Fleming is recalled as having an exacting, disciplinarian teaching style.

The feminised Warlpiri diaspora of 2009–2013 also warrants a revision of the remote settlement experience of Warlpiri women in the second half of the twentieth century. I will return to this issue later in this chapter where I draw out the implications of the phrase 'Warlpiri matriarchs'. In the concluding chapter I also consider to what extent the settlement upbringing of the Warlpiri matriarchs in the diaspora amounted to a school for boldness that was the foundation for their success in towns and cities. Many of the stories in this book tend to qualify Diane Bell's general characterisation of the assimilationist era on the settlements as one of increased subordination and marginalisation of Aboriginal women. The stories also present an alternative to her prescription of a return to landed traditionalism as the best pathway to greater autonomy for Aboriginal women on the settlements (Bell 1980, 1983; Bell and Ditton 1980). My findings have their greatest parallel in Diane Barwick's characterisation of the colonial era, based on an account of a very different time and place, as one of giving Aboriginal women unique opportunities to overturn and surpass the constricting traditional gender order (Barwick 1974).[24]

Contra Bell, there is overwhelming evidence from many sources that the pre-contact gender order in traditional Aboriginal society was one of the subordination of women.[25] This general subordination existed alongside and despite the economic primacy of women's labour, pervasive homosociality in everyday life, women's separate rituals and the growing personal autonomy of Aboriginal women as they matured. It was evident in the greater pre-eminence and scope of male rituals, the exclusion of women from the politics of male rituals, the promised marriage of young girls to much older men, and polygyny. Moreover, there was a differential use of sex in which the male was believed to have induced the maturation of the young wife through sexual intercourse with her. Sex with women was part of the broader aspect of social relations that took on various functions of punishment (rape as a punishment for serious breaches of traditional law), male hospitality (the lending of wives) and as part of various ritual performances (Merlan 1988, 1992).

Something of the tenor of the subordination of Warlpiri women in pre-contact traditional society can be extrapolated from Meggitt's account of Warlpiri marital relationships in the 1950s. It appears that a degree of violence between husband and wife was widely accepted and even expected for misdemeanours such as swearing at one's husband or failing to look after children (Meggitt 1962: 85—114). He reported that the wife's relations would enforce some limits on the degree of punishment by a husband, particularly if it drew blood or was likely to cause permanent injury. The effectiveness of such protection depended upon the presence of key kin and the state of various ongoing relationships. There was a widespread male double standard about infidelity and concomitant suspicion and close surveillance of wives.

Even fraught relationships tended to endure and over time resulted in a deep emotional attachment that was demonstrated in the concern and attentiveness shown to an ill spouse and the intense and expressive mourning for the death of a long-standing spouse. More recent analysis of marital violence, that I think is consistent with the Warlpiri material, suggests that wives were not cowed into total submission but would continue to vigorously assert themselves even though they knew the probable outcome of such physical altercations with their husbands (Burbank 1994: 133–177).

The era of the establishment of Aboriginal settlements and the continuation of much smaller Aboriginal camps on many pastoral stations coincided with a significant change in statecraft towards Aboriginal people from a reliance on rations to cash wages and cash welfare payments – what Rowse characterised as a crisis of managed consumption in central Australia in the 1960s (Rowse 1998: 118–46). The policy twists and turns and contradictions of that time, including the initial impoverishment occasioned by these changes, need not detain us here, except to register, in a summary way, the enduring changes set in motion by periodic cash welfare payments.

Although per capita incomes on settlements at the beginning of the era of cash welfare payments were low, they were above subsistence levels, partly due to the relatively inexpensive new staple of flour. This allowed for targeted savings for the purchase of motor vehicles and associated travel expenses (Peterson 1977). Improved access to transport enabled diverse projects such as the extension of catchment areas for traditional rituals; the enlarging of the pathways of some travelling rituals; and the ability to travel to regional centres where liquor was available. Some accounts of the introduction of cash welfare payments emphasise the reluctance of Aboriginal people to accept that they were now responsible for purchasing their own food (Myers 1980; 1986: 256–85). They had for many years received rations and interpreted the changes as a breach of their compact with their new bosses who, in return for Aboriginal co-operation, were supposed to look after them. From the very beginning there were also differential generational and sex role implications. To oversimplify somewhat, young men and some young women saw their cash welfare payments as their own discretionary funds which they could spend on non-subsistence items whereas cash welfare payments to old-age pensioners and to women, ostensibly intended to support their own children, were seen as appropriately applied to the provisioning of all their relations. In particular, husbands who received unemployment benefits did not necessarily view the funds as partially quarantined for the provisioning of their wife and children, and this led to early concerns about the need to split such payments between husband and wife (Bell and Ditton 1980: 94–96). More general analyses, focusing on day-to-day demand sharing, tend to emphasise the way in which cash welfare payments have been assimilated into traditional modes of exchange and how they have funded continuing ritual life and endosociality more generally. This has been described as an Aboriginal domestic moral economy that is resistant to expectations of market influence and material accumulation (Peterson 1993, 2013; Peterson and Taylor 2003).

Other analyses tend to see more gendered transformations occurring. Merlan (1991), for example, attempted to place the exchange of material objects within a broader account of traditional Aboriginal systems of value. Drawing upon Sansom (1980, 1988) and her own fieldwork, she suggested that what was traditionally valued was various kinds of service (including the provision of material goods) that could be described as help, which includes quotidian generosity, helping out in a crisis and more long-term dedicated help such as raising a child or organising a child's initiation. Alongside the valuing of help was the valuing of not feeling particularly indebted when one receives some material help upon the request of a relation ('the absence of close calculation of reciprocity'). Merlan called this 'generalised demand' and Peterson described it as 'demand sharing' and more recently as 'asymmetrical reciprocity' (Peterson 2013). While Peterson proposed it as a general trait of traditional Aboriginal culture (the pressure towards generosity among hunter-gatherers, the need for the continual enactment and testing of kin relations), Merlan saw some variation within traditional kinship systems. In particular, she thought that the more constrained and carefully monitored relationships with affines, such as bride service, had a moderating influence on generalised demand. The contemporary breakdown of contracting traditional marriages[26] removed that moderating effect and generalised demand has been refocused on women who, because of the expectations placed upon them to be the primary carers of children, regularly obtain the necessities of life which then becomes the object of demands from a wide group of kin (also see Finlayson 1991). The effect of cash welfare payments then has been to lessen the personal recognition of such women as the providers of service because of the anonymity and ubiquity of money. Legal tender broke the personal connection between traditional production (hunting and gathering) and its distribution. As we shall see in Chapter 3 (Making Alice Springs a Warlpiri Place), Merlan's account continues to be relevant to explaining the pressures on the Warlpiri matriarchs of the town camps of Alice Springs and Darwin.

Diane Austin-Broos provided a remarkably similar account to Merlan's, even though it concerned a remote settlement in a later period (Austin-Broos 2003). At Hermannsburg in the 1990s, she noted that the diplomatic skills in negotiating demand sharing requests of others and being an effective demander fell mostly to mature women. Those aged between forty and sixty became the targets for demands from the widest categories of kin. Because of the broad similarities between Hermannsburg and the Warlpiri settlement, much of Austin-Broos' account can be extrapolated to the Warlpiri. Her account helps to explain some of the increased pressures on settlement women and why a move to a diaspora location might moderate that pressure. The density of bilateral kin relations on the settlement and the constancy of demands, especially on paydays, was exacerbated by those who had lost their money in card games or who had spent it on drinking binges. She inferred from these new money pressures a fundamental rebalancing away from the pre-contact operation of the kinship system. The old system had been more embedded in country identities and the resources of the country. The contemporary system was skewed towards the kinship system and was realised more through the circulation of commodities and cash. A further context, not present in Merlan's account but quite relevant to Warlpiri settlements in the 1980s and beyond, was the competition between Aboriginal men for the desirable resources being channelled through local councils and outstation organisations, in other words, competition over allocative power and the ability thereby to fulfil kin demands (also see Macdonald 2000). The concentration of such resources, especially compared to the pre-contact dispersal of natural resources, led to conflict and feuding between different kin groupings, adding to the sense that kinship relations had become harder to manage despite the successes of land rights.

Returning to the initial years of the era of cash welfare payments, it is true to say that by 1974 any remaining juridical and economic impediments to Aboriginal migration had been removed. In 1964 the replacement of the Social Welfare Ordinance meant that Alice Springs was no longer a prohibited area and the prohibition on liquor consumption by Aboriginal people was also lifted (Rowse 1998: 201).[27] In 1968 there was the equal wages decision for Aboriginal pastoral workers and in 1973–1974 the replacement of training allowances with universally available unemployment benefits (Rowse 1998: 118, 178). These changes created one of the two big economic foundations for the Warlpiri diaspora: the portability of social security payments. The other foundation was access to welfare housing which did not overtly discriminate against those from the remote settlements, although long waiting times presented obvious difficulties with regard to interim accommodation.

The contemporary economic foundation of Warlpiri diaspora (government subventions) contrasts markedly with the wage labouring of the Torres Strait Islander diaspora in Queensland in the 1960s and 1970s (Beckett 2010), as well as the Aboriginal town campers of the late 1970s for whom seasonal pastoral work remained important (Collmann 1988).[28] Indeed, stories of exceptional Warlpiri stockmen and drovers like Old Darby (Campbell 2006), as well as the distribution of Warlpiri people on various pastoral stations in 1957 and distant job placements in the assimilation era (Giese 1966;

Smee 1966; Long 1992: 158), are all suggestive of a contemporary decline in previous work related mobility.

The Contemporary Settlement Situation

In this book I persist with the terminology of 'settlement' rather than the more contemporary 'community', some might say anachronistically, so that the initial impetus and history of these places remains in view (see Long 1970; Rowse 1998: 147–83). The word 'settlement' also carries with it less sentimental baggage than 'community' with its connotations of peaceful common purpose. Most of the Warlpiri migrants discussed in this book left the Warlpiri settlements in the 1980s and later. By then the settlements were very different places and the broader societal revaluation of Aboriginal tradition that accompanied the new national policy orientation of self-determination (circa early 1970s) was beginning to have local effects: a succession of successful Warlpiri land claims; the outstation movement; the proliferation of Aboriginal controlled NGOs; and bilingual education. In these and other projects, the Warlpiri would be 'enlisted' as the exemplars of tradition and the settlements relabelled as 'communities' and considered to be the locus of Warlpiri tradition (Rowse 1990): Yuendumu as the Warlpiri Athens.

These developments, which presented new opportunities for the bi-cultural adepts, were accompanied by seemingly intransigent problems of unemployment, alcohol abuse, the occasional outbreak of petrol sniffing epidemics and drunken violence, notwithstanding liquor restrictions that made the settlements more liveable than the towns, at least for the non-drinkers. Occupation of the outstations declined dramatically partly due to funding restrictions and policy changes (Kerins 2009) but also, I suspect, because the knowledgeable old men and women who were their most ardent supporters were dying.[29] The rate of such deaths seems to have accelerated due to epidemics of diabetes, heart disease and substance abuse. Mortuary rituals are now the most frequent ceremony performed (Glaskin et al. 2008).

The contemporary form of the traditional mortuary ritual, known as 'sorry business' (Musharbash 2008a), is typically commenced soon after the confirmation of the death. Nowadays there is also a later, fairly elaborate funeral based on Christian funeral services and elaborated in unique Warlpiri ways, such as the lining up to prostrate oneself over the coffin. This serial prostration seems to be based on the traditional chest-to-chest rubbing of the corpse (Meggitt 1962: 320). The Warlpiri embrace and development of the funeral service is of relatively recent origin and gathered momentum over the second half of the twentieth century.[30] In the first few decades of the Warlpiri settlements, up to the 1970s, Warlpiri people avoided funeral services and burials which were largely conducted by the white missionaries and white settlement staff. Now the organisation of and attendance at funerals has become a serious obligation, requiring the marshalling of resources and scrupulous attention to explaining one's absence, for example, by sending an explanatory condolence message to be read out at the funeral. Perceived options for place of burial have also multiplied since the early decades of the settlements when burials were confined to formally designated cemeteries near the settlements. While those cemeteries are still used, others choose outstations or bush locations that are within visiting range of the settlements.

Settlement living and the adoption of funeral services have presented problems for the continuation of some traditional mortuary practices, even more so for those Warlpiri people who have moved to towns and cities. The inclusive character of contemporary funeral services and their close association with burial tends to conflict with traditional practices that limit the category and sex of kin responsible for dealing with the corpse. There has been a tendency to relax such restrictions so that all can attend the funeral service and burial.[31] A bigger problem has been the traditional practice of abandoning shelters and moving to the next water source. This was relatively easy to accommodate in the early decades of the settlements when most Warlpiri people lived in makeshift humpies (the traditional *yujuku*). Even in 1978, 70 per cent of the Warlpiri people at Yuendumu lived in humpies (Young and Doohan 1989: 139). Moving residence became more problematic as more substantial houses were built and occupied. The swapping of houses or circulation through the existing housing stock was a potential solution in the era of the local administration of the housing stock. But in towns and cities, where waiting times for public housing were long, the consequences of giving up a tenancy because of the death of a close relation were more severe. How Warlpiri people dealt with this issue in the diaspora will be explored in Chapters 3 (Making Alice Springs a Warlpiri place) and 4 (Warlpiri Women of Adelaide).

Fundamental demographic changes have been taking place which mean that there are now fewer older people to care for and socialise the young, who are a growing percentage of the total population. The passing of the generation who grew up in the desert has also revealed problems in the transmission of detailed knowledge about the country and associated rituals (Curran 2010; Peterson 2008). Initiation ceremonies continue but in a somewhat truncated form. Women's ceremonies (*yawulyu*) also continue but sometimes in contexts that are disengaged from the ongoing ceremonial life of the settlements (Dussart 2004). The continuation of *yawulyu* is also threatened by transmission problems, including the inherent difficulty for the younger generation in learning the words of the songs; the declining opportunities for such learning to occur naturally; and changing mores in the younger generation of women who are beginning to feel shame about exposing their painted torsos (Barwick, Laughren and Turpin 2013).

At the same time, there has been a rise in Western Desert style painting as fine art in the international art market (Myers 2002). This has influenced other differentiated art markets, providing a possible supplementary economic basis for the diaspora. In parallel with the growth of these differentiated markets has been the growth of government sponsored arts centres on the settlements. Whatever the original impetus for artistic endeavours, the production of art for sale and self-identification as an artist has permeated the settlements. A relatively large proportion of Warlpiri people call themselves artists and the settlements can sometimes give the appearance of being one large artists' workshop as canvases are worked on at many locations around the settlement as well as at the art centre. The developing art market is thus enabling of both diaspora and continued settlement life.

Royalty payments on the other hand tend to reorient the Warlpiri back to the settlements and tradition. Such payments are one of the consequences of the successful Warlpiri land claims which brought highly prospective Warlpiri traditional country under federal land rights legislation. That legislation mandated the payment of mining royalties to traditional owners.[32] In the period of the research approximately $5 million was distributed each year to Warlpiri people from goldmines on Warlpiri land. Meetings to decide the details of such distributions are perennial topics of conversation among the Warlpiri and the meetings themselves precipitate a biannual convergence on the meeting site, including from the diaspora. As well as vindicating Warlpiri traditional relations to their land, the distributions sometimes cause bitter intra-family disputes.[33]

The language situation on the settlements was continually transforming over the second half of the twentieth century. At a national level, Warlpiri is seen as one of the strongest remaining indigenous languages with thousands of speakers (see, for example, Australian Institute of Aboriginal and Torres Strait Islander Studies, and Federation of Aboriginal and Torres Strait Islander Languages 2005: 67–88). On closer inspection, however, dramatic intergenerational changes have been taking place. Whereas the current older generation would speak classical Warlpiri to each other and a version of Aboriginal English and Standard English to native English speakers, the younger generation among themselves would more frequently use code-mixing and code-switching between Warlpiri and Aboriginal English. At Lajamanu the mixing of various source languages (standard English, classical Warlpiri, Gurindji Kriol and various forms of Aboriginal English) became standardised to the extent that the linguist, Carmel O'Shannessy, identified it as a new language which she called Light Warlpiri (O'Shannessy 2005, 2013). Such standardisation does not appear to have emerged from the constant code-switching in the other Warlpiri settlements. Even at those other settlements some older Warlpiri people identify the younger generation as speaking 'light Warlpiri', used in a non-technical sense to indicate a substantial change from classical Warlpiri. Some older Warlpiri grandmothers pride themselves on teaching the grandchildren in their care to speak classical Warlpiri. Others defer to the language variety spoken by their grandchildren. The variation in the kind of Warlpiri spoken on the settlements is one of a number of factors complicating the assertion of Warlpiri identity in the diaspora. I found Warlpiri identity typically described both in terms of descent from an acknowledged Warlpiri ancestor and competence in the Warlpiri language. Therefore, these questions arise: what degree of competence and what variety of Warlpiri language are being assumed in these pronouncements?

As well as the obvious changes already outlined, there have been more subtle changes in everyday life on the settlements. One is what could be called the informalisation of daily routines. The attempted inculcation of a daily routine of three meals, work and education reached its apogee in the 1950s and 1960s in the assimilation era of communal feeding and a siren marking the commencement of the working and school day and its various official breaks. As Rowse documents, such plans were also subject to internal contradictions which meant, for example, that punishment for breaches of requirements had to give way to the need to ensure that mothers attended health clinics and mothercraft classes (Rowse 1998: 147–83). There were also variable interpretations by individual superintendents of the required degree of compliance and the persistence of contrary Warlpiri social practices encouraging wilfulness and individual freedom of action. Nonetheless, I think there has been a general tendency over the second half of the twentieth century towards less formality in mealtimes and the preparation of food, and a decline in deference to white authority. One has only to look at the remarkable images from that earlier era, of Warlpiri people dressed in their Sunday best for church services or the disciplined march past at an early Yuendumu sports weekend (see illustrations on page 32), to gain an impression of the inculcated routines of earlier times.

While these changes seem to be synchronised in some way with changes in the broader society, some of the Australia-wide changes also tend to be amplified on the settlements. There seems to have been a broad synchronisation of tendencies towards informality in dress, meal preparation, mealtimes, the rise in takeaway food and the rise in sedentary leisure pursuits (TV, DVDs and computer games). The amplified trends range from health (increasing incidence of obesity, heart disease and diabetes) to patterns of church attendance (the decline in long-established denominations and the rise in new Pentecostal Christianity).

This kind of influence reflects an increasing awareness of the broader society by the bi-cultural adepts and the changing media landscape in the Warlpiri settlements. I have already mentioned the expanded experience of the world gained by the bi-cultural adepts through educational networks

Illustrations 1.1 and 1.2 The march past at Yuendumu sports weekend and the Baptist congregation outside the first church circa 1960s (source: the Fleming Family Collection, courtesy of Jol Fleming)

(distant secondary boarding schools, teacher education and vocational training) and church networks (distant Bible study, conventions, one trip to PNG, Thailand). The 1970s societal revaluation of Aboriginal tradition, combined with the new art market, enabled even more extensive networks to be established and travel undertaken, for example, to international exhibitions of Warlpiri art opened by a traditional ritual performance or sand painting (Paris, New York). Various institutional and personal networks facilitated the travel of traditional Warlpiri women's dancing troupes to various venues around Australia. The introduction of Australian Rules football to the Warlpiri also facilitated travel to regional competitions and later on an ongoing relationship with a large Melbourne club. In most cases the travel and connections have been assisted by white people who go to the Warlpiri settlements to work on the various government and NGO projects mentioned. After 1987, connections with the broader world accelerated through the introduction in the Warlpiri settlements of telephones, TV, fax, videos and eventually Internet access (Hinkson 1999: 56–58).

The influence of the broader society should not, however, be overestimated. The geographic remoteness of the settlements, as well as continuing tendencies towards endosociality among the Warlpiri and their lack of economic integration beyond welfare payments, all mean that the settlements remain culturally distant from mainstream white society. Even if we choose for comparison the white underclass[34] concentrated in public housing in the outer suburbs of large cities, where inter-generational unemployment and intensive engagement with the welfare system and prisons would produce a greater statistical equivalence with the Warlpiri, wide cultural differences remain. One of the more startling cultural elements to have survived missionisation and the projects of tutelage of the assimilation era has been the continuing belief in the ubiquity and efficacy of sorcery. I found this to be true even of the bi-cultural adepts, although in their case, they tended to be more circumspect in initially revealing such beliefs to their white acquaintances until a trusting relationship had been established.

Moreover, for the majority living on the settlements, their day to day interactions are with their close relations. As one would expect of the legacy of a fully functioning kinship system of the pre-contact era, these relationships tend to be multifaceted and dense. Austin-Broos has suggested that under contemporary conditions there has been a contraction of such dense kinship relationships to an inner circle of those who are regularly depended upon for help (2003: 123–24). As will be seen in the unfolding of the diaspora story, my research offers some support for a similar tendency among the Warlpiri. It seems to me that a further consequence of kinship-based endosociality and sedentisation in the relatively large enduring settlements (compared to the pre-contact mobile bands) has been the layering of history of interactions between residential kin groups. This history is not only one of help, service and successful joint undertakings such as marriages and rituals. It is also a history of competition, deliberate infliction of illness and death through sorcery, maiming and manslaughter in fights, and arguments about the distribution of mining royalties. Further legacies of the kinship system are self-help policing and group responsibility for crimes committed by individual members of the kin group. Among other things, these features provide fertile ground for the accumulation of grievances between kin groups and are the means of rapid escalation and ramification of disputes.

The broad differences between contemporary settlement culture and mainstream society can be dramatically illustrated by imagining the transposing of a Warlpiri household on the settlements into a middle-class suburb of a town or city. Leaving aside for the moment the diversity and stratification I have been asserting as the result of intercultural history on the settlements, one can imagine the surprise and apprehension about the new, dark neighbours. They would be observed speaking their own incomprehensible language amongst themselves and conducting their conversations at a very loud volume. They might have frequent and numerous visitors staying with them. They might not make a priority of maintaining the grounds of the house and might occasionally abandon an old car in the yard. There might be occasional loud parties and frequent absences for attending funerals. These kinds of stereotypes, although also based on observation, are only useful to set out some broad parameters of the scale of difference. They do not prepare us for the diversity of actual cases. For example, the white neighbours in a northern suburb of Adelaide were pleased when a Warlpiri woman artist and her white partner took over public housing next to them, since the previous tenants were young white men who grew marijuana in the backyard and held frequent, loud drunken parties. In their relief, they embraced the Warlpiri artist's quiet productivity and agreed to place an article in their Neighbourhood Watch bulletin about her paintings. I was not able to discover what they thought about the steady stream of Warlpiri visitors and the various family crises the artist had to deal with.

While this story of a positive reception by relative strangers challenges some available stereotypes, it also suggests a gendered and a generational differentiation in the ease of reception. I wondered whether the reception would have been so warm and immediate if the new neighbour had been a young Warlpiri man. Perhaps with the abstemious, middle-aged Warlpiri women artists there is something relatively safe, comprehensible and worthy of support compared to the less predictable and potentially dangerous young men. In any event, this issue of gendered reception will be revisited throughout this book at different diaspora locations.

Indigenous Diaspora and its Precursors under Other Guises

Although the idea of an Australian indigenous diaspora is novel, anthropological studies in Australia, the USA and Canada have traversed similar ground, if under alternative guises of 'fringe camps', urbanisation or internal migration. Kerin Coulehan's 1995 unpublished doctoral dissertation on Yolngu women who left remote settlements in Arnhem land to reside in the city of Darwin is the closest in spirit to my Warlpiri study and I will be referring to her thesis for comparative purposes throughout this book (Coulehan 1995). Some of the earliest works on Aboriginal migration to cities in the 1960s and 1970s introduced themes that I have found relevant to my research. Diane Barwick's 1960s work on previously rural Aboriginal people who had moved to Melbourne raised questions of the persistence of particular regional affiliations notwithstanding the tentative formation of an overarching Melbourne Aboriginal community that was socially segregated from urban white society (1962, 1963, 1964). Fay Gale's research on Aboriginal migration into Adelaide in the 1960s and 1970s revealed the significance of Aboriginal women who had married white men (Gale 1966, 1972; Gale and Wundersitz 1982). John Taylor's research on Aboriginal migration to the Northern Territory town of Katherine developed a list of push-pull factors (social tensions, location of family, availability of jobs, services and alcohol) (Taylor 1988, 1989; Taylor and Bell 1996, 1999, 2004). The theme of a competitive politics of identity between the migrants and those who stayed at home was first raised by Jeremy Beckett about the Torres Strait Islander diaspora: should the stay-at-home Islanders have consulted the migrants about the location of the new airstrip on Murray Island (Beckett 1983)? Beckett also introduced the differing diaspora experience of male and female Islanders, noting the reluctance of some female migrants to return to the harder grind of domestic work and continual surveillance by other families back on the islands (1987: 213).

George Morgan's more recent work, *Unsettled Places: Aboriginal People and Urbanisation in New South Wales* (2006), pursues the theme of the resistance of rural Aboriginal migrants to abandoning their culture in urban centres as was expected in the modernising ethos of the assimilation era. Instead, there occurred the ethnogenesis of an urban pan-Aboriginality, inspired by radical black protest movements in America. The new pan-Aboriginality insisted upon Aboriginal control of their political engagements and of their own service NGOs (legal aid services, medical services and the like). The new nationally framed identity and political agenda raise the question of the terms on which the Warlpiri migrants might be drawn into the new overarching identity as Aboriginal (or Indigenous) or retain more of their regional distinctiveness as Warlpiri people. Possibilities for collaboration between the two kinds of Aboriginal groupings would seem to exist, especially considering the more accessible traditionalism of the Warlpiri migrants and the traditionalist elements of the national Aboriginal identity. An alternative model of this kind of intra-indigenous encounter is provided by older ethnographic accounts of the movement of Western Desert Aboriginal peoples out of the desert into the country of their weakened Aboriginal neighbours (Doohan 1992; Kolig 1981; Petri and Petri-Odermann 1970; Young and Doohan 1989). Such encounters raised issues of intra-Aboriginal competition and cultural chauvinism of the migrants. Just how such various possibilities play out in practice with the Warlpiri migrants will be explored in relation to Katherine (Chapter 2), Alice Springs (Chapter 3) and Adelaide (Chapter 4).

Fringe camp studies, such as Collmann's 1970s Alice Springs study (Collmann 1979b, 1979a, 1988) and Sansom's 1970s Darwin study (Sansom 1980) would seem to require some analysis of the relationship between the town dwellers and their hinterland culture. But this connection did not emerge fully until much later (Merlan 1998; Rowse 1998; Sansom 2010). Sansom's attention to everyday practice is much more suggestive of diasporic themes: the deliberate adoption of the new modes of conduct ('that Darwin style we got') in response to the need for a new cultural *modus vivendi* among the diverse Aboriginal groups attracted to the city and the adoption of Aboriginal English as the *lingua franca*. Darwin itself presented new exigencies and opportunities, especially for drinking liquor. Sansom also identified a unique kind of Aboriginal cultural entrepreneur of the diaspora, those 'Masterful Men' who could market their superior knowledge of Darwin to their visiting hinterland relations. The Masterful Men demanded loyalty from the visitors and payment for a safe experience of the town that only the Masterful Men could ensure. Quite unexpectedly, I found in Adelaide an analogous group of Masterful Warlpiri Matriarchs who had accumulated seemingly arcane knowledge of urban survival and prospering (see Chapter 4, Warlpiri Women of Adelaide).

In addition to comparisons that could be made to global diasporas, there is more directly relevant comparative anthropological literature on the internal migration of indigenous minorities in other First World countries.[35] One of the earliest was Joseph Mitchell's study of the involvement of Native Americans of the Caughnawaga Reservation in high altitude construction work all over the United States: *The Mohawks in High Steel* (Mitchell 1959). Another strand of the North American literature arose out of the Bureau of Indian Affairs relocation and employment assistance programmes between the 1950s and 1970s that were specifically designed to encourage permanent migration away from reservations to urban centres.[36] Similar relocation programmes existed in Canada and Edgar Dosman made a detailed study of one of them: reservation Indians moving to the city of Saskatoon (Dosman 1972). He gained remarkable access to the files of the government agency administering the Canadian relocation programme and was able to document in detail how the pre-existing social stratification on the reservations broadly predicted the successful and unsuccessful relocations.[37]

A more recent examination of the cultural politics of such urbanisation is Renya Ramirez's *Native Hubs: Culture, Community and Belonging in Silicon Valley and Beyond* (2007) (in a similar vein, see Nagel 1996; Weibel-Orlando 1999; Lobo and Peters 2001). Ramirez's focus is on the urban-based pan-Native American NGOs and organised cultural events (her 'hubs') where, for complex historical and juridical reasons, homeland tribal identity is still prominent. Rather than attempt a comprehensive overview of this diverse and fragmented literature here, I will refer to it, as appropriate, in the course of this book.

Special mention should, however, be made of Nancy Fogel-Chance's study of North Slope Inupiaq women living in Anchorage in the 1980s, 'Living in Both Worlds' (1993). There is a remarkable similarity between her findings and my research on the Warlpiri diaspora: the feminised indigenous diaspora; indigenous social stratification and outmarriage; matrifocal households as the stable nodes in remote-urban kin networks; the conscious fashioning of the new configurations of traditional identities; and the emergence of a native two-way ideology. All are suggestive of deeper, structural logics being played out in broadly similar Fourth World situations.

Miniaturising Diaspora

Rather than terms such as 'internal migration' or 'urbanisation', I prefer 'diaspora' as the overarching description of this project. It could have been called 'the cultural implications of internal indigenous migration', but the concept of diaspora gives appropriate prominence to the continuing importance of the traditional homelands to those Warlpiri people who have moved away and it is suggestive of original questions and themes. Before coming to those questions and themes I want to outline some of the implications of my miniaturisation of the concept from transnational diasporas to an indigenous diaspora within a nation state. The extension of the concept well beyond the paradigmatic example of the Jewish diaspora can sometimes be problematic. Following Brubaker (2005: 7–10) I also wish to distance myself from some of the hyperbolic claims of diaspora studies, namely that they always represent a radical reimagining of previous theoretical orientations. The Warlpiri diaspora project builds upon existing sedentary ethnography. Similarly, following Friedman (2002, 2012), I want to distance myself from the sometimes breathless celebration of diaspora as an inherent antidote to supposed assumptions in previous studies about national cultural uniformity, boundedness and single territorial affiliation.

The early efforts to define modern diaspora, such as William Safran's in the first volume of the new journal *Diaspora* (Safran 1991), followed fairly closely the paradigmatic case. Safran emphasised 1) a history of dispersal, 2) memories and myths of the homeland, 3) alienation in the host country, 4) a desire for eventual return, 5) ongoing support for the homeland and 6) a collective identity that was defined in significant ways by the relationship to the homeland. Subsequent efforts, such as Cohen's (1997: 23–25), deployed more fine-grained historical understandings of the Jewish diaspora to suggest voluntaristic reasons for the initial dispersion, for example establishing commercial trading networks, and that the experience of diaspora was not only fraught but often a creative and enriching experience. Cultural studies of the African diaspora in the Caribbean had already anticipated the latter move, especially in relation to music, dance, film and literature (see, for example, Hall 1990; Gilroy 1993) and added an ambivalence about an actual physical return. James Clifford's influential survey of diaspora research (1994) endorsed these various extensions from the paradigmatic case and, significantly for the Warlpiri diaspora project, raised for the first time the applicability of diaspora to indigenous peoples encapsulated in First World countries. The Warlpiri diaspora project is the first research project to actively take up Clifford's suggestion.

Clifford admits that tribal cultures are not literally diasporas because their sense of rootedness in the land is precisely what global diasporic people have lost (1994: 310). His argument is that indigenous people may claim diasporic identities in as much as their distinctive sense of themselves is orientated towards a lost or alienated home defined as aboriginal and thus outside the surrounding nation state (1994: 309–10). He uses the situation of Native Americans to explain the unique travel circuits that imply both autochthony and trans-regional worldliness. He refers to older forms of tribal cosmopolitanism (travel, spiritual quest, trade, exploration, warfare, labour migration, visiting and political alliance) as being supplemented by more properly diasporic forms: the practices of long-term dwelling away from home. Some of these forms do resonate with the Warlpiri situation. But contemporary Warlpiri circumstances make the analogy with global diasporas more direct and even more plausible. This is because the Warlpiri homeland is, in certain significant respects, like a separate nation. The legal title to most of the extensive traditional Warlpiri lands has been secured for Warlpiri traditional owners under federal land rights legislation. By virtue of that legislation welfare incomes are supplemented by royalties from gold mines on Warlpiri land. The government-supported Warlpiri settlements on or near Warlpiri traditional country comprise a local majority Warlpiri population who share the same original language and culture. Moreover, notwithstanding the porousness demonstrated by intercultural history, there is something like a border, defined broadly in geographic and cultural terms. There are large tracts of sparsely populated land that have to be traversed before reaching the Warlpiri homelands and there is still a very noticeable cultural boundary with the encapsulating society.

Accordingly, although the concept of an indigenous diaspora is clearly an extension of the concept of transnational diasporas, in the case of the Warlpiri, the extension does not have the conceptual diluting effect of the extension of the concept of diaspora to cover any geographic dispersion of broadly defined religious or ethnic groups (see, for example, Brubaker 2005 on the need to refocus sprawling diaspora studies on those who are actively pursuing the ideal of diaspora; and see Tölölyan 1996 on diaspora as 'a promiscuously capacious category'). The extension that may be most contentious in proposing indigenous diaspora as a field of enquiry, at least in the Warlpiri case, is its relatively small scale, short history and the, as yet, limited self-consciousness as a unified grouping separate from the Warlpiri homeland. Butler, for example, suggests that to be called a diaspora it should have been in existence for at least two generations, otherwise it might only reflect a temporary exile (Butler 2001: 191). Generally speaking, the second-generation Warlpiri diaspora is only now arising. Despite the emergent quality of the Warlpiri diaspora, I do think that the term diaspora is justified, not least because of the number of Warlpiri people I encountered who had positively decided never to return permanently to the Warlpiri home settlements. Such people do represent a distinctive cultural configuration significantly defined by the divided belonging to home and away (Kalra, Kaur and Hutnyk 2005: 8–27). Whether they also reflect a kind of consciousness or a distinctive mode of cultural production (as in Vertovec's typology of kinds of diaspora, 1999) remains to be seen. I do acknowledge that the extension or miniaturisation of transnational diaspora to indigenous diaspora is somewhat experimental. I shall return to the evaluation of the experiment in the conclusion of this book.

For the moment, I simply point out that adopting diaspora as the overarching concept provides a novel ethnographic agenda and a novel angle from which to explore the intercultural. The ethnographic agenda common to all diaspora studies includes: 1) reasons for and conditions of dispersal, 2) relationship with the homeland, 3) relationship with the host land and 4) inter-relationships within communities of the diaspora (adapted from Butler 2001: 195). I have already begun my exploration of the intercultural by introducing the idea of the bi-culturally adept Warlpiri person and the key role such individuals play in the emergence and maintenance of the Warlpiri diaspora. In the looser terminology employed in the transnational diaspora literature, the bi-cultural adepts may be dealt with under the rubric of cultural hybridity or cosmopolitanism, provided cosmopolitanism does not necessarily entail elite rootlessness (see Werbner 2008 on the 'new cosmopolitanism'). I will be furthering the intercultural agenda by developing the idea of Warlpiri matriarchs and the way they expand their personal social networks beyond their Warlpiri kin (see below, this chapter). More generally, I will explore whether new forms of personhood are emerging in diasporic conditions.

In adopting the concepts of homeland and diaspora from transnational studies, some terminological clarification is required. In this book the term 'Warlpiri homeland' refers to the traditional country of the Warlpiri in the Tanami Desert, plus the four main Warlpiri settlements and Ali Curung, which has a large Warlpiri minority but is not considered to be a Warlpiri settlement. Ali Curung and three of the Warlpiri settlements are, strictly speaking, on the margins or just outside of traditional Warlpiri country. It makes sense to include the settlements in the Warlpiri homeland because they have become the primary residential locus for most Warlpiri people and for Warlpiri cultural orthodoxy. Therefore, 'Warlpiri diaspora' refers to those Warlpiri people permanently living away from Warlpiri traditional country plus the four main Warlpiri settlements plus Ali Curung.[38]

Degrees of Social Embeddedness

I have used the term 'embedded' to describe one of the central aspects of traditional Warlpiri personhood: the self as embedded in networks of kin. However, I do not see the degree of embeddedness in kin networks as requiring an essentially different concept of Warlpiri personhood in contradistinction to Western personhood as is sometimes asserted in Melanesianist anthropological theorising about partible personhood and the 'dividual' (for similar caution about importing the dividual, see also Glaskin 2012; Keen 2006). Consistent with the intercultural approach, I see personhood as porous to changes in general social conditions (see Burke 2018 for more details of my reasoning). The concept of social embeddedness can also be used to encapsulate the variety of ways in which some cultural practices become ingrained and relatively difficult to change. The obvious relevance of this concept to indigenous diaspora lies in the question of how physical relocation away from the density of face-to-face relationships on the settlements may facilitate social distancing from aspects of Warlpiri culture. There are a number of ways of thinking about social embeddedness that are all relevant to indigenous diaspora. These include the power of the taken-for-granted presuppositions of all social life that are inculcated through socialisation; the limited space for reflexivity about these presuppositions (to step outside the system and to see it as a whole); and specific cultural forms that reproduce themselves in robust ways.[39]

As outlined earlier in this chapter, in traditional Warlpiri society the kinship and marriage system built up multiple reciprocal obligations of bride service and promised marriage within the same language group. Reinforcing these networks were economic, ritual and security interdependencies that produced a dense network of kin who were continually interacting with each other. While it was dense, it was also loose in the sense of the inculcation of personal assertion, the absence of a permanent ruling class and a self-help style of justice. Colonial conditions are inevitably intercultural, producing variable changes in traditional socialisation, personhood and the scope for the active and constructive agency of individuals. Despite the multiple challenges to the traditional system, many of its deeply ingrained features continued under the settlement conditions, albeit with varying degrees of enforcement and the bi-cultural adepts who might take a different view of them. These relatively robust features include the already mentioned persistence of demand sharing, initiation ceremonies, mortuary rituals and belief in the pervasiveness and efficacy of sorcery.

These features are reflected in the cultural practices the Warlpiri take to the diaspora, the reasons they temporarily return (explored in chapter 5) and in the widespread family feud that coincided with this research project (see below in this chapter under the heading 'The immediate context'). The feud, although likely aggravated by current circumstances, demonstrated the persistence of ideas of collective responsibility for transgressions by individual kin and the principle of self-help. Significantly, it drew some, but not all, of the bi-cultural adepts in the diaspora back into violent forms of action that they had previously chosen to disavow. Thus, one general question of indigenous diaspora research is to what extent and in what way does geographic distancing from the dense sociality of the home settlements enable social distancing from settlement culture? Drawing on the terminology of transnational diaspora, a related question is to what extent does the spiritual emplacement in the country of the 'deterritoralised' Warlpiri in the diaspora become attenuated?

Warlpiri Matriarchs

Looking back, Bell's work can be seen as a product of an earlier era of feminist anthropology, now characterised as the anthropology of women, which was concerned with reversing the relegation of women in previous androcentric ethnography to a domestic and non-sacred domain.[40] It was characterised by its universalising categories ('women', 'status', 'domestic versus public spheres') and a strong agenda of repatriating ethnographic examples to help critique the gender order in Western countries.[41] Hence the interest in more egalitarian hunter and gatherer societies, matrifocal or female-headed families and so-called matrilineal societies. Bell purported to provide ethnographic validation of one of the emerging tenets of the anthropology of women – the reversal under colonial conditions of the traditional equal status and autonomy of hunter and gatherer women – particularly drawing inspiration from the work of Eleanor Leacock (1978, 1980). Metropolitan theorising in feminist anthropology moved on to focus on the social construction of maleness and femaleness and the relationship between them. One wonders whether Bell's ethnographic account would have produced such a benign picture of pre-contact complementarity and interdependence had she systematically followed a gender relations approach (as inferred in Merlan's influential review, 1988).

Later trends in metropolitan theorising, reflecting dissatisfaction with universal categories, began insisting upon the intersection of class, race, sexual orientation and other relevant social differences within the category 'women', in other words, intersectionality and, more generally, difference. Poststructuralist inspired approaches questioned the stability of the categories of gender and sex, implying that these were the result of repetitive performances of discursive regimes that provided the impression of naturalness that could easily be subverted, such as in drag theatrical performances (Butler 1990). Sexuality came more into focus through the various challenges to heteronormativity.

The clarification I take from this brief excursus is that the Warlpiri diaspora project is not primarily an investigation of how the particular social construction of Warlpiri gender categories came about. Gender attributes will come into play in the broad differences between men's and women's stories of leaving the home settlements (Chapter 2) and in the various ways the Warlpiri matriarchs of the diaspora have sought to modify the settlement gender order (see, for example, the story of 'Natalie' in Chapter 3 and her comprehensive inversion of that order). Having read Marilyn Strathern's account of the 'detachability' of the attributes of male and female genders in PNG (1978), I did wonder whether 'Natalie's' story and other cases of Warlpiri women pursuing projects of religious leadership and economic independence in the diaspora would tend to alter their gender designation, in other words, whether their male-like qualities would be accompanied by other designations of them being 'like men'. But I did not find any evidence of this. From the perspective of feminist theorising, the Warlpiri diaspora project is more about the intersection of women, race and class and in particular about social mobility within and beyond those categories and the reception of a particular stratum of Warlpiri women (bi-cultural adepts, matriarchs) by white people in a variety of class positions.

As suggested previously, the project does have something to say about some of the long-standing debates, in particular about the changing status of Aboriginal women during the process of colonisation. Part of the problem with Bell's account was the generality of the question, for it will become apparent in the course of this book that there are a variety of social trajectories open to Warlpiri women because, as a category, they are highly differentiated. As will be seen, some of these trajectories allow certain Warlpiri women greater social mobility within the encapsulating society than most Warlpiri men.

The other debates concern the status of the domestic sphere (Yanagisako 1979) and female-headed or matrifocal households (Smith 1996, 2001; Blackwood 2006; Tanner 1974). The value and sexual division of labour within the domestic sphere continues to be a touchstone issue in our own society. In an earlier era of universalising feminist anthropology, the following question was raised: whether the widespread distinction between the domestic/private sphere and the political/public sphere was everywhere implicated in the subordination of women. The salience of the question formulated at that high level of generality tended to dissipate under the weight of contradictory circumstances around the world. Anthropological theorising about matrifocal households, based primarily on Afro-Caribbean ethnography, tends to emphasise how broader social hierarchies and economic marginalisation have undermined the claims to authority within the household of the husband-father (for a critical overview, see Barrow 1996). This literature reinforces the desirability of attempting to link the emergence of matrifocal households in the Warlpiri diaspora to the broader societal marginalisation of Warlpiri people, although the availability of welfare to the Warlpiri represents a significant contrast with the Caribbean situation. Indeed, Collmann attributed the appearance of the Aboriginal matrifocal household in the town camps of Alice Springs in the 1970s to the introduction of welfare (especially child support payments directed to mothers) (Collmann 1988: 106–25). I hope to demonstrate in this book that a critical achievement for many of the matriarchs of the Warlpiri diaspora was the maintenance of functioning households of varying degrees of order and vulnerability. In diasporic circumstances, these welfare-supported households not only worked as sites of provisioning and the raising of children, they became prized assets within kinship networks and launching pads for personal projects beyond the domestic sphere.

The reconsideration of Bell's work also prompted a conceptual clarification of what is meant by personal autonomy since it became clear to me in light of the prevalence of the theme of escape in the feminised Warlpiri diaspora (see Chapter 2, 'Getting Away') that Bell had emphasised only one aspect of personal autonomy, the mastery of social relationships, and neglected the more obviously feminist connotation of personal autonomy as an escape from constraining relationships (see, for example, Meyers 1997: 46). Apart from this observation, the reconsideration of personal autonomy by feminist philosophers cannot be applied to the Warlpiri matriarchs of the diaspora in any straightforward way because of cross-cultural complications. Marilyn Friedman, for example, while acknowledging that autonomy is a matter of degree, tends to define it in terms of capacities for reflective agency relating to the pursuit of 'deeper concerns' (2003: 17–18). As indicated earlier, traditional Warlpiri personhood emphasises spiritual emplacement and social embeddedness which leaves little room for sustained individual reflection about deeper concerns. This raises the question of whether hitherto unimaginable kinds of personhood and personal autonomy will arise among the Warlpiri matriarchs of the diaspora. I will pursue this question initially in my reflection on the limits of life history methodology among the Warlpiri (see below in this chapter under 'Methodology') and in the concluding chapter where I consider the degree to which the Warlpiri matriarchs of the diaspora have refashioned their traditional culture.

Given the above, some clarification is required of the term 'Warlpiri matriarchs' and its particular usage in this book. It is not suggesting rule by women in traditional Warlpiri society or in broader Australian society, both of which can be accurately characterised as patriarchal. The phrase 'Warlpiri matriarchs' does, however, partake of general characterisations of traditional Warlpiri society as gerontocratic and the enlarged status of middle-aged women. The tendency of women to acquire greater autonomy and authority as they become older has been noted in many tribal societies around the world (Kerns and Brown 1992; Counts 1992; Lee 1992). This tendency is sometimes compared favourably to Western notions of women's middle age as a time of relegation, dependency and decline (see Brown 1992 for an overview). An additional contrast is that Warlpiri women do not feel that their advancing years reduces their desirability to the opposite sex (Bell 1983: 166; Dussart 1992: 340). As we shall see, this characteristic has implications for the nature of the adventurousness of some of the Warlpiri matriarchs in the diaspora.

Although many of the matriarchs of the Warlpiri diaspora possessed detailed traditional knowledge and traditional skills, none were ritual leaders (*yamparru*) in the sense described by Dussart (2000: 85–138). Nevertheless, they were able to deploy that knowledge and skill to their advantage in the diaspora. As will be seen when the stories of this book unfold, the claims to authority of the Warlpiri matriarchs of the diaspora also relate to sustaining and controlling functioning households in difficult circumstances and in their successful deployment of non-traditional networking skills. Their authority also relates to their ability to undertake projects on their own account in religious, educational and economic spheres by mobilising their newly established social networks. 'Household' also needs further specification because in most situations they were not isolated households but nodes in kinship networks that became sites for the management of their continuing obligations to kin and their desire to pursue their own projects.

All of the Warlpiri matriarchs were bi-cultural adepts in the sense I have used it above, although a few of them lacked the relatively high level of formal education that I have associated with the typical bi-cultural adept Warlpiri person. What those Warlpiri matriarchs lacked in formal education, they tended to make up for in the boldness of their networking. However, the exercise of the authority of the Warlpiri matriarchs must be viewed against the background of the general economic and political marginalisation of Aboriginal people in Australia. I am not suggesting that the Warlpiri matriarchs of the diaspora have totally evaded such pervasive power structures, only that certain inroads have been made. The focus on the Warlpiri matriarchs also raises the question of the intersection of Warlpiri women's life-cycle and the diaspora. The relevance of the stage in the life-cycle when the women leave the settlements will become more apparent in the next chapter on reasons for leaving (Chapter 2) and Chapter 5 (Ambivalent Homecomings) which covers reasons for returning.

The Expansion of Personal Social Networks: White Spouses, Friends and Contacts

One of the key attributes of the matriarchs of the Warlpiri diaspora was their capability to extend their personal social networks beyond the existing networks of their Aboriginal kin. Indeed, this could be seen as one of the prominent features of this indigenous diaspora. For the purposes of exposition, one could imagine a broad comparison between traditional modes of the extension of personal social networks and new modes that had to overcome a long-ingrained tendency towards endosociality. These new modes had to be acquired through boldness and trial and error. Ethnographic descriptions of traditional Aboriginal society suggest the extension of social networks via the co-operation of senior men in large regional ceremonies and the sharing and exchange of esoteric knowledge (see, for example, Myers 1986: 219–55). In addition, shared section and subsection systems provide a mechanism for the attribution of particular kinship relationships to distant Aboriginal contacts who have no known genealogical connection. These kinds of networking could be contrasted with social networking in contemporary Western society with its more limited kinship networks and the emphasis placed upon relatively impersonal interactions within a complex, large-scale economy and bureaucracy. Thus, one of the particular characteristics of indigenous diaspora is the interaction of two radically different forms of social networking. Again, there are obviously some overlaps in mutual recognition of basic ideas about kinship and marriage.

One of the empirical findings of the Warlpiri diaspora project is how many of the Warlpiri diaspora locations are attributable to Warlpiri women forming long-term relationships with white and non-Warlpiri Aboriginal men. Despite some quite different connotations of marriage in traditional Warlpiri culture as compared to the encapsulating white society, there are certain shared basic ideas about marriage that probably help to bridge some of the cultural differences. I have already mentioned some of these differences above: the contractual arrangement between kin groups, the nature of violence within the relationship as well as affective bonds. What may be relatively new to Warlpiri tradition are ideas about romantic love and companionate marriage.

Following Delaney (1996) I take the Western ideal of romantic love to be a desire to unite with another person in profound psychological and physical ways, to take another's needs and interests to be your own and to wish that the other person does the same. The advancement of the other's interests and securing of their needs is held to be directly connected to a lover's well-being. It approximates a confederation of two independent states the terms of which are worked out on an intimate level because people only want to be loved for the properties that they take to be central to their own self-conception. 'Falling in love' gives rise to romantically loving and the accumulation of a shared history which involves mutual longings for sexual intimacy and a heightened delight in each other's physicality. Romantic love may endure over the longer term depending on responsiveness to changes in the other's self-conception, or loving commitment may continue beyond the end of romantic love as a sentimental attachment. Companionate marriage is an overlapping concept and is equally a Western ideal. It is characterised by a prior romantic relationship, individual choice of spouse, monogamy, expectations of sexual fidelity, a nuclear family household, neolocal residence, married sex as a form of emotional attachment and, more generally, the assumption that the marriage partners will be the primary source of emotional gratification for each other (Wardlow and Hirsh 2006: 4–5). While a narrower idea of romantic love (romantic seduction and passion) probably did exist in traditional Warlpiri society, the broader ideals sketched here for both romantic love and companionate marriage were quite foreign.

One could imagine a broad transition from traditional, relatively egalitarian Warlpiri endogamy towards hypergamy as the emerging bi-cultural adepts 'marry up' to higher status white partners. But, as we shall see, the white partners in fact occupied a variety of different class positions. How the Warlpiri women negotiated these different class-inflected expectations and understandings of marriage within long-term inter-racial relationships will be one of the continuing themes of this book. As will also become apparent, however, some Warlpiri women were not looking for replacement long-term relationships when they extracted themselves from traditional marriages on the settlements, but instead the freedom to experiment with a variety of conjugal relationships.

The making of friends is another significant aspect of the Warlpiri matriarchs extending personal social networks beyond kin. The broad differences between kinship and friendship have long been recognised (Pitt-Rivers 1973). Kinship ties can be characterised as inflexible, involuntary, immutable, established at birth and subject to pervasive norms of behaviour (1973: 90). Friendship can be seen as the direct opposite: informal, open-ended, voluntary and the concern only of those involved. Thus, as with romantic love and companionate marriage, but even more so with the movement beyond kindred to personal networks that include friends, there may be a movement into the relative unknown.

There are perennial problems in defining exactly what friendship means for the purposes of cross-cultural comparison.[42] For the purposes of this book, however, a decidedly Occidental idea of friendship will have more heuristic value in assessing just how far from settlement norms some Warlpiri people have travelled. Accordingly, friendship is taken to mean an intimate personal relationship of mutual concern for the well-being of the other. Friends typically help each other and do not engage in personal bonding for strategic or instrumental reasons and thus friendship can be distinguished from a client-patron relationship. Friendship is a relationship of trust that usually involves some degree of mutual personal revelation. I have to accept the ethnographic difficulties occasioned by these sometimes opaque characteristics and be as open as I can about interpretive ambiguities. In this Western idea of friendship there is also perhaps an underlying assumption of equality and homophily. This means that true friendship between Warlpiri and white people will typically, but not invariably, face significant cultural and class hurdles. Moreover, patron-seeking interactions may be culturally ingrained since a legitimate basis for hierarchy is looking after people (Myers 1986: 219–85). This means that there is not only great scope for cross-cultural misunderstanding, there is also interpretive fluidity about the nature of the relationship.

What I frequently observed in the Warlpiri diaspora was an exploratory movement from acquaintanceship to something approaching friendship. Sometimes acquaintances were initially made in relatively impersonal contexts such as official meetings with the staff of schools or welfare agencies. The willingness of some Warlpiri to personalise such encounters sometimes coincided with that of exceptional government employees, for example, teachers, social workers and Aboriginal liaison officers, who were willing to exceed their formal roles and embark upon something more. To be clear, I am not fixated on friendship as some pinnacle of bi-cultural success. Such exploratory relationships, which tended towards friendship, coexisted with other kinds of non-kin bonding and so-called 'weak ties' that were nevertheless important to the sustainability of the diaspora location. It has long been recognised that 'weak ties' can be critical for expanding one's personal social network and thriving in our own relatively anonymous society (see Granovetter 1973, 1983 on the network significance of weak ties). Chapter 3 provides an example of an important weak tie in the form of ongoing relationships with particular friendly taxi drivers. Chapter 4 provides examples of the receptive government employees and also of an art wholesaler who resisted continual pressure from his Warlpiri artist to expand their relationship well beyond its economic core. Relationships within a particular religious congregation also provide an interesting special case involving an overarching quasi-kin ideology (brothers and sisters in Christ) within which possibilities of acquaintanceship, friendship, leadership and patronage coexisted.

Most contemporary social network analysis tends to focus on the pattern of connections between people rather than the single, ego-centred personal social networks I have explored above. The Warlpiri diaspora project was not designed for this other kind of social network analysis. However, in my travels I have observed enough parts of some socio-centric networks to infer the existence of Aboriginal drinkers' networks, in which Warlpiri people participate, and multiple, overlapping travelling circuits based on geographical distribution of kin. Such travelling circuits have long been identified in 'settled' Australia, referred to as 'beats' in Jeremy Beckett's analysis of mobility in western New South Wales (1965) and 'runs' in Chris Birdsell's study of the Nyungar people of the south-west region of Western Australia (1988). One research question, then, is how do these kinds of social networks interact with the personal social networks of key Warlpiri people in the diaspora? The more general question, though, is how do the expanding social networks beyond kin contribute to the sustainability and permanence of the diaspora locations and distancing from traditional cultural practices?

Origins of the Warlpiri Diaspora • 49

Demographic Overview of the Current Warlpiri Diaspora

The statistics on which the accompanying maps 1.4 and 1.5 are based were collected via forty-four genealogies of varying degrees of completeness as well as lists of known Warlpiri migrants from long-term Warlpiri residents at all the major locations discussed. Both sources fed into a Warlpiri diaspora census of individually named people who were verified as permanently living there. In this way, I hoped to discount those who were merely visitors.[43] To be clear, the focus of this book is not on the highly mobile Warlpiri travellers. A study of Warlpiri travellers would be interesting, if difficult to do, since my impression is that a relatively large proportion of the Warlpiri population are travelling somewhere at any point in time. This reflects a variety of cultural imperatives and the location of service centres as outlined in Young and Doohan's mid-1980s study (1989). It also reflects the Warlpiri love affair with motor vehicles and the pleasure they take in travelling in company to new destinations.[44] While the desire for vehicles and travel appears to

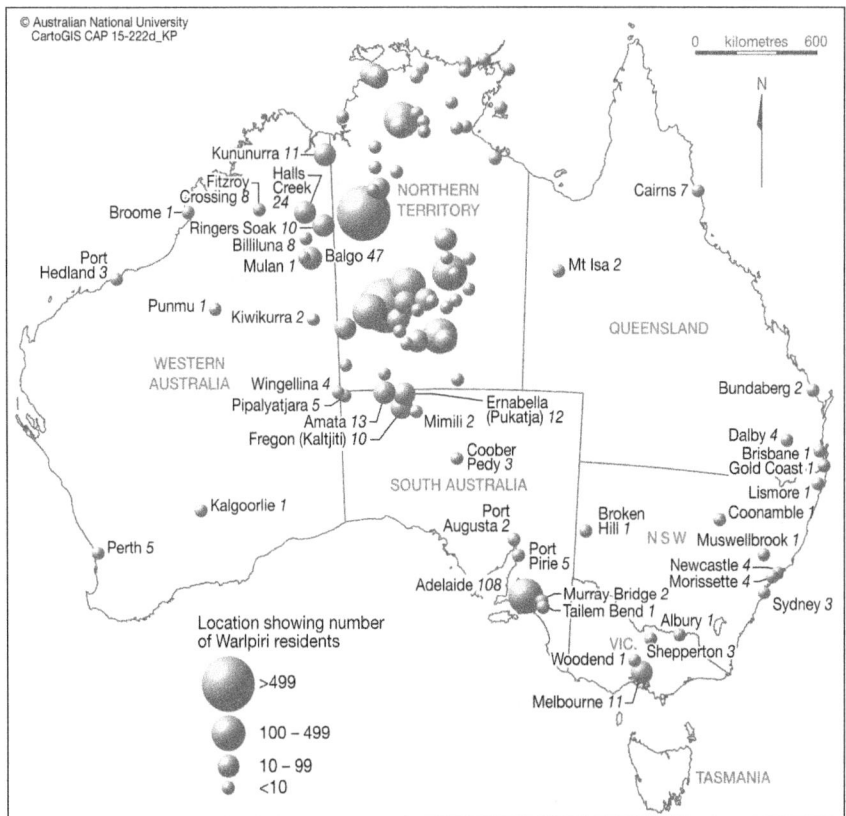

Map 1.4 Location of the Warlpiri in Australia

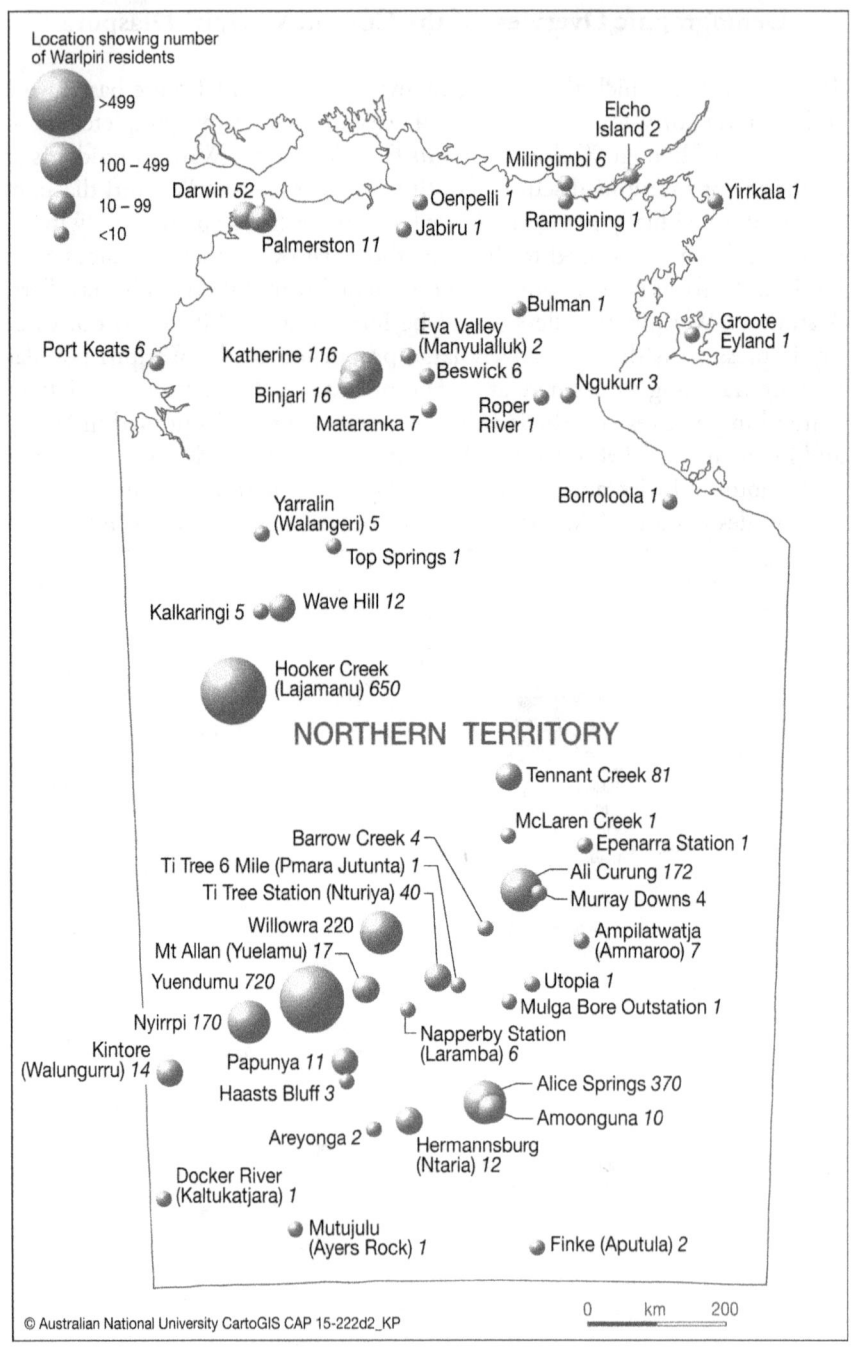

Map 1.5 Location of the Warlpiri in the Northern Territory

be evenly distributed among the Warlpiri, actual car ownership and journeys tend to reflect the settlement gender order of the predominance of male prerogatives. Private vehicles and other forms of transport supported many Warlpiri people travelling around their preferred circuits of kin and supported some inveterate Warlpiri travellers who always seemed to be on the move to new locations. For the purposes of the survey of the Warlpiri diaspora, I have attempted to disregard those people in favour of the more permanent residents. The results cannot claim to be absolutely definitive. The continual discovery, right up to the end of the research, of more Warlpiri people in the diaspora suggests undercounting. On the other hand, the tendency of Warlpiri informants to claim the descendants of tribally mixed marriages as Warlpiri suggests probable overcounting. The claim I make for them is that the figures are, nevertheless, broadly indicative of the scale and distribution of the current Warlpiri diaspora.

What these maps show is that approximately 56 per cent of the Warlpiri population still live in the four main Warlpiri settlements of Yuendumu, Lajamanu, Nyirrpi and Willowra. A further 16 per cent of the Warlpiri population live in numerous remote Aboriginal settlements and about 28 per cent of the Warlpiri are to be found in majority white towns and cities. This percentage includes the involuntary diaspora (boarding school students, prisoners, inmates of drug and alcohol rehabilitation facilities, dialysis patients, those in aged care facilities). Taking away the involuntary diaspora, I would say that about 23 per cent of the Warlpiri people have moved to towns and cities. Many of these town and city dwellers (40 per cent) are to be found in Alice Springs, in effect making Alice Springs the site of the third largest concentration of Warlpiri people, after the Warlpiri settlements of Yuendumu and Lajamanu.

In presenting these overview maps I do not want to give the misleading impression that the concentrations of Warlpiri people necessarily indicate integrated diasporic communities. The extent of such integration and collective identity is a question explored throughout this book. As will become apparent, kin connections die hard and sometimes the closest kin are in multiple different locations. If it were possible to graphically represent the close kinship relations of all the Warlpiri people at their various locations in Australia, I imagine the final result would look like complicated overlapping spider webs. This panoptic view would show connections from all over Australia back to the four main Warlpiri settlements plus Ali Curung, the main geographical nodes of Warlpiri kinship networks. There would also be smaller nodes in the nearby Aboriginal settlements of Mount Allen, Ti-Tree and Balgo, and bigger nodes in Alice Springs, Tennant Creek, Katherine, Darwin, Port Pirie and Adelaide. The networks would then dissipate to smaller outposts of the relatively isolated Warlpiri diaspora locations like

Melbourne, Sydney, Newcastle, Muswellbrook, Cairns, Kununurra and so on. Such a geographical representation could be further complicated with an overlay of the location of accessible public housing and government services as well as the travelling drinkers' network of unofficial drinking haunts and drinker-friendly households. As will be demonstrated over the course of this book, the location of such services tends to shape the Warlpiri diaspora and the points of intersection between the social networks of the sober matriarchs and the drinkers' networks become sites of complex negotiation of relatedness and autonomy-preserving distancing.

The Immediate Context: The Intervention and Family Feud

The Warlpiri diaspora project was formulated well before the dramatic imposition of Australian Government policy changes on the Northern Territory government in 2007 which collectively became known as the Northern Territory Emergency Response or 'the Northern Territory intervention', or simply 'the Intervention' (Altman and Hinkson 2007, 2010; Department of Families Housing Community Services and Indigenous Affairs 2011; Northern Territory Emergency Response Review Board 2008). Concerns about the declining social conditions on remote Aboriginal settlements across northern Australia had been rising throughout the last decades of the twentieth century (Neill 2002; Pearson 2000; Sutton 2001; Trudgen 2000). But it was the uniquely vulnerable constitutional position of the Northern Territory that enabled the Australian Government to impose its legislative will on that self-governing polity. A politically viable justification for the Intervention arose in 2007 with the release of a Northern Territory government report on Aboriginal child sexual abuse which described it as an issue of urgent national significance (Merlan 2010a; Wild and Anderson 2007).

Some of the key policy changes included the quarantining of 50 per cent of welfare payments for spending on food and necessities (excluding cigarettes, liquor and gambling); winding down the remote work-for-the-dole scheme; compulsory medical checks for children; funding for more police in remote communities; Commonwealth takeover of the alcohol restriction legislation governing remote settlements and adding restrictions on pornography; the removal of the permit system on Aboriginal land allowing freer access by outsiders; and the compulsory acquisition of leases to build houses on Aboriginal land. The new regulatory regime applied to remote Aboriginal settlements and Aboriginal town camps, all of which were exhaustively designated with boundaries delineated in the legislation. All the Warlpiri settlements were included. This new regime was introduced in dramatic fashion with the help of the army under the slogan 'stabilise, normalise, exit'. In general, the policy changes were consistent with the then conservative Liberal-National Party Government's approach of extending ideas of mutual obligations for welfare recipients and of winding back the institutions of the previous policy era of self-determination and the so-called Indigenous rights agenda. The policies have been continued by subsequent Australian Labor governments and Liberal-National Party governments. Given the continuing bipartisan support at the national level for the Intervention measures and how much they seemed to infringe upon the previous bipartisan, liberal consensus of the self-determination era, some say that Australia has entered a new era of Indigenous policy that can be given an overarching characterisation of the era of normalisation (Sullivan 2011). Others have noted that the new policy measures are also consistent with a wider trend in neo-liberal government policy. The Intervention measures were highly contested in the political arena, including by Aboriginal service NGOs in central Australia and prominent Warlpiri leaders, but to no avail. The polarising political debate about the Intervention had its counterpart within Australianist anthropology.[45]

While the implementation of the Northern Territory Intervention measures occurred throughout the entirety of this research project (2009–2014), it has proven to be less of a preoccupation of the Warlpiri than originally expected. Many Aboriginal people in remote areas, with the significant exception of some of the bi-cultural adepts, are disengaged from national political processes. Moreover, in their everyday lives the Aboriginal people who are subject to the most intrusive restrictions, such as income management, seem capable of adjusting to them or evading them through the sharing with kin of their welfare debit cards and the supposedly secret pin numbers. Some commentators have asserted that the Intervention measures have caused an increase in the migration of Aboriginal people to towns and cities.[46] I have not found much evidence of this. The scale of the diaspora seemed to me to be relatively stable over the research period.

A precursor to the suite of Intervention measures was Noel Pearson's policy proposal of orbiting (Pearson 2009b: 60–61, 2009a: 294–95). Under this proposal, rather than permanent migration, Aboriginal people would leave their remote home settlements to take up opportunities for education and jobs in distant locations while remaining in touch with the home settlements and returning there for important ritual events and holidays, leaving open the possibility of eventual return. Although not initially orientated to this policy debate, the Warlpiri diaspora project can make a critical contribution to it because the Warlpiri people I describe in this book left their home settlements well in advance of any targeted government policy overtly encouraging them to do so. Thus, while the debate about the Intervention is now highly politicised, the analysis of the pre-existing diaspora may assist in evaluating the likely consequences of such policies. I will return to the issue of policy implications in the concluding chapter of this book.

By far the more immediate and pervasive influence on people's movements during the period of the research was a family feud that arose out of the death by stabbing of a young Warlpiri man at Warlpiri Camp in Alice Springs in September 2010.[47] Both the victim and the young Warlpiri men accused of involvement in the death came from prominent Warlpiri families at Yuendumu. Following a well-attended 'sorry business' ceremony held at a town camp in Alice Springs directly across the highway from where the incident had occurred, the victim's family took violent revenge upon the families of the perpetrator at Yuendumu in the form of a riot in which people were threatened with axes and machetes, cars were torched and houses ransacked. These events attracted national media attention that continued when 100 Warlpiri people from Yuendumu temporarily relocated to Adelaide to escape the violence.[48] While there have been a number of seemingly insoluble feuds at Willowra and Yuendumu in the recent past, this latest one was more intense, more widespread and longer lasting. The disruption to every aspect of life at Yuendumu carried over to Alice Springs, especially during the court cases of the accused, and the frequent eruptions of rounds of retaliation at Yuendumu sparked a similar action between the same sets of relations in diaspora locations as far away as Adelaide. Some in the diaspora returned to temporarily participate in the fighting, most notoriously the Warlpiri former AFL star Liam Jurrah.[49]

Methodology for the Anthropologist Who Is Mistaken for a Missionary

This project required the adoption of multi-sited ethnography in the mode of 'follow the people' (Marcus 1995). Original enthusiasm for the methodology among anthropologists is now tempered with more world-weary evaluations of its limitations, namely having to rely largely on interviews and having to curtail the pull into 'thicker and stickier' interactions with informants (Hage 2005). Informants' editing of their life story in order to present it in the best possible light is probably universal (cf. Holly Wardlow's account of triumphalist shaping of life stories among her Huli informants in PNG, 2006: 89–90). One of the more dramatic examples of self-editing I encountered was the initial omission of a ten-year period which one woman had spent in jail in Darwin for manslaughter. Others attempted to hide their well-known addictions to poker machines. Moreover, many middle aged Aboriginal women I dealt with were adept at quickly divining what was expected of them from a variety of white interlocutors, whether it be a missionary, a schoolteacher, a land council lawyer, a welfare worker, a visiting politician or an anthropologist, and responded with tried and tested formulations.

My impression is that most Warlpiri people are uninterested and unpractised in autobiography. The strongest narrative traditions are the song cycles of the foundational activities of ancestral beings. There was no strong tradition of oratory about personal vicissitudes and triumphs. There is certainly no tradition of bildungsroman. On the contrary, the impression one gets from the literature and my own interactions with Warlpiri people is that those who talk about themselves are more likely to be considered egotistical blowhards who need to talk about themselves because they lack the knowledge, courage and effort required to actually gain respect and renown. Taciturn competence in the performance of tasks and delivery upon kin obligations is more rewarded. This means I had to be aware that in questioning Warlpiri people about their life story I may have been corralling them into an unfamiliar form.

Of course, there were variations among the Warlpiri people I encountered. As one would expect from the bi-cultural adepts, many of them were aware from their interaction with white people that processes of introduction and befriending often involved some recounting, however summary, of one's present occupation and personal history. Some had become unusually adept at elaborating to new white contacts their own personal history, personal qualities and past triumphs. But I never witnessed similar discourse among Warlpiri people themselves and I surmised that such talk would not have been well received. Those who became involved in Pentecostal churches did adopt the narrative tradition of the personal testimony of conversion and the power of God that formed the centrepiece of many a Pentecostal service. This practice was not so well-developed among the Warlpiri Baptists, but as we shall see below, personal redemption stories did provide something of a narrative framework for a number of the Warlpiri Baptists I interviewed.

Because of the nature of this project, some informants found me difficult to place initially, especially when I did not express much interest in being taken hunting, in talking about ceremonies and in visiting sacred sites which seemed to satisfy most of the previous anthropologists they had known. My relatively mature age and attendance at Baptist Church services provided another possibility for their classification of me as a sympathetic missionary type who might respond to stories of victimhood, redemption and the eventual achievement of respectability. And indeed, this was to be one of the underlying structures of many of the life stories I was told. One can never completely escape from these sorts of ingrained expectations, although the ubiquity of mutual surveillance and backtalk ensured that no outrageous pretence was maintained for very long. As much as possible, I also tried to triangulate the life stories I was offered with the views of knowledgeable others who have been my Warlpiri associates for more than thirty years. The engagement of a few of these associates with the research project has been essential for moderating the self-editing distortions mentioned above. They have given me access to the Warlpiri backtalk and Warlpiri common knowledge of personal histories. The use of some of them as paid research assistants on my initial visits to diaspora locations facilitated the acceleration of a typically more sedate snowballing technique by providing introductions and, in effect, vouching for me. I do not wish to oversell or undersell the results of such a methodology. My claim is that the involvement of my long-term Warlpiri associates has enabled a high degree of participant observation in Alice Springs and in other locations it has facilitated some degree of participant observation and contextualisation of interviews. This variability will be apparent in the qualifications used in presenting some aspects of the results.

I based my fieldwork in Alice Springs where I initially spent two and a half months in 2009 and conducted fieldwork intermittently at various locations over the following five years (eighteen months in total). Once initial contacts were made in Darwin, Adelaide, Newcastle and Muswellbrook with my research assistants, I made repeated visits to those locations on my own, although I did employ the woman I have called 'Barbara' as my occasional research assistant in Adelaide. Thus, the process of confidence-building and gaining trust proceeded more intermittently and over a longer period than would be the case in more sedentary fieldwork.[50]

Outline of the Book

It is possible to imagine three broad phases of any process of diaspora: 1) the original displacement from the homeland; 2) dealing with an uncertain welcome in a foreign location; and 3) reconfiguring the relationship with the homeland and the traditional culture it represents. I have adopted these phases in structuring the book. 'Displacement' covers a multitude of possibilities, including expulsion, escape and the more sedate playing out of the various social and economic push-pull factors. To what extent there is an active and constructive agency in the initial movement to the diaspora location will be one of the underlying issues of Chapter 2 ('Getting Away': Reasons and Pathways). Among this diversity of reasons and pathways certain gender and generational patterns emerge. Although the focus of this chapter is on the journey away from the Warlpiri settlements, it also provides an account of what the theme of escape entails for some Warlpiri women who take up the exuberant but precarious life in the unofficial town camps of Darwin and a loose sorority of Warlpiri women who experimented with relationships with white men in Alice Springs. The chapter concludes by suggesting a general model of how the larger Warlpiri diaspora locations are founded and grow and, in one case, decline.

Dealing with an uncertain welcome by forming diaspora communities, and thereby raising issues of assimilation, hybridisation and resistance, is common to most studies of diasporas. With indigenous diaspora there is the added inflection that it is sometimes other local indigenous people who may be unwelcoming of the new indigenous migrants. This was notoriously the case in Katherine in the 1980s when the rising number of Warlpiri people in the town was the cause of some alarm to the local Aboriginal people and it became a contentious political issue in the town (Merlan 1998: 42–43). Defensive community formation and the degree to which diaspora locations encourage greater engagement with the wider society will be the focus of Chapters 3 (Making Alice Springs a Warlpiri Place) and 4 (Warlpiri Women of Adelaide). Separating the case material in this way will also allow a comparison to be made between the different opportunities and challenges presented by the more manageable scale of a town as opposed to the potentially intimidating vastness of a city. Both locations have potential for the expansion of personal social networks. Thus, one of the aims of Chapters 3 and 4 is to be attentive to how some 'weak ties' may increase through emotional intensity, trust, time spent together and reciprocity to become strong ties.

Chapter 5 (Ambivalent Homecomings and the Politics of Home and Away) examines the question of the relationship between the Warlpiri diaspora and the home settlements through the issue of return. A significant context for return is an emerging Warlpiri politics between those who have remained on the home settlements and those in the diaspora. This is revealed in mutual stereotyping between the two kinds of locations, mythologising stories about the dangers of distant locations, and tensions around the proper location of particular Warlpiri funerals and burial sites. Both return visits and permanent return are explored through actual examples. While individual Warlpiri families will never disown their distant kin, from the stories of return there emerge differing degrees of attenuation from home settlement culture and engagement with Warlpiri kin. This sometimes makes it difficult for those with abstract genealogical connections to reintegrate themselves into Warlpiri affairs.

Finally, I will conclude this book by revisiting the questions raised in this chapter and consider the policy implications of this research, in particular of the proposal to encourage 'orbiting'. This will involve re-examining the idea of social embeddedness through the prism of the various ways in which the Warlpiri matriarchs expanded their personal social networks. As a contribution to anthropological theorising about the matrifocal household, I will present a model of the distinctive aspects of such households in the Warlpiri diaspora. As for the Warlpiri matriarchs, I will respond to the challenge of intersectional analysis by exploring the interaction of the personal quality of boldness, their formative experiences on the home settlements, and the broader historical factors shaping their reception in the diaspora. This will involve a consideration of whether new forms of personhood emerged in the diaspora and to what extent there has been a refashioning of tradition. Following my consideration of 'orbiting', I will evaluate the experiment of using diaspora as the overarching framing device.

Notes

1. With some misgivings, I have adopted the terminology of 'white' (rather than 'non-Indigenous' or 'Anglo-Australian') to take advantage of developments in Whiteness studies. As Kowal, drawing upon Frankenberg (1993), explains, it is not intended to refer to a natural category based on skin colour, rather a structure of cultural dominance that is naturalised and allows those who can be classified in this way the privileges associated with the dominant culture without necessarily having to overtly identify as such (Kowal 2011: 327, note 1). My misgivings centre on the inherent Occidentalism of such a concept and its potential to falsely attribute privilege to even the most marginalised members of the white underclass. As will be seen in this book, some members of the white underclass sought to improve their lot by attaching themselves to the Warlpiri people they encountered.
2. Unless specified otherwise, throughout this book I use the word 'kin' in a non-technical sense to encompass consanguineal relatives and affines.
3. 'Town camps' refers to a variety of small Aboriginal residential areas, typically on the fringes of towns in outback Australia, especially the Northern Territory. Their historical antecedents are the makeshift shelters of Aboriginal people who relocated themselves from more remote areas to be near white towns from which they were socially, and sometimes legally, excluded, hence the alternative term of 'fringe camp'. Generally, they could be distinguished from official Aboriginal reserves or mission settlements. Many habitual fringe camps near the main towns in the Northern Territory were formalised and housing was upgraded in the 1970s and 1980s so that a distinction between official town camps (with secure tenure, substantial dwellings, etc.) and unofficial town camps (no tenure, makeshift accommodation) is justified.
4. I am using the phrase 'community studies' in this context to refer to village ethnographies. The potential need for clarification arises because the phrase 'community studies' is sometimes understood as referring to ethnographic studies of small towns in Western countries (see, for example, Barrett 2010: 113–14).
5. A complete list of non-linguistic research on the Warlpiri can be accessed on the Internet at www.anu.edu.au/linguistics/nash/aust/wlp/wlp-eth-ref.html. Some of the anthropological highlights include: Mervyn Meggitt 's classic *Desert People* (1962), Nancy Munn's *Warlpiri Iconography* (1973), Stephen Wild's ethnomusicology of the Warlpiri (1975), papers by Nicolas Peterson on Warlpiri ritual (1969, 1970), Barbara Glowczewski's French structuralist account of the Warlpiri of Lajamanu (1991), Eric Michaels' action anthropology approach to the introduction of new media at Yuendumu

(1986; with Kelly 1984), Francoise Dussart on the internal politics of women's ceremonies (2000), the revision and extension of Eric Michaels' work on the new media by Melinda Hinkson (1999, 2005) and, more recently, Yasmine Musharbash's close examination of quotidian life at Yuendumu (2003, 2008b) and Eirik Saethre's account of the persistence of chronic diseases at Lajamanu (2013). As to theorising the idiosyncratic development of a regional, specialist literature, see Fardon's 'Localising Strategies' (1990). My own attempt to explore the implications of applying different anthropological theoretical frameworks to the Warlpiri was my Master of Letters sub-thesis (Burke 1998).

6. Many of the references to the literature on the emotional attachment of Aboriginal people to their estates have been collated by Peterson (1972: 24).

7. See, for example, Elkin (1964: 80): 'It is this spiritual bond which explains the reluctance of most Aborigines to remain away for very long periods from their own "country"; they desire to revisit it from time to time to be near the home of their spirits as well as to see some of the places in it sanctified by a mythological "history"; and finally they like to die in it so that their spirits will not be lost when they sever their connection with the body. Many an old Aborigine would be better off some distance away at some mission station or government feeding depot, but no! "That is not my country, this is my country," he says, and he will not find peace until he settles in the latter and there awaits death'.

8. Kolig, working with a Western Desert diaspora in the 1970s, Wolmadjeri who had migrated north of their traditional country and settled at Fitzroy Crossing, imagined their previous life in the desert precisely in terms of a parochial ethnocentrism which either despised or feared (or both) alien Aboriginal traditions. He emphasised the importance of conception Dreaming and the multiplicity of 'patriclan lodges' with esoteric knowledge about localised sacred landscapes. He imagined traditional ceremonies conducted by spiritual leaders in a mode of serious austerity, congruent with their world-sustaining purpose, and that the ritual leaders would have a wide authority beyond the immediate ritual sphere. Thus, in his survey of the contemporary situation he characterised as new a variety of regional extensions: the knowledge of many Dreaming tracks with their expansive regional linkages; the acquisition of new rites through trading with sometimes distant groups; the rise of the cultic broker in acquiring those new rites; and well-travelled religious leaders and the tendency towards eutrapelia in the presentation of ceremonies (1981: 64, 156–57).

9. Wave Hill Station and Victoria River Downs were established in 1883, Gordon Downs Station in 1886 and Sturt Creek Station in 1887 (Smith 2000; Meggitt 1962: 16–29).

10. The overland telegraph line had been constructed in 1871–1872, with stations at Alice Springs, Barrow Creek and Tennant Creek (Taylor 1980).

11. 'The Coniston massacre' refers to the killing of Aboriginal people near Coniston Station and along the Lander River by a police expedition led by a white policeman and including two Aboriginal police trackers. The expedition was in response to the killing of an old white prospector named Brooks at a water source near Coniston Station and the wounding of a lone white settler further to the north on the Lander River in the same year (Hartwig 1960; Meggitt 1962: 24–25; Rowse 1998: 55; Wilson and O'Brien 2003). Ostensibly the police action was aimed at arresting the Aboriginal perpetrators although it also had the hallmarks of a punitive raid by outraged and outnumbered white settlers, with the surviving settlor and other pastoralists being part of the expedition. In an official enquiry into the affair members of the expedition admitted to shooting and killing thirty-one Aboriginal people, although Aboriginal accounts suggest many more were killed. The enquiry exonerated the police on the basis of self-defence when they were attacked trying to effect arrests and specifically rejected the accusation that the police

action was a reprisal or punitive expedition. The events of those years were remembered and memorialised by Warlpiri eyewitnesses and their descendants, including through their testimony in various Warlpiri land claims and, most recently, through the making of a film about it (the 2012 film *Coniston* directed by David Batty and Francis Jupurrula Kelly and produced by PAW Media and Rebel Films).

12. Thus we have the case of actual cousins identifying as Luritja and Warlpiri respectively because their fathers, two actual Warlpiri brothers, settled in the quite different settlements of Papunya and Yuendumu. In a few cases the Warlpiri ancestry of some of their descendants became obliterated with the passing of time and only came to light in recent times due to intensive genealogical research undertaken by the Central Land Council to delimit the rightful recipients of Warlpiri mining royalties. Upon receiving the news of their distant Warlpiri ancestry some chose to continue following their Arrernte or Luritja identities as they had been doing for the previous few generations.

13. The terminology of 'wards' when referring to Aboriginal people of the Northern Territory came from the Welfare Ordinance of 1953. That Ordinance was one of the first awkward steps away from a government policy of protection to a policy of assimilation. The idea was that rather than focus on a racial category, such as 'natives', a non-racial welfare law should simply refer to any person who was in need of special state care because of their manner of living and inability to manage their own affairs. Such persons could be declared wards of the state with the Director of Welfare becoming their legal guardian. Under the Ordinance, which only lasted until 1964, the Director of Welfare could gazette the names of those who had been declared wards. This is what happened in a blanket, non-individualised way to all the full blood Aboriginal people of the Northern Territory, hence the gazetted Register of Wards. Curiously, the Register of Wards included Aboriginal people at Gordon Downs and Ord River Stations in Western Australia, technically outside the scope of the relevant legislation. It did not pick up any of the Warlpiri at other locations in Western Australia.

14. David Nash, a long-term linguist of the Warlpiri language, reported (personal communication, 2015) that another isolated Desert Walnut tree (*Owenia reticulate*, known to his informants as *marrawaji*) near the Ali Curung turnoff on the Stuart Highway had also been used for the purpose of indicating Warlpiri heartland territory to the west. He emphasised that the Desert Walnut was one of a number of species used to identify the Warlpiri heartland.

15. I have derived this impression of early Yuendumu from an account I collected from a young eyewitness, Cecil Japangardi Johnson (born circa 1940, interviewed 16 October 2010), an early missionary account (Steer 1996), a contemporaneous account of an early Native Affairs superintendent (reconstructed from personal letters and official reports in O'Grady 1977: 110–26), Meggitt (1962: 26–29) and discussions with Mary Laughren, a long-term linguist of the Warlpiri language, who made her own enquiries of Warlpiri people who had lived through that era. In the description of historic Yuendumu I use the word 'camp' to refer to both the Aboriginal makeshift shelters located at some distance from the centralised European infrastructure (missionaries' house, school, clinic, etc.) and a designation of a separate social domain where the Aboriginal people felt freer to act according to their own cultural practices (see also Trigger 1986 on the explicit use of Whitefella and Blackfella domains in managing remote race relations)

16. In stating the nature of traditional egalitarianism this way, I am following the conventional anthropological wisdom derived from many sources about the traditional quarantining of ritual authority to the ceremonial ground and it not being extended to secular domains (in relation to the Warlpiri, see Meggitt 1966: 71). However, I am also aware that T.G.H.

Strehlow, who had some early contact with the Warlpiri, was critical of Meggitt on this point, suggesting that the lack of extension of ritual authority to other domains was a result of changed colonial circumstances and did not adequately take into account the likely undermining effect on traditional authority of the terror and marginalisation of the early contact period (Strehlow 1963). I also note that Dussart, based on her fieldwork in the 1980s, explicitly challenged Meggitt's view, writing of the 'tentacular' nature of ritual authority extending into other domains (2000: 110).

17. For the most detailed biography of another of these early intermediary Warlpiri figures, see Liam Campbell's *Darby: One Hundred Years of Life in a Changing Culture* (2006).
18. Some of the bi-cultural adepts have been mentioned in passing in other works such as the mini-portraits of Ned Jampijinpa Hargraves and Robin Japanangka Granites in Andrew Stojanovski's *Dog Ear Café* (2010). Nicholas Rothwell has published a brief portrait of Andrew Japaljarri Spencer, long-term police aide and aspiring preacher (2007: 115–24). Melinda Hinkson's *Remembering the Future* includes some compelling vignettes of Neville Japangardi Poulson, Tess (Sarah) Napaljarri Ross and Jeanie Nungarrayi Herbert (Hinkson 2014: 22–30, 88–92, 93–99). Some have left their own literary footprint, for example Jeanie Egan's contribution to the *We Are Bosses Ourselves* volume (Egan 1983) and co-authored papers of Steve Jampijinpa Patrick (Patrick and Box 2008a, 2008b).
19. For a further explanation of 'two laws talk' in relation to a neighbouring language group, see Austin-Broos (1996). For 'two-way Aboriginal education', see Harris (1990).
20. See, for example, Eric Michaels' *For a Cultural Future: Francis Jupurrula Makes TV at Yuendumu* (1989).
21. Wendy Baarda, interview, 29 September 2009. Wendy Baarda is a very long-term white resident of Yuendumu who has been directly involved in bilingual education over a lengthy period. Her length of residence and involvement make her an exceptionally knowledgeable informant.
22. *Purlapa* means a category of traditional ceremony open to all, not restricted by gender, ritual status or age (described as 'entertainments' in Meggitt 1962: 209). I also note that Dussart in her brief description of the Christian *purlapa* saw it as marginal to other traditional rituals and as being mainly the concern of two kin groups that were particularly closely aligned with the Baptist missionaries (2000: 80–81).
23. Tonkinson revised his account of missionary failure in a later paper that took a less combative attitude and provided details of developments in the decades after his initial fieldwork in 1963 (Tonkinson 1988). What emerged at Jigalong in the 1980s that was so different from the earlier missionary era (1930s–1969) was an Aboriginal Christian ideology of rapprochement and complementarity between traditional law and Christianity that to me seems closer to the Baptist model at Yuendumu under Rev. Tom Fleming. Tonkinson traces the origins of the new ideology back to the 1970s when a less conflictual relationship to Christianity emerged after formal control of the mission was ceded to the government in 1969. According to this account, the burdens of self-management of the settlement in the self-determination era were beginning to be felt along with an Aboriginal nostalgia for the strict domain separation of the missionary era when responsibility for some of the more intrusive actions to curb social problems had been taken by the missionaries. The more significant influence, however, was the 1979 evangelical Christian revival movement that spread through the Western Desert region under an influential Aboriginal leadership and incorporated popular country and western style gospel songs.
24. This suggested trajectory of Warlpiri women over contact history is consistent with Dussart's report of Warlpiri women taking on a more prominent 'ambassadorial' role in

the presentation of traditional rituals (2000: 213–28) and Biddle's throwaway suggestion of a recent feminisation of the Dreaming (2007: 11).

25. For reasons of limited space I do not wish to rehearse in all its detail the evidence presented to counter Bell's most disputed claims about the relative autonomy and equality of Aboriginal women in the pre-contact era and refer readers to the sceptical reactions of other regional specialists (see, for example, Berndt 1989: 14; Hamilton 1986: 9; Keen 1989: 29–30; Merlan 1988: 26–30; Tonkinson 1990: 141–43). Merlan has provided a balanced and scholarly review of the issue and has been at pains to untangle the conflation of homosociality and equality (Merlan 1988, 1992). Bell has never made a detailed or convincing reply to the critiques of her view of the pre-contact era (but see her more general reply to her critics, Bell 1993: 273–306). To be clear, I am not trying to engage with all of Bell's arguments about the marginalisation of Aboriginal women in Australianist anthropology, many of which were justified, or the benefits of raising the profile of Aboriginal women in recuperative government projects by mirroring traditional forms of homosociality in having parallel, sex-segregated organisational structures and consultation processes.

26. For an account of the transformations and continuities of Warlpiri marriage since the 1950s, see Musharbash (2010).

27. In noting that the Social Welfare Ordinance 1964 removed legal controls over Aboriginal people's movements within the Northern Territory, it should be understood that it is unlikely the previous laws had much practical impact on Warlpiri migration. The first legislative apparatus relating to Aboriginal people in the Northern Territory during the period of South Australian administration (1863–1911) was the belated Northern Territory Aborigines Act 1910. That Act allowed for a protection and segregation regime under a Chief Protector with powers to remove Aboriginal people from towns that were declared as prohibited places and also to keep non-Aboriginal people out of declared Aboriginal reserves. However the scale and the reach of state apparatus was tiny and focused on Darwin, leaving the Warlpiri largely uncontacted and unhindered. During the initial Commonwealth era of administration, the Aboriginals Ordinance of 1918 continued the protection regime and segregation from towns with the most intrusive controls focused on part-Aboriginal people. Again, protective regulation of employment contracts was not matched with administrative capability. Paradoxically, it was assimilation-inspired legislation, the Welfare Ordinance of 1953, which was potentially most intrusive since it was accompanied by the administrative capacity to individually identify all of the Warlpiri people in the Northern Territory (included in the 1957 Register of Wards) and to set up and staff the training settlements, such as Yuendumu. The Director of Welfare and superintendents of the settlements had the legal authority to restrict the movements of Aboriginal people under their control but it seems that enforcement of such a restriction was rarely required. Workable cultural accommodations, continuing economic dependency, the relative isolation of Aboriginal people, and the lack of transport at their disposal all seemed to be relevant factors in this sedentisation and continued to be so after the legal apparatus of control and tutelage was dismantled in 1964. For a general overview of the changing legal and administrative framework, see Heatley (1979: 131–59), Rowley (1970: 222–45, 305–40; 1971: 35–54, 285–348), Tatz (1964) and Chesterman and Galligan (1997: 142–50, 172–77). For a much richer account of the intimate practice of statecraft over the same eras, see Rowse (1998).

28. The contemporary Warlpiri situation also contrasts with the situation of the North Slope Inupiaq women in Anchorage in the 1980s, most of whom had jobs (Fogel-Chance 1993: 95–96).
29. For a brief account of the early enthusiasm for outstations from Yuendumu in 1978, see Kesteven (1978). Notable in her account were the very rough conditions on the proto-outstations, mostly consisting of humpies and windbreaks; the justification of the choice of location of outstations in terms of Dreaming stories and associated subsection names; and the tendency to view the outstations as an answer to the settlement problems of feuding, drunken fighting and illicit love affairs. For a more general account of the early outstations movement, see Coombs et al. (1980) and for an account of the policy rationale and particular histories of various outstations, see Peterson and Myers (2016).
30. A similar history of the gradual embrace and adoption of funeral services as a quasi-traditional Aboriginal ritual has been provided by Brian McCoy in relation to Balgo mission in Western Australia over the same historical period (McCoy 2008a). While McCoy encompasses both traditional mortuary practices and funerals under the umbrella of the phrase 'sorry business', among the Warlpiri a distinction is maintained between 'sorry business' (referring to traditional mortuary ritual) and the funeral (a point also noted in Musharbash 2008a: 21, fn 1).
31. Also noted by Musharbash (2008a: 21, fn 1).
32. For convenience I have used the vernacular term 'mining royalties' even though it is technically a misnomer and covers a variety of payments to traditional owners. The Land Rights Act does not give ownership of minerals to the traditional owners. Instead, the Australian Government pays the traditional owners and their land councils royalty equivalents. What are known as 'mining royalties' include payments to Aboriginal people affected by the mining (not just the traditional owners); payments negotiated with mining companies as part of the agreement to allow mining (traditional owners only); and negotiated payments for compensation for mining exploration (traditional owners only). For an account of the process of identification of Warlpiri traditional owners and distribution of mining royalties, see Elias (2001: 207–28).
33. I should make it clear that not all the royalties are distributed to individuals or families directly. Some funds have been set aside for investment, for the Warlpiri Education and Training Trust and for community development programmes (Jagger 2011).
34. In using the term 'underclass' in this book I am not aiming for technical specification, rather a broad identification of the social milieu of marginality associated with long-term welfare dependency, drug addiction and criminality, something more like the American terms 'skid row' and 'white trash' (Hartigan 2005). There are obvious problems of stereotyping, reification and unacknowledged moral judgements creeping in to the analysis (cf. Vincent 1993; Maxwell 1993; Cowling 2002), but 'underclass' seems to be more neutral than some of the alternatives. Needless to say, in adopting this usage I am not seeking to entangle myself with the debate in the USA about anti-poverty programmes that is sometimes undertaken using the term 'underclass' as a distinct cultural group along similar lines to previous 'culture of poverty' debates (see, for example, Gans 1995). Untangling those debates and their relationship to marginalised indigenous peoples would be an interesting project but one well beyond the scope of this book.
35. See, for example, Fogel-Chance on North Slope Inupiat women in Anchorage in 1986 (1993); Fienup-Riordan on the Yup'ik migrants in Anchorage, Alaska (2000); Janovicek on a native Canadian women's NGO for urban migrants at Thunder Bay Ontario in the 1970s and 1980s (2003); Krouse on traditional dances organised by Iroquois living

in Rochester, New York State in the 1990s (2001); Ablon on Native American Indian migrants in the San Francisco Bay area in the 1950s (1964).

36. For a concise summary and overview from a human geographer, see Neils (1971); for more recent overviews by ethnohistorians, see Fixico (2000) and Miller (2013); for a more focused ethnohistorical study of Indian migration into Chicago, see Lagrand (2000).

37. Dosman's identification of the social strata on reservations is evocative if somewhat arbitrary (1972: 56–76). At the top are the 'leading families' who occupy official positions in local organisations. They are able to benefit from government ameliorative programmes and, it is hinted, receive favoured treatment by the authorities. Members of this stratum have a relatively unproblematic, planned relocation to the better suburbs of the city, becoming the 'affluent Indians', 'the native aristocracy in the city'. The next stratum is the reservation families with full-time jobs, the 'self-supporting families'. Those with only occasional work he classified as the third stratum, the 'semi-dependent'. Those with no paid work he classified as the 'confirmed indigent', the fourth and lowest stratum characterised by extreme dependence, peripheral status, as being relatively unacquainted with the outside world, shy and retiring in the face of superior status whites or Indians. The bottom two strata comprised the majority of the reservation population and typically their relocation to the city was to skid row.

38. Potential confusion arises because the Warlpiri outstations, which are quite small residential outposts from the main Warlpiri settlements, are also sometimes referred to as Warlpiri homelands. The outstations are deliberately located on Warlpiri traditional country and represent a return to tradition both in their smaller scale and their assertion of traditional connection to the country. Accordingly, some thought that the term 'outstation' was too redolent of the pastoral era and did not accurately portray the intentions of the movement: hence the term 'homeland movement'. So, to be clear, in this book I use the phrase 'Warlpiri homeland' in a different sense drawn from the literature on transnational diaspora. 'Warlpiri homeland' in this book includes Warlpiri traditional country, Warlpiri outstations, Warlpiri settlements plus Ali Curung, in order to set up a broad distinction between the majority of Warlpiri people who remain on or close to their traditional country and those who have moved away from it.

39. In its ordinary sense 'embeddedness' is a feature of all societies through socialisation, socially constructed subjectivity and normalisation of existing circumstances and presuppositions, as in Bourdieu's theorising about *habitus* and *doxa* (1977: 72–95, 164–71; see also the various extensions and modifications of these ideas in Bourdieu 2000). 'Embeddedness' is sometimes used in a summary way to refer to debates about the nature and extent of individual reflexivity in social action. For example, in Lewandowski's critique of Bourdieu's theory of practice, he suggests that reflexivity can extend beyond the context sensitivity recognised in practice theory to reflexivity about context transformation (Lewandowski 2000).

40. The periodisation of feminist theorising I adopt here is based on various reviews by Henrietta Moore (1988, 1999, 2006, 2010) and other influential reviews and collections (di Leonardo 1991; Mukhopadhyay and Higgins 1988; Quinn 1977; Reiter 1975; Rogers 1978; Rosaldo 1974).

41. One of the earliest and most famous examples of the critical repatriation of ethnography must be Margaret Mead's *Coming of Age in Samoa* (Mead 1928) and the most explicit, programmatic explanation of the concept would be Marcus and Fischer's *Anthropology As Cultural Critique* (Marcus and Fischer 1986). In between these bookends, feminist anthropologists used ethnography of diverse cultures to question the universality of male

dominance (Leacock 1981) and reconstruct broad social evolutionary pathways from primitive equality to modern inequality (Sanday 1981; Leacock 1983). An essential part of this project was the critique of colonialism as an instrument of transforming the former sexual equality of subject peoples to conform to patriarchal norms of the colonising power (Etienne and Leacock 1980).

42. I do not wish to delay this overview of the means of extension of personal social networks by reciting the various positions on defining friendship taken in the recent anthropological literature, but see Paine (1974), Bell and Coleman (1999), Killick and Desai (2010) and the masterly conspectus of the anthropology of friendship by Beer and Gardner (2015).

43. I have not adopted the multiple sub-categories of permanent migrant that have been developed in Migration Studies since they seemed overly specific for a relatively small-scale study such as this: see Brettell's discussion of different formulations of typologies including, in relation to economic migration, 'seasonal', 'temporary non-seasonal', 'recurrent', 'continuous' and 'permanent' and other categories of 'conflict migration', 'refugees', 'involuntary migrants', and 'return migration' (Brettell 2000: 99–102).

44. David Nash rightly observed that for Aboriginal people of central Australia, the motor vehicle was the most sought after durable product of Western society (Nash 1986).

45. The immediate negative reaction of anthropologists and others to the Intervention can be gauged in the collection of papers under the title *Coercive Reconciliation: Stabilise, Normalise and Exit Aboriginal Australia* (Altman and Hinkson 2007). In 2008 investigative journalist Paul Toohey provided an extended account of the early implementation of the Intervention (Toohey 2008; see also Moran 2016 for an account of the implementation of the Intervention measures in one remote Aboriginal settlement from a community development perspective). Toohey's account provoked some interesting commentary from experienced observers of the remote Aboriginal scene, revealing greater ambivalence about the measures (see, for example, Mahood 2008). A more considered range of anthropological views are to be found in the second collection of papers by Altman and Hinkson, *Culture Crisis: Anthropology and Politics in Aboriginal Australia* (2010). At the risk of oversimplifying the polarised debate among Australianist anthropologists, there emerged two broadly opposed views: 1) those giving priority to a state-centric, denial of human rights framing of the issue; and 2) those who would relativise such a framing and be open to some ongoing government interventions to address vulnerability, dependency and marginalisation, while not agreeing with all elements nor the heavy-handed implementation of the Intervention. Merlan was the first to publicly articulate the latter position (Merlan 2009b) with which I broadly agree (see also Edmunds 2010). Along with others adopting a similar position, they were caricatured as conservative dupes to neo-liberal forms of racial governance (Morris and Lattas 2010; see also Merlan's response 2010b). Diane Austin-Broos tried to untangle the debate by distinguishing between cultural difference and inequality (2011).

46. See, for example, Sabine Kacha's report for the Stop the Intervention Collective, *The NT Intervention: Does the Ends Justify the Means* (2009: 18), accessed at www.stoptheintervention.org on 10 February 2015.

47. Some Warlpiri relate the 2010–2012 feud to the previous feud at Yuendumu and Christine Nicholls goes further to suggest that enmity between the same families goes back to the initial disputes when Yuendumu was founded in 1946 (Nicholls 2011: 34–35).

48. Nadja Hainke, '11 Held After 2 Day Rioting', *Northern Territory News*, 18 September 2010, p.8; Sarah Aitken, 'Feud Group's Exit Sparks New Row', *Centralian Advocate*,

24 September 2010, p.2; Michael Owen and Mark Schliebs, 'Exodus Families' Ordeal to Last a Week', *The Australian*, 24 September 2010, p.2; Sarah Aitken, 'Payback Call in Feud', *Centralian Advocate*, 1 October 2010, p.2; Rosemary Neill, 'A Sorry Tale of Sorcery and Payback at Yuendumu', *The Australian*, 2 October 2010: Dale Fletcher, 'Yuendumu Out [of the Australian Rules Football Competition because of the feud]', *Centralian Advocate*, 6 May 2011, p.68; Cameron Boon, 'Yuendumu Man Fears for Family', *Centralian Advocate*, 6 May 2011, p.4; Cameron Boon, 'Six years' Jail for Watson Stabbing', *Centralian Advocate*, 28 February 2012, p.3.

49. Anthony Dowsley, 'I Can't Forgive Jurrah, victim says', *Northern Territory News*, 10 March 2012, p.4. It should be noted that Liam Jurrah was ultimately acquitted of the charges relating to the feud.

50. For example, I made five trips to Adelaide, catching up with many of the same people over a five-year period during blocks of fieldwork that lasted between ten and thirty days, totalling three months over the entire period. Some locations I only managed to visit once (Kununurra, Halls Creek, Balgo, Cairns) or twice (Katharine, Coober Pedy, Ti-Tree). I spent a total of eighteen months conducting fieldwork at various locations between 2009 and 2014. Towards the end of the project I visited the various Warlpiri diaspora locations and went through the draft text of this book as it related to the individuals concerned. Most seemed pleased with the draft. Some corrected factual errors and others requested minor clarifications which I have identified in the text or in footnotes. One Adelaide woman, who I have called 'Rosie' (Chapter 4), entered into a line by line negotiation with me.

Chapter 2

'Getting Away': Reasons and Pathways

Introduction: Layered Reasons and Multiple Pathways

In adopting the phrase 'getting away' from one of my Warlpiri informants, I will initially focus on just one kind of assertion of personal autonomy in the mode of disrupting constraining relationships. It is most clearly exemplified in a young woman's elaborate plans to escape promised marriage through a risky long-distance relocation. As other stories of leave-taking are layered onto this archetypal example, it will become more apparent that other kinds of personal autonomy, more in the mode of the skilful enactment of relationships, have also been at play. Some widows took their beatings and left. Others saw out their period of mourning before they left. Some married women, whose assertion of personal autonomy had been growing with their age and responsibilities, sought the right cultural moment to leave in a way that would minimise any potential backlash. Otherwise they would seek to deflect such a backlash by deploying conventional, justified modes of action, such as to help look after grandchildren already in town or by simply remaining part of information sharing networks so that they would know when the immediate threat of retaliation had passed. These later examples hint at the more complicated motives and pathways that in individual cases are multiple, layered and sometimes difficult to discover. There may be a tendency when looking at individual agency for assumptions about rational decision making to become too pervasive. In order to present a more accurate picture I will juxtapose the active and constructive agency of an escape plan with the risks awaiting them at their destination. Warlpiri women in the makeshift itinerant camps of Darwin and an informal Warlpiri sorority in Alice Springs often led haphazard and contingent lives of experimentation. The middle-aged women I met in Darwin for this project were the survivors of the rigours of this kind of free-form living. Many others, they told me, had died.

In relation to the predominance of Warlpiri women in the diaspora, I will attempt to tease out in this chapter[1] the interaction of the historical moment with exceptional personal qualities and life cycle dynamics. I will also try to identify some of the historical developments that contributed in varying degrees to individual stories of permanent relocation in the 1970s and early 1980s. Improvements in communication and transport enabled settlement dwellers to link up with earlier pioneering Warlpiri migrants. Decades of investment in settlement education came to fruition in the emergence of a small group of well-educated bi-cultural adepts. Houses were built for Aboriginal people in the town camps of Alice Springs, Tennant Creek, Katherine and Darwin and some of them were occupied by Warlpiri people. In the broader society, influential developments included a general revaluation of Aboriginal tradition, a less accepting attitude to the quarantining of domestic violence as a private matter, and liberalising attitudes towards inter-racial marriages. All these developments contributed towards certain exceptional Warlpiri women feeling the constraints of settlement life more keenly. Some circumstances tipped their emotional identification with the settlement from a place of supportive kin to a place of victimhood. Accompanying these changes was a new openness to a readjustment of their relationship to traditional law. In a number of instances, the move from settlement to town and beyond reflected key events in this process of readjustment.

The problematic leave-taking of the women seems to contrast with the relative ease of the young men slipping away for an adventure, suggesting that they are subject to quite different settlement expectations and that double standards still abound. The other stories of men in this chapter, however, seem to conform to a common trope about migration away from home providing an opportunity to reinvent the self. This was the case with a man escaping his drinking companions. It was also the case with a couple escaping a closing net of welfare workers and law enforcement officers so that their problematic relationship could be given a second chance. Finally, it was the case with the Warlpiri man specifically seeking personal transformation through an involvement in distant religious sects.

Foundational Couples and Pioneers of the Early Diaspora

The Warlpiri people I encountered in diaspora locations from 2009 to 2013, mostly women, were not all exceptionally brave, bi-cultural individuals who set off to become strangers in a strange town. An earlier era of Warlpiri pioneers meant that, in a number of locations, later Warlpiri migrants could call upon already established Warlpiri people in the major service centres of Alice Springs, Tennant Creek, Katherine and Darwin. These service centres had become familiar to the later migrants, in some respects at least, through their more official visits for health and educational reasons.

One Warlpiri man, Kim Jangala Ross, who had married an Aboriginal woman from the northern part of the Northern Territory (the 'Top End') and had lived at Bagot Reserve in Darwin since the early 1970s, was mentioned in so many stories of Warlpiri people settling in Darwin in that era and beyond that it gave credence to the idea of a foundational couple. At the height of the assimilation era in the 1960s, he had been sent with Warlpiri men from Yuendumu to work on the forestry plantation at Snake Bay on Melville Island, north of Darwin. It is unclear how he managed to do so in an era of relatively strict surveillance, but after his stint of work on the plantation, he stayed on in Darwin rather than return to Yuendumu. His wife was from the Darwin hinterland and they set up house in one of the sheds on Bagot Reserve.

It is no accident that the first Warlpiri pioneers found themselves on Bagot Reserve in the 1960s. It was originally a relatively large area (200 hectares) that had been reserved in 1938 for the concentration, segregation and administration of 'full-blood' Aboriginal people in Darwin. They were mostly from the Darwin hinterland, but also included some local Larrakia. They had previously been permanently residing in unofficial camps around the predominantly white town of Darwin, then with a population of less than 2000 people. At the time, the site of the reserve was conspicuously distant (about 5 km) from the town. The precinct of the reserve was also the location of the 'half-caste' children's institution, moved from its previous location in the town; reflecting the policy anxieties of the times, the children were strictly segregated from the 'full blood' residents in another part of the same reserve. In the 1960s, approximately 300 Aboriginal people lived at Bagot and in line with the new policy of assimilation, it was styled as a training settlement, along similar lines to Yuendumu, with a superintendent, administering staff, school, basic housing for the Aboriginal people (although with fewer humpies than at Yuendumu), a health clinic, work and training regimes, church, sporting teams and so on.[2]

Kim Ross's shed at Bagot became one of the first ports of call for visiting Warlpiri people; this was the case for well over a decade, indeed until it was blown away by Cyclone Tracey in 1974. His willingness to help his visiting Warlpiri kin became widely known. At some point he was joined at Bagot by Cecil Japangardi Johnson ('Crocodile Dundee'), a Warlpiri man also from Yuendumu, who had become very involved in the Baptist Church and was asked to undertake lay missionary and welfare work for the Baptist Church in Darwin. He married a Top End woman from the Tiwi Islands and raised a family in Darwin.

There was another much younger Warlpiri pioneer in Darwin from Lajamanu at the time and she played a significant role at various points in the lives of other young Warlpiri women arriving there. 'Annie' seemed to have been an exceptionally bright and assertive young teenager who had been sent to Kormilda College in 1967 aged fourteen after aggressively resisting cohabitation with a much older promised husband. While she excelled academically at Kormilda College, she rebelled and evaded the school principal's attempts to control her social life. Before the age of sixteen she had had two babies, both given up for adoption, and had travelled around Australia with her white boyfriend before arriving back in Darwin. There, she was soon recognised by the welfare authorities as an absconder. Under tighter welfare control she finished her education and became the first Warlpiri person to be accepted into the public service in Darwin where she remained for her early working life.

There is a story of a foundational couple in Alice Springs. Some of the Aboriginal workers, who had been learning to build houses at Yuendumu, were sent to Amoongana in the early 1960s when it was established 15 kilometres outside of Alice Springs; this was the closest Aboriginal settlement, having replaced The Bungalow that was only 4 kilometres north of Alice Springs. One of these Warlpiri workers, Dennis Japanangka Williams, stayed on in Alice Springs after the construction work at Amoongana had been completed and he eventually married a local Arrernte/Anmatjerr woman and raised a family there. Unlike Darwin, however, the permanent Warlpiri presence in Alice Springs goes back to the end of the Second World War. Many Warlpiri men and at least one Warlpiri woman served in the Aboriginal Corps in Alice Springs and in Darwin and in army camps inbetween along the Stuart Highway. It seems that some Warlpiri men stayed on in Alice Springs after the Second World War. They were later joined by Warlpiri/Anmatjerr men who had been working on pastoral stations to the north of Alice Springs. There was a similar story with regard to Katherine, where some of the earliest and most senior Warlpiri migrants had married local women (see below).

Escape from 'Dry' Areas

As anticipated in the previous chapter, the portability of new, individual social security payments in the late 1960s, and the early scrapping of legislative restrictions on movement and drinking alcohol away from the settlements, set the scene for an acceleration of Warlpiri travel for alcohol.[3] Typically, this involved trips by groups of men to the liquor outlets nearest to the settlements or longer binges in the nearest towns of Alice Springs, Tennant Creek and Katherine. Sometimes there would be a return trip to the settlement with the liquor supplies, 'a grog run'. Such boisterous exploits at Yuendumu were celebrated in a Warlpiri song of the time: the 'flagon wagon song'.[4] Eventually, a new phenomenon emerged: the option of an adult Warlpiri individual or a husband or wife deliberately leaving the settlement to take up the drinking life permanently in town. Among the life stories I collected, there also emerged a pattern of recently widowed Warlpiri women taking up the drinking life. For example, one recently widowed Warlpiri woman from Lajamanu initially went to live at the drinking camp at Top Springs, the nearest liquor outlet 265 kilometres to the north-east, and thence to the Warlpiri camp at Katherine and eventually to Bagot in Darwin. While other widows nurtured their new-found independence among their fellow widows of the *jilimi* on the settlements, I gained the impression that among the widows who left to become drinkers there were a variety of motives and circumstances. Some in their sorrow sought escape and oblivion. Others felt unjustly treated by in-laws in the semi-ritualised beatings they received upon the death of the husband for their failure to look after him.[5] Generally, other Warlpiri people seemed to take a relatively benign attitude towards the widows who became drinkers, particularly if they had been formally released from a period of mourning. Perhaps this was due to an acknowledgement of their growing independence as they got older and more experienced. In any case, there was tolerance of their self-destructive behaviour because it was seen as an expression of sorrow for the loss of a husband. However, such tolerance did not apply to the young women seeking escape from their first promised marriage, as will be outlined below.

The rise of the Aboriginal drinking camps created a new kind of network spread out over Australia that intersected at certain nodes with the more abstemious and sedentary parts of the Warlpiri diaspora which are the focus of this book. Major nodes in the drinkers' network were the unofficial camps (in Darwin known as 'long-grass' camps) and the official town camps of Alice Springs, Tennant Creek, Katherine and Darwin. During my fieldwork in Bagot reserve in Darwin there was also one unique node in the drinkers' network: a large, abandoned galvanised iron building known as 'the Gurindji shed' where many groups of drinkers could easily be accommodated.[6] More minor and more distant nodes of the drinkers' network included the camp at Top Springs; the drinkers' camps at Mount Isa and Cairns; several unofficial camps near official Aboriginal town camps in Coober Pedy and Port Augusta; individual drinking households in suburban Adelaide; and various locations in the parklands near the city of Adelaide, such as one just outside the cemetery on West Terrace. Although the more adventurous drinkers also followed their Warlpiri kinship networks to distant locations, the unofficial drinking camps in the cities of Darwin and Adelaide did not seem to be exclusively Warlpiri. Rather, they included numerous language groups which were sometimes referred to by overarching names like 'desert mob' (Warlpiri, Arrernte, Pitjantjatjara) in contradistinction to 'Top End mob' in Darwin and the local Aboriginal people in Adelaide. The less adventurous and less resourceful drinkers seemed to have more limited beats (cf. Beckett 1965). All the drinkers seemed to belong to what could be called a fraternity of the shameless. Such a fraternity was much more open and cosmopolitan than traditional kin networks (cf. Merlan 1998: 205–206).

The Politics of Arrival

Most of the Warlpiri travellers and migrants followed predictable pathways of geographical convenience, for example, from Lajamanu, to the nearest liquor outlet at Top Springs, thence to the nearest regional service centre of Katherine, and thence a relatively short distance to Darwin. This Warlpiri highway with its northern orientation was naturalised and reinforced through the use of medical and educational services in Katherine and Darwin and, in the 1970s, the arrival of a Lajamanu team in an annual Darwin Australian rules football competition. A notorious fight in Katherine involved a Warlpiri football team returning from Darwin around 1974. In one version, the fight was instigated by some white abattoir workers who were initially victorious. However, the Warlpiri football players soon returned to Katherine from Lajamanu with reinforcements and proceeded to wreak havoc on the whole town. This incident set the tone for the most contentious reception of Warlpiri people of any town in the Northern Territory. The Warlpiri presence in Katherine, particularly in unofficial transient camps, became a political issue for the local Aboriginal people. In coalition with the white local council, they objected to the disruption caused by drunken Warlpiri people and together they resisted calls to improve the conditions of the so-called 'transients' camp'. It was still a live issue at the time of Merlan's and Bauman's fieldwork in the Katherine region in the 1980s (Merlan 1998: 42–43; Bauman 1998). What the locals objected to was the aggressiveness of the Warlpiri and their riotousness when drunk. Influential

Warlpiri men who had married local women tried to mediate particular disputes but without assuaging the overall resentment towards and suspicion of the Warlpiri. That resentment was in part based on local perceptions that the Warlpiri also possessed stronger sorcery. As indicated in Chapter 1, the theme of the cultural intimidation of local Aboriginal people by assertive desert migrants has been explored at various locations of Western Desert migrants. During the period of my fieldwork (2009–2013), intra-Aboriginal tensions in Katherine had been somewhat defused as more frequent inter-marriage between the different language groups in the younger generation produced ramified kinship connections between the groups. From my own genealogical work, it appears that a significant lessening of language group endogamy is a general trend in the whole of contemporary central Australia (also see Vaarzon-Morel 2014: 243).

Warlpiri migrants from Ali Curung typically headed for the relatively close service town of Tennant Creek. Although Tennant Creek was clearly within Warumungu traditional country, the intra-Aboriginal tensions of the intensity seen in Katherine did not develop to the same degree in Tennant Creek. This may have been because of the long history of co-residence of Warlpiri, Warumungu and other language groups initially at Phillip Creek Mission settlement (1945–1956) and then at Ali Curung (1956 to the present). There has also been significant intermarriage. Nonetheless, Diane Bell's account of Ali Curung in the late 1970s reported residential separation based on language group and underlying tensions with the numerically weaker traditional owners, the Kaytej (Bell 1983: 28, 74–75, 78–79, 101–103; see also Christen's account of a confrontation in 2000 between Warlpiri and Warumungu over the traditional ownership of Marlamarla and railway corridor compensation, 2009: 168–72). From the Warlpiri settlements of Yuendumu, Nyirrpi and Willowra, the Warlpiri highway heads to Alice Springs (see next chapter).

Escape from Marriage

Perhaps the most dramatic story was of two young women who secretly saved up their wages from teacher assistant jobs (or, according to another version of the story, their winnings from card games) and booked a direct flight from Lajamanu to Darwin, a distance of 890 kilometres. In the execution of their plan they had enlisted the help of their school principal and the settlement bookkeeper, both of whom were sympathetic to the young women as the victims of fairly sustained physical violence from their promised husbands, particularly when their husbands were drunk. One of them had sheltered in the principal's house on several occasions. The secrecy of the plan, the lack of direct involvement of most of their Aboriginal kin, and the swiftness of its execution was intended to limit any retaliation against their kin and also to avoid alerting those who would try to stop them.

The brutality of beatings typically played a part in arousing the sympathy and support of key kin, usually a mother or sister, and also the support of white settlement staff. A relevant broader context for the white staff was probably the slowly changing attitudes to domestic violence in the broader community during the 1970s and 1980s (Laing 2000). This meant that in one case, after a long series of violent incidents, one young woman at Lajamanu was given a police escort to a waiting plane, then flown to Darwin and delivered to a women's shelter there. Other stories revealed more opportunistic, zigzagging routes to the diaspora location, for example, getting a lift with a sympathetic visiting truck driver, hitchhiking with white strangers or sympathetic young Aboriginal men heading for a Darwin adventure, staying for a short time with relations along the way, and making sometimes repeated attempts after recapture by relations.

Yet another story of escape to Darwin commenced at Papunya in the early 1970s. A twenty-year old Warlpiri woman became the second wife of her promised husband, living away from her own family in Yuendumu where she had grown up. She was lonely and sick of the continual beatings she received from her husband after his drinking binges. When she spotted some of her relations travelling through, she immediately got in the car and returned to Yuendumu and thence to Lajamanu where she worked in various jobs. Her experience of marriage as loneliness and violence inoculated her against any thought of remarriage: 'I had too much lesson from Jungarrayi', she recalled bitterly forty years later. In Lajamanu she came under renewed pressure to remarry. This time her relations helped her to avoid the man by paying for her flight to Darwin, where she stayed with Kim Ross until the man concerned married someone else and moved to another settlement.

The dual aspects of personal autonomy (competent enactment/repudiation of constraint) were nowhere more apparent than when those who had escaped their promised husbands in Lajamanu arrived in Darwin. The accomplishment of their escape plan was rarely matched by any detailed plan about how they would live in Darwin. Instead, they sought out the few kin, like Kim Ross, who were already there. He sometimes offered shelter in his own modest house at Bagot and, critically, his network of local in-laws allowed the Warlpiri strangers to be introduced and transformed into quasi-kin – a potentially momentous joining of two separate kin networks. In the terminology of social network theorising, Kim Ross became a 'bridge' in the enlarged social network.

A number of young Warlpiri women were attracted to the lifestyle of the Aboriginal migrants to Darwin who lived in unofficial camps around the city.

The migrants were known as 'long-grassers' after the typical terrain of such camps. The lifestyle of the long-grassers included a free attitude to sexual partners and liquor. The long-grassers made a precarious life for themselves, in true bricoleur fashion, out of the bits and pieces that were around. The drinking partner would become a 'husband', whose relations in Darwin shared food and liquor with them when they could. One could get a shower at the YMCA. A friendly taxi driver might give credit. A scrounged scrap of plastic could be used as a tarpaulin to protect a second-hand mattress from the rain. Scarce food would be supplemented by the occasional gift of fresh fish from anonymous white people and lunch at the soup kitchen run by a charity. Moreover, their quotidian existence would be enlivened by wild drinking and dancing nights at 'The Dolphin', a hotel favoured by Aboriginal people. Income could be supplemented by the occasional sale of a painting. In other words, this was a much less ordered existence than the one described by Sansom at a different unofficial camp on the outskirts of Darwin in an earlier era (Sansom 1980, 1988, 2010).[7] At one stage some of the escapees from Lajamanu joined the well-educated foundational woman, 'Annie', at a relatively well-organised long-grass camp near Mindil Beach. She insisted upon an unusual degree of neatness and a routine of washing clothes, both of which she had learned at Kormilda boarding school and the welfare institutions of her late teenage years. Her assertiveness and fighting prowess also proved valuable when unwelcome white men approached the camp in search of sexual liaisons. Looking back, she was proud of her neat camp which I imagined to have been exceptional among the long-grassers who usually had more immediate priorities.

Although drinking partners and 'husbands' changed often, some of the intertribal relationships did endure and part-Warlpiri children would be raised back on their fathers' settlement in Arnhem Land. Generally, though, among the long-grassers relationships seemed to be more negotiable. The whole raison d'être of the long-grass camps was to be free of all sorts of inhibiting restrictions, although some traditional prohibitions die hard. One Warlpiri woman enjoying the newfound freedom of being able to select her own partners could not quite bring herself to have a permanent relationship with an unrelated man from another desert tribe. He happened to have the same subsection name as her, in theory standing in the same relationship as a classificatory brother (cf. Bauman 2002 for a detailed account of the sometimes awkward meshing of different subsection systems in the Aboriginal melting pot of Katherine).

Other instances of 'getting away' involved a Yuendumu woman leaving after a beating inflicted by her in-laws who she felt had falsely accused her of 'running around' (having adulterous affairs) and a Willowra woman who left after her husband took a second, younger wife. Sometimes the women simply wanted to end a constraining relationship and pursue other more exciting possibilities. These separations tended to be the most difficult to achieve because, as in the case of the younger escapees, they required a degree of boldness, orchestration of support, tenacity and, ideally, having receptive close kin already established in the diaspora location. One woman's departure to Alice Springs from Yuendumu followed her husband's non-attendance at her brother's funeral, an unforgivable solecism in the view of her kin, and which therefore ensured their support for her. Another managed a potential backlash for leaving a husband by attaching herself to her daughter's household in Alice Springs and helping her look after her young children, her own grandchildren.[8] This woman, who I will call 'Dulcie', joined other Warlpiri women of her age in Alice Springs, where they felt under fewer constraints preventing them from pursuing their own interests. In 'Dulcie's' case this involved pursuing her facility for adventure and fun and expanding her interest in experiments in friendship with white people (see Chapter 3: Making Alice Springs a Warlpiri Place).

Education and Getting Away

I now wish to turn more systematically to the variety of ways in which education has been implicated in 'getting away'. In Chapter 1 I outlined how decades of the major governmental project of education on remote settlements had resulted in a stratified Aboriginal population in which the more successful were encouraged to further their education and became key intermediary figures and bi-cultural adepts. In the 1970s and 1980s male and female Warlpiri students who excelled in their primary education on the settlements were encouraged to take on further education at Kormilda College, a secondary boarding school in Darwin, and later shorter residential courses at Batchelor College just outside of Darwin to become teacher assistants.[9] This experience allowed them to become familiar with Darwin and to broaden their horizons. While many of these figures remained on the settlements, some Warlpiri women, with the support of their fathers, were able to indefinitely postpone promised marriage and pursue distant education. I met two such women from Ali Curung in Adelaide where they had been living for more than twenty years: 'Valmae' and 'Rosie' whose life in Adelaide will be described in more detail in Chapter 4 (Warlpiri Women of Adelaide).

Reconstructing the earlier period of their leave-taking as best I can, there seemed to have been a particular confluence of significant historical factors. An important factor at Ali Curung in the 1970s was the rising tide of alcohol abuse and domestic violence following the granting of drinking rights in the mid-1960s and the extension of unemployment benefits to Aboriginal people in the early 1970s (Bell and Ditton 1980; Bell and Nelson 1989; Brady 1988; Wright 1997). The two women had grown up during this period and were first-hand witnesses to the devastated scene, even though their own parents were not part of it. Their fathers represented an abstemious traditionalism. They were non-drinkers and ceremonial leaders at the forefront of the land rights and outstation movements. They were also the heads of households whose children were doing well at school. As the girls became older they began to realise that their promised husbands were part of the drinking scene. One of the girls had learned about an Aboriginal College in Adelaide where one of her relations was also doing a course. She sought her father's approval to study there and he gave it. It is now difficult to recover the possible conditions the father may have placed on his approval and the possible ambiguities and differing expectations between father and daughter that may have attended such decisions. No doubt the inevitable disappointed expectations of the promised husbands had to be managed in some way. Whatever the conditions, her father's support was forthcoming and she moved to Adelaide, determined not to marry any man but rather to further her education.

Another account of such pivotal support from a Warlpiri father came from Bess Nungarrayi Price, who was later to become an outspoken conservative politician in the Northern Territory. Speaking of Yuendumu in the 1960s and early 1970s, she noted a particular constellation of compromises and adjustments to the regimented settlement routines and the strong influence of the Baptist missionary, Rev. Tom Fleming.[10] As she recalled for a newspaper profile (Rintoul 2012), all the Warlpiri people had a job they were expected to do, there were communal meals, visits to outstations on weekends, and return for the schooling of children during the week. Traditional rituals continued alongside conversion to a Baptist version of Christianity that took a broadly non-confrontational stance vis-à-vis the rituals. Unusually, Bess summarised her father's attitude as one of respect for all things European.

The Warlpiri diaspora has sometimes been unwittingly fostered by Aboriginal secondary boarding schools where Aboriginal teenagers from disparate language groups would be brought together. Initially, from 1968, the focus was on Kormilda College in Darwin and then, from 1973, on Yirara College in Alice Springs.[11] In 1968 Kormilda College was also running a teacher training course for Aboriginal people and this is where Peggy Napurrula Anderson, a young Warlpiri woman from Ali Curung, met her future husband, James Gurrwanngu Gaykamangu from Milingimbi, who was also doing the same course.[12] After their marriage they lived at Milingimbi, where they raised a large family, and they lived at various locations in the Top End of the Northern Territory as they followed James' working career as a land council field officer and later office administrator and various other high-status, intermediary jobs open to the bi-culturally adept. While some of their adult children joked about being 'salt water Warlpiri' people, it was also clear that Peggy had been incorporated into James' extended family, clan and Yolngu culture more generally. She worked as a teacher at the bilingual school and gradually learned to speak and write the local language (Gupapuyngu). He asserted the prominence of his family within the wider eastern Arnhem Land region based on his knowledge of the sacred landscape of his traditional country and its associated ritual. His ritual status and connections enabled him to become something of a guarantor of the safety of the few other Warlpiri people scattered around the settlements of eastern Arnhem Land.

In a later period, a similar process took a young Warlpiri man from Ali Curung to Ernabella on the Anangu Pitjantjatjara Yankunytjatjara (APY) lands in South Australia. He had met his sweetheart, a Pitjantjatjara woman from Ernabella, when they were high school students together at Yirara College (in strictly sex-segregated dormitories). He moved to Ernabella to raise a family with her, and in addition two of his brothers from Ali Curung also found wives at Ernabella through the connections he established. Thus began a little Warlpiri outpost that was occasionally augmented by Warlpiri people from other Warlpiri settlements. During the research period, the Warlpiri outpost at Ernabella facilitated the easing of tensions at Yuendumu by providing something of a sanctuary for a key protagonist in the family feud (the mother of one of the young men accused of manslaughter).

Finally, there are the grandmothers who see towns and cities as desirable locations in which to inculcate school attendance in their grandchildren. In the two instances where this seemed to be a significant factor, one grandmother was in Darwin (originally from Ali Curung) and the other was in Adelaide (originally from Yuendumu). Both grandmothers had themselves attended schools on remote settlements and had become convinced of the value of education. They had witnessed the contemporary decline in school attendance on the settlements. Both had become the primary carers of young grandchildren, one after the untimely death of her daughter and the other following her daughter's incapacity to care for her young children because of her tempestuous relationship with her partner at Yuendumu and her drinking problems. These circumstances also gave rise to other reasons for their decisions to stay in the diaspora locations: to assuage the grief of a family tragedy on the settlement and to keep grandchildren away from the uncertain care of a jilted son-in-law at Yuendumu. Both, however, developed strong relationships with the staff of the schools their grandchildren were attending in Darwin and Adelaide.

More directly, though, government projects of education on the settlements brought young male teachers into contact with relatively well-educated

Warlpiri women working in the schools. Some inter-racial relationships arose from this contact and created opportunities for further geographical spread.

Romantic Love and Inter-racial Marriage as Vectors of Indigenous Diaspora

In Chapter 1 I outlined changes in the status of women on the Warlpiri settlements that have resulted in a decline in the fulfilment of promised marriages, even though the preferred marriage categories of kin seem to persist when contemporary Warlpiri women choose more transient partners (Musharbash 2010). There have been reports, not only among the Warlpiri but in many accounts of remote Aboriginal settlements in the 1970s and 1980s, of the assertion by adolescent girls of their free choice of marriage partners and resistance to traditional marriage arrangements (Burbank 1988; Tonkinson 1990).

One aspect of this has been the rise in marriages to non-Warlpiri men (and a few non-Warlpiri women), who are by definition outside the Warlpiri kinship universe, at least initially. The early protectionist era prohibition against inter-racial marriage was gradually dismantled in the 1960s so that there were no legal consequences for Warlpiri women 'marrying out', in contrast to the loss of the legal status as an Indian in Canada in comparable situations.[13] I became aware of 24 long-term inter-racial relationships in the Warlpiri diaspora, representing approximately 3 per cent of all Warlpiri marriages. Many of the inter-racial relationships were implicated in the distribution of Warlpiri people around Australia and the establishment of diaspora locations. Inter-racial relationships have also been a significant factor in the migration of other Aboriginal groups at other times.[14] One recurring pattern among the Warlpiri was of the inter-racial couple meeting on one of the settlements or nearby towns and eventually returning to the home town of the non-Warlpiri partner. This was the case for one of the long-term Warlpiri residents of Adelaide; for a young Warlpiri boy in Muswellbrook in country New South Wales; for another in Melbourne; for the large Warlpiri diaspora location of Murray Bridge, counting around 50 people in its heyday (now largely dispersed); and one Warlpiri woman in Wagga Wagga (no longer there). In four other cases the inter-racial couple moved to the more neutral locations (neolocal residence after marriage) of Kununurra, Katherine, Alice Springs and Cairns.

Some of the white male teachers who arrived at the settlements in the 1970s were delighted by the women they met working in the school as teacher assistants. One of them told me later: 'It's the combination of old fashioned girl femininity, physical and emotional toughness, incredible sexiness and a refreshingly natural and untroubled attitude to pregnancy and motherhood'.

The cold sociologist in me also sees the continuing influence of social endogamy as the teachers become attracted to the local educated elite. Perhaps inevitably on such small settlements, the male teachers, particularly single ones, also became the objects of curiosity, gossip and flirting by young Warlpiri women. In this sexually combustible atmosphere it is not surprising that some inter-racial relationships commenced and that some developed into long-term relationships that were easier to manage away from the settlements. In one case, the Warlpiri woman was already married with two children and the new couple secretly eloped, initially to Darwin, to avoid the inevitable backlash from her Warlpiri husband and his family, and possibly some of her own family. In another case, the Warlpiri woman was unhappily married to the father of her young son (not her actual promised husband) and arranged a more negotiated leave-taking with the support of her family and the conditional support of the promised husband. The promised husband was assured that his prior claim would be recognised should the new relationship not endure. After some years in the Top End of the Northern Territory and a stint in a remote Aboriginal community in Western Australia, the couple returned to Alice Springs to live.

There were other instances of inter-racial relationships in the diaspora that commenced with visiting white men on the settlements (a building contractor, a union organiser), but other Warlpiri women met their future white partners in nearby towns like Alice Springs or distant cities like Adelaide. Alice Springs in the 1980s seems to have been a site for the re-congregation of Warlpiri women who had taken various pathways out of the settlements. The dynamics of this group, including their engagement with town camps, newly emerging Aboriginal NGOs and churches, will be described in greater detail in the next chapter. Part of this 1980s moment of expanding possibilities for Warlpiri women in town was the arrival of a few Warlpiri women who had extracted themselves from marriages to Warlpiri men on the home settlements. They encouraged each other in their new-found freedom and a number of them entered into relations with white men they met in Alice Springs. I knew some of these Warlpiri women at the time (1983–1991, when I was living in Alice Springs) and I have since interviewed others about that era for this project. My impression now is of a unique and propitious time of experimentation by some Warlpiri women that did not have a direct counterpart in Darwin, except for 'Annie', the runaway schoolgirl I have already mentioned. As in Darwin, the experimentation included the freeform lifestyle of drinking and gambling, but in Alice Springs it also included the discovery of individual non-Aboriginal men, and sometimes friendship networks of such men, who were willing to enter into publicly acknowledged, ongoing relationships with them. Among the small group of relatively well-educated Warlpiri women, such relationships seemed to become a recognised measure of their boldness and distinction: a sorority of the successful hunters of white men. On occasion they also became competitive, such as when two of the Warlpiri women fixed their attention upon the same white man.

In suggesting Alice Springs as a happy hunting ground for non-Warlpiri sexual partners, I am not proposing a radical revision of general race relations, which remained largely segregated. Rather, the scale of Alice Springs compared to the much smaller remote settlements would simply allow such men to be found. I am also aware of the tendency towards *post hoc* mythologising. Accordingly, some balancing comments are in order. One is that not all the white partners treated with equanimity the continued involvement of their Warlpiri partners in the drinking, gambling, carousing scene that the sorority sometimes became. A particularly well remembered incident from the early 1980s is of one such white husband intervening in a drinking and gambling session and angrily retrieving his Warlpiri partner. One non-drinker participant in this scene justified her own participation as providing the service of a watchful friend ready to intervene in case others, in their inebriated state, placed themselves in danger. This role recalls the slow-drinking camp bosses and Masterful Men of Sansom's account, whose job it was to keep a supervisory eye on the other drinkers of their mob (Sansom 1980: 65). Another balancing comment is that some of the women were theoretically encumbered by young children whose care became haphazard during drinking sessions. Evidence of the wanderings of such hungry children was provided by a white foster mother who lived in Alice Springs in the 1980s and who adopted some of the children and fed many others.

I also do not want to give the impression that the search for new sexual partners in town was a predominantly female phenomenon. I gained enough reliable information to indicate that, for a number of Warlpiri men, towns were associated with the possibility of extramarital affairs. One Warlpiri man I met in Darwin was explicit about this. Warlpiri women shared information about such male exploits although they were usually circumspect about not causing unnecessary antagonism by keeping such information from the relevant Warlpiri wife back on the settlement. Some Warlpiri women reasoned that a few Warlpiri men who had bad reputations as wife-bashers were forced to travel further afield to find sexual partners because no Warlpiri woman would have them.

Some of the inter-racial couples in Alice Springs who came together in the 1980s remained there but others moved on following the kin networks of their white partners to Port Augusta and Adelaide. Similar patterns of movement occurred in the few instances of Warlpiri women's relationships with Aboriginal men from eastern Australia. I only gradually learned to make this distinction when I actually interviewed these women since many of the other Warlpiri people I spoke to referred to the men, a little carelessly, as white men.

The couple that moved to Adelaide had been living in Alice Springs for a number of years and had two children together. As in most cases, the seemingly simple fact of their relocation was attended by all sorts of reasons and interpretations. The white partner had grown up in Adelaide and, although his Aboriginal art dealing business was based in Alice Springs, his parents in Adelaide were getting older. He wanted to spend some time with them and allow them to get to know their grandchildren (his children). There were concerns about raising children in Alice Springs because it was a place of manifold distractions and bad role models in terms of the drinkers. Personal tragedies had also tainted the place with sadness. One of their close Warlpiri friends had died mysteriously on a remote road with two of his children. It left them feeling bereft and eager to make a new start in Adelaide. The whole family began to look forward to the move with some excitement. The couple's commitment to living in Adelaide became foundational for the expansion of Warlpiri diaspora in the northern suburbs of Adelaide.

Other relationships with underclass white men did not necessarily lead to this kind of geographic relocation and to the possibility of some sort of distancing from settlement culture. Instead, alcoholic white men, whose ties to their own relations had broken down, were incorporated into the more tolerant and inclusive Warlpiri kinship networks in town camps, unofficial drinking camps and drinking households in cities. Even in these relationships there was a wide variety of circumstances. Some Warlpiri women set their sights on a drinking and sexual adventure and had the strength of character and physical robustness to carry it through. These relationships, centred on drinking alcohol, tended to be announced with an aggressive possessiveness on the part of the male partner, to which the Warlpiri woman would acquiesce (sometimes very uncharacteristically) if they wished to pursue the relationship. The course of the relationships tended to be characterised by fairly intense jealousy, violence and the rough physical conditions of their sometimes makeshift accommodation. The assertiveness of these women sometimes came as a surprise to the white partners, one of whom referred sarcastically to his Warlpiri ex-partner as 'the Prime Minister'. Often the Warlpiri women involved were more educated than their white partners and more socially adept at dealing with the welfare and housing authorities which they relied upon. It sometimes seemed that the Warlpiri women were toying with their partners, easily outmanoeuvring them, feigning emotional engagement and enjoying the inversion of the gender relations they had experienced on the home settlement where the idea of male superiority was well entrenched.

Semi-professional Careers as Vectors of Indigenous Diaspora

Thus far I have emphasised addictions, life crises, education and inter-racial marriage as vectors of the Warlpiri diaspora. Now I wish to turn to semi-professional and professional careers that take Warlpiri people to diaspora locations. These include the professional Australian Rules football players, semi-professional musicians and artists and what might be called cultural entrepreneurs. During the research period there were three professional football players in Brisbane/Gold Coast teams and one high-profile player, Liam Jurrah, playing for Melbourne (Mackinnon 2010). In the same period, there were three Warlpiri bands whose typical orbits included Battle of the Sounds competitions at sports weekends on remote settlements, the occasional gig in Alice Springs or interstate tour and, for some, recording contracts with the Central Australian Aboriginal Media Association (CAAMA) (Ottosson 2016). A select few, but currently no Warlpiri, became known nationally and graduated to fully professional careers in music, although none of them moved permanently to the city.

A select few renowned Warlpiri artists had individual exhibitions in State capital cities and became the object of interest for private gallery owners who would arrange exhibitions or residencies and who developed a close personal relationship with a particular artist that would enable the occasional visit to the city (see, for example, the cases of Dorothy Napangardi and Judy Watson: Watson et al. 1996; Watson and Martin-Chew 2009; Museum of Contemporary Art 2003; Nicholls 2003). Closer to home, in Alice Springs, the visits of some Warlpiri people were financed by shady art dealers who would lock the artists in their workshops until they had completed the paintings. Of course, there was also some mutuality here since the artists would be temporarily shielded from the demands of their kin and hidden away from random acts of drunken violence. Moreover, the renewed worldwide interest in Western Desert dot style painting, spearheaded by the acceptance of selected masterworks as fine art, encouraged the development of other less elite markets. These other markets allowed a much broader group of Aboriginal artists, beyond the few internationally renowned ones, to financially support their travel and to provide a positive means of interacting with strangers and institutions they encountered in the diaspora.[15] Despite the ubiquity of artistic endeavour in the diaspora, only a few raised it as the major reason for their permanent relocation. Another documented example of how artistic endeavour enabled migration is Lorna Fencer's relocation from Lajamanu to Katherine for some years (Nicholls 2011; West 2011). In her case, and in the case of a Warlpiri man from Willowra living in Albury in New South Wales, the support of community Aboriginal art centres was important. The most interesting group, however, comprised several Warlpiri women in Adelaide who had the same private art wholesaler. Their remarkable story will be told in more detail in Chapter 4. The leader of this group was a Warlpiri woman from the remote Warlpiri/Anmatjerr settlement of Mount Allan (also known as Yuelumu or Wariyiwariyi). She had initially taken up her semi-professional life as an artist in Alice Springs attached to an Aboriginal art gallery there, before eventually moving to Adelaide with a white boyfriend. In Adelaide, she met up with her old Mount Allan art adviser who introduced her to his friend who eventually became her art wholesaler and the economic foundation of her life in Adelaide.

The existing approaches to the engagement of remote Aboriginal settlements with Australian rules football tend to focus on the re-enactment of traditional roles, sex segregation (McCoy 2008b: 145–66) or re-masculinisation of marginalised indigenous men (cf. Diaz 2002 for a remasculisation approach to football on the Pacific island of Guam). The intercultural perspective highlights what these approaches underplay: football as a means of engagement with the broader society. Suffice it to say that an interest in Australian Rules Football, including following the national competition (the Australian Football League), is a major feature of contemporary Warlpiri culture on the settlements. It is the single most important weekly activity for many young Warlpiri men. The game takes centre stage at the proliferating weekend sports carnivals on numerous remote settlements and the movement of players and fans following the competition is the proximate cause of much of the regional mobility of Warlpiri people.[16] As outlined above, the long-standing involvement of a Lajamanu team in the Darwin AFL competition is implicated in the history of the Warlpiri diaspora in Darwin and Katherine. Some of the early Warlpiri migrants to Darwin played for the Wanderers Football Club which thus provided a point of contact with a non-kin social network. In Alice Springs, the 2000 reorganisation of the AFL competition, which abandoned the previous country competition among Aboriginal settlement teams in favour of a single integrated competition centred on Alice Springs, was seen by local residents at Yuendumu to have a significant impact on the drift to Alice Springs. Certainly, welfare NGOs in Alice Springs were aware that Warlpiri households in Alice Springs came under additional pressure from visitors each time the Yuendumu team played there since some of the travelling supporters would stay on in town after the game. The games became a gathering point and opportunity for solidarity between the visiting Warlpiri and the Warlpiri diaspora in Alice Springs. Moreover, the first grade AFL stars became emblems of Warlpiri pride, like Liam Jurrah, before his fall from grace.

The Involuntary Diaspora

While the focus of this book is on those Warlpiri people who have voluntarily left the home settlements, the overview of the Warlpiri diaspora would not be complete without mention of Warlpiri students in boarding schools; prisoners in Alice Springs and Darwin jails; the inmates of alcohol rehabilitation institutions; the dialysis patients; those in aged care facilities; and Warlpiri children (some disabled) in foster care. Exact numbers were difficult to discover and variable over time. However, the approximate scale of the involuntary diaspora is indicated by the following figures collected during the course of the research: 12 Warlpiri people in Darwin jail (October 2012); 31 in Alice Springs jail (March 2012); 10 dialysis patients in Katherine and Darwin, 41 in Alice Springs (January 2015); 5 in alcohol rehabilitation (various locations, 2012); 12 in aged care in Katherine (2013), 11 in Alice Springs (2014); 12 children in white foster care (various locations, 2013); and 10 children at secondary boarding schools in Darwin, Alice Springs, Townsville and Melbourne (for varying periods of time, 2009–2014).[17] The sum of these figures represents about 4 per cent of the total Warlpiri population. The involuntary diaspora occasionally overlaps with the voluntary diaspora and the two become integrated to varying degrees at different nodes. Thus, some dialysis patients live with kin in the town camps of Darwin and Alice Springs. Prisoners in the jail become the focus of visits by Baptist and Pentecostal Warlpiri women in the town camps. Some town dwellers are confirmed in their choice of residence by the nearby presence of an elderly parent in a nursing home. Proximity and visiting allows them to fulfil their duties to look after an elderly parent. As will be seen in the next chapter, the difference of orientations of the involuntary diaspora back to the home settlement and the voluntary diaspora towards their life in town sometimes results in an awkward proximity for the two groups.

Warlpiri Men's Pathways to the Diaspora

While the Warlpiri diaspora I encountered in 2009–2013 was largely feminised, I also encountered a few Warlpiri men and heard the stories of others who had been away from the settlements for a long time. As always, the committed drinkers were difficult to get to know. At Bagot in Darwin I interviewed some long-term Warlpiri female residents on verandahs while their brothers, whom I never saw, slept off the previous night's drinking inside. In suburban Adelaide, I encountered one long-term resident a few times but never sober. Improbably, he was allowed to continue his occupation of welfare housing which had become a port of call in the travelling

Warlpiri drinkers' network. Another less committed drinker had started a seven-year trip to Western Australia as a young man at Yuendumu when he accepted a lift to Hall's Creek with friends who had stolen a car. Relying entirely upon friendships, which he formed with Aboriginal people along the way and while incarcerated in Broome jail, his journey eventually took him to Roebourne, 1,500 km west of Yuendumu across the Great Sandy Desert. This last leg of his journey was again accomplished via an impromptu offer of travel from recently befriended Aboriginal drinkers. He stayed for some years in Roebourne and became integrated into the local Aboriginal community through a long-term relationship with one of his female drinking partners. His integration into the Aboriginal people of Roebourne prompted an unusual serial migration when he returned to Willowra briefly with his new Yindjibarndi 'brother-in-law' who he introduced to his sister. She eventually returned to Roebourne with this man and raised two children there with him before his untimely demise in a motor vehicle accident. She returned to Willowra and explained that her children still spoke Yindjibarndi in their house, and Warlpiri outside. While the small Warlpiri outpost at Roebourne lasted, it was also buttressed by the presence of another Warlpiri 'sister' who was coincidentally working nearby with her white partner on the pearl farms of Dampier Peninsula. Both accounts of Yindjibarndi–Warlpiri marriage provide a variation on the stories of some of the Warlpiri women long-grassers of Darwin. All such stories have a common theme, namely the norms of behaviour regarding traditionally acquired spouses being brought to bear upon relationships formed via non-traditional procedures in circumstances deliberately sought out as an escape from the constraints of tradition (cf. Collmann 1988: 121–22 on the distinction between 'firestick', 'kangaroo' and 'proper' marriage).

Other Warlpiri men I met in Katherine had also married local non-Warlpiri Aboriginal women and had been accepted into their families. They tended to contrast the friendliness and relative peace of their new circumstances with the incessant family feuds, fighting over royalties, and sorcery on the Warlpiri settlements. In relation to sorcery, one long-term Warlpiri resident of Katherine assured me with some relief that 'they don't do that sort of thing around here'. Another explained his positive attitude to Katherine in these terms:

> It looks nice and beautiful here. I got used to it. I found a new wife here 7 years ago. She's from Barunga area. I don't think about going back to Yuendumu because I heard of all the fighting and trouble with my kids. My kids fighting and drinking. Kids expecting me to go back and get involved. I heard about it and decided not to go back. I exercise my free choice. I don't get homesick. I

got used to this place. They got to know me and they look after me. I stay at my mother-in-law's house.

One Warlpiri man, 'Abraham', who spent the last decade of his life in a Queensland coastal town, had a story which represented the gender inverse of the inter-racial marriages already mentioned. From a relatively young age at Yuendumu, he had been interested in exploring the broader society and as an adult had become interested in joining the police force or the state emergency services. Having been rejected by the Northern Territory police force, he moved to Broome where the Western Australian authorities were eager to employ him. There he met an older white woman who was already separated and had young children. She eventually became his partner and they returned to Yuendumu for some years. At Yuendumu her financial activities caused some consternation and, following a brief stint for both of them in Darwin jail for fraud, they moved to a Queensland coastal town. Some of his Warlpiri relations eventually joined them there and became the object of anxious concern by relations back on the settlement; this story is developed in more detail in Chapter 5 (Ambivalent Homecomings).

A few Warlpiri men told me they had left the Northern Territory specifically to change their lives. I had known one of them in the 1980s as a regular client of the Aboriginal legal aid service. He spent much of his early adult life in a familiar pattern of leaving Yuendumu to go to Alice Springs to drink with his Warlpiri age-mates and there he would inevitably become involved in serious fighting and car theft. He spent much of that period of his life in jail. His journey to the west, through Fitzroy Crossing thence to Broome and Port Hedland, was not the impromptu seven-year drinking adventure of the young Warlpiri man already mentioned. Rather, it was a deliberate effort to extract himself from his circle of drinking friends and in that he was successful because he encountered few Warlpiri people and some years later he returned to Yuendumu having quit drinking.

The mother of another adult man was the original Warlpiri pioneer of the Warlpiri outpost at Murray Bridge and when he visited her there he liked it and saw it as an opportunity to radically reorient his life. He was baptised into the Mormon Church there and stayed with them for a few years, even participating in their missionary work ('walking around with a tie'). When the Murray Bridge outpost collapsed, he moved to suburban Adelaide where he was drawn 'like a magnet' to a small Pentecostal church.

Also in Adelaide at the time was a Warlpiri couple who had left the Northern Territory with a plan to construct a different life for themselves. The proximate causes of their departure were the husband's health crisis (hospitalisation in Darwin due to excessive drinking) and the closing of the net involving their drinking friends and the welfare authorities: the drinking friends were intent on continuing their drinking lifestyle with the couple, and the welfare authorities were seeking to remove a young boy from the couple's care. The police were also determined to enforce the restraining orders the couple had against each other for domestic violence. In Adelaide, they had both given up drinking, maintained a neat public housing flat, and were dealing with some of the difficulties their young fostered boy was having at the local school. They were socially very close to another Warlpiri household in the neighbouring suburb. They managed to sustain this life for a number of years before one of them returned to the drinking life in Alice Springs.

I do not wish to imply that the vast expansion of the geographical canvas on which the male projects of diaspora took place (the drinking camp network, the individual adventures and projects of redemptive exile) was an exclusively male phenomenon. Some exceptional Warlpiri women also projected this sense of expanded geographical possibilities through their own personal history in various distant diaspora locations and in their intrepid travelling. One woman in particular explained to me that Adelaide was a strategically acceptable location for her from whence she could travel north to Alice Springs and Yuendumu or east towards Wagga Wagga in New South Wales and then to Bundaberg in northern Queensland. She had spent long and happy periods of her life with in-laws in both of these places and was still confident of their welcome.

Impenetrable Reasons

Particularly difficult to investigate were the cases of two Warlpiri men, both falling into the category of bi-cultural adepts, who had in the past occupied responsible jobs, including that of police aide at Yuendumu, over a long period of time. Both eventually took up similar jobs in the settlements of other Aboriginal language groups in the region. The jobs provided plausible rationales for their relocation as did the fact that in one case the man's new spouse came from the other settlement. Having known the family of the two men for a long time, however, I had become aware of some other undercurrents but I was never sure I discovered the deepest motivating factors. I was aware, for example, of rarely articulated feelings of personal rejection and of frustration at the monopolisation of key decision-making positions by bi-cultural adepts from other powerful families at Yuendumu. It seemed to me that their relocation had a number of potential advantages for them, in addition to the prized jobs. They would not be confronted every day with the same density of relationships and the accumulated history of interactions that existed for them at Yuendumu. The relatively lower relational density in their new locations would make the performance of their jobs a little easier because of fewer kin demands. Finally, they would be removing themselves from the constituency of the powerbrokers at Yuendumu. This meant that they would no longer have to deal with the men who were their competitors or enemies at Yuendumu. Their previous presence at Yuendumu could no longer be misinterpreted as some sort of endorsement of how the powerbrokers were running Yuendumu. The departure of the two men was noted, particularly by the few long-term white residents and NGO executives. Just as the ranks of the hard-working and sober bi-cultural adepts were thinning, there were many critical jobs to be filled, as well as positions on the boards of an increasing number of Aboriginal service NGOs, and ongoing community and political issues to respond to.

One of the remaining bi-cultural adepts reflected on such departures as presaging a greater workload for her and a weakening of 'the community'. For those invested in the concept of the settlements as a community with a history, pride and reputation to protect, such departures, and even more so other departures which had no plausible rationale, were an unsettling development.

The Balance of Family, Visiting and Serial Migration

Once established, the distant locations of the Warlpiri diaspora became another node in the various kinship networks of the Warlpiri settlements. Every Warlpiri genealogy I transcribed during the research project revealed a unique spread of locations which invariably included some quite distant ones. For example, the Warlpiri family I know best had members permanently established at the Warlpiri settlements of Yuendumu, Lajamanu and Nyirrpi; the non-Warlpiri Aboriginal Northern Territory settlements of Kintore (Walangurru) and Papunya; the Northern Territory towns of Alice Springs and Darwin; the remote South Australian Aboriginal settlement of Ernabella; and the parklands in the city of Adelaide. Another Warlpiri family was well established in Yuendumu, Lajamanu, Alice Springs, Adelaide, Katherine, Darwin, the West Australian Aboriginal settlement of Balgo, and the West Australian towns of Fitzroy Crossing and Broome.

The existence of close kin with houses in the distant locations precipitated visits from their relations from the settlements in what has been called in Australia 'beats' (Beckett 1965) or 'circular mobility' (Taylor 1988, 1989) and, in the transnational literature, 'global pathways'. A widespread love of travel among the Warlpiri and the adventure of travelling to unfamiliar places combined with other ingrained practices of caring for kin and continually testing relationships through demand sharing. For some young men the possibility of an impromptu road trip adventure was irresistible. One young man, when released from Alice Springs jail, stole his girlfriend's car and travelled 1,500 km to Adelaide where he arrived unannounced at his aunt's house. The threat posed by such impromptu long-distance Warlpiri visitors to the viability of the Warlpiri outposts will be outlined in the next two chapters.

Visiting occasionally led to more permanent serial migration, sometimes unexpectedly, as in the case of the grandmother already mentioned who went to Adelaide following concerns about her holidaying daughter and her daughter's young children. When she took charge of the grandchildren she decided on reflection that Adelaide would be a better place for their upbringing. The gradual build-up of a Warlpiri diaspora location is most clearly illustrated by the historic case of Murray Bridge (circa 1995–2005) and that story brings together many of the factors already mentioned. It started with 'April' Napanangka (now deceased), a relatively well-educated Warlpiri woman in her late thirties, attending a course in Darwin where she met and formed a relationship with a white abattoir worker who was from Murray Bridge, a small South Australian town (population 19,000) 75 km south-east of Adelaide. 'April', whose own children were grown up and living back at Yuendumu, went to live with her new boyfriend when he returned to Murray Bridge. Initially she was the only Warlpiri person in the town but she was soon joined by an old school friend from Yuendumu who also found a white partner in the town. Later 'April' convinced her sister at Yuendumu to come to Murray Bridge 'to keep her company'. The next to arrive was an aunt who took to drinking. Eventually, 'April's' mother and 'April's' son and his family also moved there. The son has already been mentioned as the man who wanted to change his life and became involved with the Mormons at Murray Bridge. Back at Yuendumu, 'April's' sister, who had been an assistant teacher at the school for thirty years, began to feel isolated from her close family and also decided to move to Murray Bridge with her son, his wife and family, and her mother. She told me, 'I wanted to get away from Yuendumu and to be with my sister. I wanted to see a different environment. The main thing I was worried about my kids' education'. When they arrived the total Warlpiri population was about 50 which included around 20 school-age children (including a young Liam Jurrah). Quite fortuitously, the principal of the local primary school had worked at Yirara College in Alice Springs and knew them. He offered 'April's' sister a job teaching the influx of Warlpiri children. At its height, there were six Warlpiri households in the town. The houses were organised through the Aboriginal liaison officer at Housing South Australia, the State public housing authority, and a sympathetic local Aboriginal social worker at

Centrelink, the Commonwealth government welfare payments shop front. The Warlpiri people would regularly gather in the park to keep each other company and their households became the destination for visitors from as far away as Hermannsburg, Papunya and Yuendumu in the Northern Territory and other Warlpiri people who happened to be nearby. One of the nearby Warlpiri people included a mute Warlpiri woman who had married a white farmer not far from Murray Bridge and a Warlpiri woman married to a New South Wales Aboriginal man living and working in Adelaide. An anthropologist en route to Yuendumu made a brief visit to Murray Bridge but found the white partners 'a bit scary'.[18] A Warlpiri female relation from Yuendumu made a respite visit to Murray Bridge following the death of her daughter. She too felt uneasy about the white partners whom she felt were 'staring at her' too much in her emotionally fragile condition. She also wondered why the Warlpiri women handed over the money made from the sale of their paintings to them so readily.

During the course of my research there was only one Warlpiri person at Murray Bridge and I heard various stories of their declining presence. 'April's' sister was one of the first key figures to return to Yuendumu when one of her elderly 'mothers' requested her return to care for her, and she also received a request from the principal of Yuendumu school to return to work there. Eventually 'April's' partner, who was a heavy drinker, died and she returned to Warlpiri Camp in Alice Springs and later lived in an Aboriginal hostel when she became a dialysis patient. Not everyone returned to the Northern Territory. Some transferred their public tenancies to Adelaide and remained there. Others who had experienced life in Murray Bridge later returned to the northern suburbs of Adelaide for extended periods of time.

The shifting geographical balance of supportive kin sometimes combined with the changing emotional valence of the settlement for the women. Some deaths made the settlement a sad place to be. The death of husbands has already been mentioned, but the death of parents, siblings and grandparents figure prominently in many of the stories as providing further impetus to leave. In one instance, the beloved grandparents had raised the woman concerned after her own father had died when she was ten years old. They were her main link to the traditions of the past and of a time before the appearance of flagons of wine and the inevitable fighting on the settlement and, she ventured, before swearing became so pervasive. Their death left her particularly bereft and their prominence in her life led her to say things like 'there is nothing left there for me now' despite many close relations remaining on the settlement.

Conclusion: Stages in the Development of Diaspora Locations

The stories in this chapter allow us to see some of the characteristics of chain migration that may be peculiar to indigenous diaspora and are largely unheralded by existing ethnography. There appears to be a three-stage process of the historical expansion of the Warlpiri diaspora: 1) exceptional foundational individuals; 2) chain migration; and 3) critical mass. The male examples of early foundational individuals discussed in this chapter travelled long distances on pathways that had been established by the practical exigencies of service delivery to the remote settlements. Their initial travel had been underwritten by larger government projects: the Aboriginal corps in the Second World War in one case and in another, the circulation of construction gangs from the training settlements of the assimilationist era. Although they initially had jobs in the towns, they also secured their residency and social life there through marriage to local Aboriginal women. For both partners to the marriages, this involved an extension beyond traditional marriage arrangements. Traditions tended towards language group endogamy and they were regionally variable as to categories of marriageable kin and the proper procedures to follow for arranging the marriage. Thus, the marriages between distant language groups involved an adjustment and extension of traditional kinship networks even though the two systems had many common features. They were not as much a leap into the unknown as marriages to white people and the relatively unfamiliar ideas of romantic love and companionate marriage. Significantly, from the point of view of diaspora, the long-term marriages were a step towards permanent relocation and away from temporary exile.

As individual Warlpiri people married into another Aboriginal language group, the early pioneers of the diaspora may have simply been absorbed into the other language groups, leaving little trace of their Warlpiri antecedents. But as we have seen in this chapter, this did not always happen. There were a multitude of reasons why geographically stretched kinship ties were activated in chain migration. Even those Warlpiri people who did not originally travel to towns specifically to reunite with their Warlpiri kin there were drawn together by traditional obligations of generosity towards kin and the fact that there were few other points of contact in a town of strangers. Despite their quite different local histories, the town camps of Darwin, Katherine and Alice Springs, segregated as they were from the white population, also encouraged this initial congregation of kin. In this way a critical mass of Warlpiri people developed in town locations.

In using the term 'critical mass' I am gesturing towards some sort of numerical preconditions for the formation of an identifiable Warlpiri group in the new location, the requirement of some minimal scale for the processes of mutual support to enable survival in a sometimes dangerous or uncertain environment. The adventures of the Warlpiri sorority of Alice Springs may not have come to pass without a critical mass of mutual support. Then there are questions of minimal requirements for the assertion and recognition of group identity and for the reproduction of a Warlpiri cultural identity, albeit in very different circumstances from the home settlements. In Katherine, Warlpiri local group identity and recognition became apparent in the defensive reaction of the Warlpiri migrants to the widespread antagonism of the local Aboriginal people. The transients' camp became known as the Warlpiri camp. Speaking the Warlpiri language and ensuring that it is reproduced requires a group, and, in the case of the Murray Bridge outpost, the fortuitous enlisting of sympathetic school personnel. And, as we shall see in the next chapter, performing Warlpiri mortuary rituals requires more than a few knowledgeable participants. Having outlined in this chapter the various pathways to diaspora locations and the heterogeneous Warlpiri personnel it delivers to them, I will now focus on particular projects that seemed to sustain these diaspora locations and on the dynamics of the interaction among the Warlpiri and their new co-residents.

Notes

1. Some material in this chapter was previously published in Burke, 2015, 'Rupture and Readjustment of Tradition: Agency and Autonomy in the Feminised Warlpiri Diaspora in Australia', in *Strings of Connectedness: Essays in Honour of Ian Keen*, edited by P. Toner, pp.215–34. Canberra: ANU E Press. Reprinted with permission.
2. There is no easily accessible account of the history of Aboriginal people in Darwin. I have derived this thumbnail sketch of Bagot from a variety of sources (Woodward 1974; Bauman 2006; Day 1994, 2008, 2012; Wells 1995; Cummings 1990). Bagot has since been through as many incarnations as there have been policy regimes. As elsewhere in the Northern Territory, the legislative liberalisation of 1964 saw the beginning of the end of enforced, sober tutelage. The 1970s were characterised by the reassertion of Larrakia traditional ownership and their successful land rights campaign for title to a living area of their own, Kululuk, to the north-west of Bagot. This may have had the effect of further enhancing Bagot's reputation as an accessible point of contact for non-local Aboriginal people planning to travel to Darwin. Since the 1970s the Larrakia have consolidated their position under the corporate masthead, 'Larrakia Nation', and although their bid for recognition under the Native Title Act 1993 was unsuccessful (Scambary 2007), they have taken on numerous state-like welfare functions (Fisher 2013). Both Kululuk and Bagot have now been rather engulfed by the expansion of the city of Darwin (population 136,000). Bagot, now referred to as 'Bagot Community' and reduced to 23 hectares, has become a conspicuous enclave that over the years has been derided as an anachronistic eyesore and has been subject to calls for its redevelopment. In the

Intervention period, post-2007, Bagot was classified with the town camps, presumably because of its concentration of Aboriginal public housing, its enclave appearance and the ongoing concerns about unemployment, alcohol abuse, violence and the dilapidated housing stock. The projected transformation of Bagot into a 'normal suburb' proceeds in piecemeal fashion.

3. Escape from alcohol restrictions and other irksome monitoring by white authorities on missions and cattle stations seems to have been a central motivator of the town campers described by Sansom, the Wallaby Cross mob of the outskirts of Darwin in the 1970s (Sansom 1980). In retrospect, the project of the Wallaby Cross mob seems to have been a unique and overt attempt to combine aspects of hinterland traditionalism (the cache of sacred objects, the holding of initiation ceremonies, practices for looking after drinkers) with the drinking life in Darwin (Sansom 2010). In this respect, the Wallaby Cross mob were distinguishable from the excessive and uncontrolled drinkers who had no pretensions of pursuing traditionalism alongside of their drinking life (1980: 69–70). Hinterland alcohol restrictions also play a part in Merlan's account of the drinking scene in Katherine in the 1970s and 1980s, but more as an exploration of the continuation of an Aboriginal social order that has a spatial basis so that Aboriginal drinking and attempts to respond to it have a unique spatial inflection, for example, in declaring certain locations as 'dry areas' and attempts to give up drinking as 'moving away' from grog (Merlan 1998: 196–207).

4. The flagon of the time was a large (2 litre/4 pint) glass container of liquor, typically sweet fortified wine. The Warlpiri hand sign for drinking liquor relates to this era when the neck of the flagon was grasped with one hand and raised directly to the mouth.

5. Mary Laughren, personal communication, 2013. Mary Laughren is a linguist specialising in the Warlpiri language. She lived and worked at Yuendumu between 1975 and 1988 and has continued her involvement with the Warlpiri language and people since then. These comments rely on her direct observations.

6. Gurindji is the name of the Aboriginal language group spoken immediately to the north of traditional Warlpiri country. The Warlpiri settlement of Lajamanu is located on traditional Gurindji country and there has been considerable intermarriage between the Gurindji and the Warlpiri. Thus the name of the drinking shed evokes some sort of transplanted familiarity.

7. To be clear, a close reading of *The Camp at Wallaby Cross* does suggest that the camp leaders at Wallaby Cross were relatively exceptional leaders with good contacts in the broader community who could help them. Sansom is explicit about the diverse range of circumstances of other mobs who did not necessarily have such skilful or well-connected leaders or who had chosen unpromising camping sites (1980: 185–91). Moreover, there were seemingly numerous 'silly drunks' who had placed themselves outside the protection of any mob and had the scars of victimhood to show for it (1980: 69).

8. Coulehan's study of Yolngu women in Darwin includes a similar example of a mature woman, Darrpa (pseudonym), leaving a remote settlement to join her son and his family who had established themselves in Darwin, where the son had a steady job. The relative peacefulness of her life in Darwin, contrasting with the pressures on her in the settlement to help her large extended family, settle intra-family disputes and look after many grandchildren, made her return trips to the settlement less and less attractive (Coulehan 1995: 139–40).

9. Even earlier, in the 1960s, some young Warlpiri men, such as Harry Jakamarra Nelson from Yuendumu and Maurice Jupurrula Luther from Lajamanu, achieved educational success and went on to play prominent leadership and intermediary roles in settlement

administration and broader politics. They were the first two Warlpiri men to be mentioned in the *Specials Schools Bulletin*, a publication of the Education Section of the Welfare Branch in the 1960s and 1970s. In 1964 they both received certificates for attending a residential course as part of their training to be assistant teachers (*Special Schools Bulletin* 1[1]: 9) and in 1968 a photo of Harry Nelson teaching in Yuendumu school appeared on the front cover of the publication (*Special Schools Bulletin* 5[3]).

10. As to the limits of the actual adoption of imposed settlement routines, see Rowse (1998: 147–83). The name Bess Nungarrayi Price is not a pseudonym since the information in this paragraph comes from a publicly available newspaper profile in which she voluntarily participated.
11. For an account of Kormilda College in the early 1970s, see Sommerlad (1976).
12. Peggy Anderson and James Gaykamangu have approved the use of their real names in this book. James has given an account of their unusual courtship in his recently published autobiography (Gaykamangu 2014: 83–88).
13. During the period 1869–1985 the Canadian Indian Act provided that an Indian woman who married a male who did not have Indian status (registered as an Indian under the Indian Act) ceased to be an Indian and lost all rights related to status as an Indian, as did her children. The long history of these provisions is recounted by Kathleen Jamieson (1978). Janet Silman has published the personal accounts of some of the women involved in the ultimately successful political campaign in the 1970s and 1980s for the removal of the provisions (1987). However, it seems that the complex drafting of the provisions to reinstate the so-called 'non-status Indians' has left open the possibility of the loss of status for some categories of descendants (for a legal overview, see Napoleon 2001; and for a broad historical overview, see Van Kirk 2002).
14. Smith and Biddle, for example, in their study of Aboriginal migration to Brisbane in 1965, reported that 38 per cent of all Aboriginal migrants had non-Aboriginal partners and that three quarters of such couples consisted of an Aboriginal woman and a white man (1975: 32). Fay Gale's study of Aboriginal migration to Adelaide in 1965, while not stating numbers or sex, referred to the older arrivals of a group of 300 Aboriginal people from the Northern Territory as having married white partners (Gale 1966: 29–32). There is no exact statistical breakdown for the 25 Inupiaq women in Anchorage in 1986 in Fogel-Chance's study but inter-racial relationships again seem to have been significant, with 9 of the 25 moving to the city with a 'Euro-American boyfriend, husband, or parent' (1993: 95).
15. See Myers's *Painting Culture* for an account of the transformation of Western Desert painting into a high art (Myers 2002). Some idea of the high rate of engagement in art production among the Warlpiri and neighbouring language groups can be gleaned from Vivian Johnson's biographical dictionary, which, among other things, includes biographies of two of the Warlpiri matriarchs described in this book (Johnson 1994).
16. This assessment is based on my own intermittent observation and a 2009 personal communication from Dr Georgia Curran, who undertook long-term fieldwork at Yuendumu during 2005–2008. The contemporary significance of Australian Rules Football to Warlpiri people is also well demonstrated in Liam Campbell's film *Aboriginal Rules* (2007, PAW Media).
17. I compiled the jail figures from regular Warlpiri visitors to the jails who were able to name the Warlpiri people they had seen in jail or knew from other sources were there. I consider those figures to be reasonably accurate, if subject to some undercounting because of inevitable limits on their knowledge of distantly related Warlpiri people. The dialysis figures come from a well-placed administrator, Sarah Brown, the CEO

of The Purple House in Alice Springs and are, I think, highly reliable. The Purple House is the name of the headquarters of a central Australian Aboriginal NGO (Western Desert Nganampa Walytja Palyantjaku Tjutaku Aboriginal Corporation) dedicated to supporting dialysis patients in towns and developing dialysis services in remote settlements. The aged care numbers I consider reliable since they were compiled from visitors, locally generated lists and genealogies, but there are gaps for Tennant Creek and Darwin. Thus, I suspect undercounting. The alcohol rehabilitation and fostering figures have been gleaned from my own Warlpiri Diaspora Census via lists generated by long-term local residents and genealogies; therefore, I suspect undercounting. The figures on secondary boarding schools need to be treated with some caution since the length of stay varied remarkably (in one case a day, in another a term, in other cases the full year). The current proliferation of boarding school destinations suggests undercounting in my figures since I was only able to identify a few locations.
18. Yasmine Musharbash, personal communication, 2005.

Chapter 3

MAKING ALICE SPRINGS A WARLPIRI PLACE

Introduction

In this chapter[1] I will be suggesting ways in which Alice Springs has become naturalised to Warlpiri people: through their intermarriage with local Aboriginal people; through their long-term residence; through the holding of mortuary rituals there; through the assertion of their traditionalism over the locals; and through their engagement with Aboriginal-run NGOs. Together with the increasing ease and frequency of visitors from home settlements, these are the ways in which Alice Springs can be considered to be a Warlpiri town, notwithstanding their relatively small numbers and their lack of orthodox traditional claims to the country. Although the Warlpiri women I describe in this chapter all seemed secure in their sense of belonging in Alice Springs, the relatively recent reassertion of the continuing Arrernte traditional ownership of Alice Springs, through a successful native title claim, belatedly intensified the issue of the uncertain Indigenous welcome for the Warlpiri migrants. This issue will be explored via a comparison with the reception of the Warlpiri in other Northern Territory towns and via an account of the recent politicisation of Aboriginal visitors to Alice Springs.

Another additional resonance of the uncertain welcome for indigenous people in the diaspora, particularly the Warlpiri diaspora, is the sheer degree of difference in modes of living between the Warlpiri from the home settlements and the majority of the white and some long-term Aboriginal residents of Alice Springs who had jobs. As we shall see in this chapter, the differences often gave rise to conflict around the expectations of welfare housing authorities that its tenants would lead neat and contained lives and would maintain houses and yards to a high standard. However, such high standards were rarely achieved on the home settlements. In town, the Warlpiri tenants were also expected to limit the number of visitors to their houses and to limit disturbance to neighbours from noisy gatherings. These expectations conflicted with pervasive Warlpiri values of generosity to kin. These difficulties resulted in a familiar pattern for Warlpiri people, including a number of the exemplary Warlpiri women of Alice Springs described in this chapter, moving from temporary residence in town camps to welfare housing in suburban Alice Springs, only to return to the town camps when the suburban tenancies proved too difficult to maintain.[2] Notwithstanding this familiar pattern, quite a few Warlpiri women in Alice Springs, Katherine and Darwin did manage to maintain suburban public housing tenancies, sometimes with the assistance of NGOs specifically funded to support 'vulnerable tenancies'. In the town camps, the relatively low rents and the permissive attitude to the maintenance of the buildings and yards made them more amenable for most would-be migrants from the remote settlements. Each of the nineteen town camps of Alice Springs has its own history and hinterland Aboriginal affiliation, although they could all be described as small, residential villages outside of the predominantly European suburban areas, typically in some semi-secluded location which in the past had been used by Aboriginal visitors to the town from remote settlements as unofficial camping areas. They also had a reputation as sites of vandalism, alcohol abuse and violent crime. As such, they became one of the prime targets for the Australian Government's Intervention in the Northern Territory in 2007 and by the end of the research period their formal administration had been taken over by the Northern Territory Government's public housing authority, Territory Housing, which was pursuing a policy of 'normalisation' (to make them more like suburbs).[3]

The other major difference with transnational diasporas is the relative unimportance of economic imperatives and the labour market. Only a few Warlpiri women in Alice Springs had jobs or economic opportunities via painting, which tended to structure their lives in Alice Springs. Two held important intermediary positions. One was an Aboriginal Liaison Officer in the hospital, invariably a busy crossroads of Warlpiri patients and visitors, and the other was a field officer with the Central Australian Aboriginal Legal Aid Service. Both of these women had married local Aboriginal men and lived in the town camps, although in relatively well-maintained houses.

But the story I wish to tell in this chapter is not primarily about housing or jobs. It is about the particular ways in which a few exceptional middle-aged Warlpiri women have expanded their personal autonomy and social networks in town settings and how group formation both reproduces settlement norms and transforms them as new opportunities that are only available in town are taken up. I will pick up the story of 'Dulcie', mentioned in the previous chapter as one of the Warlpiri women whose move to town coincided with her disentanglement from a Warlpiri husband. She became the exemplar *par excellence* of the exuberant town life; freed from some of the irksome constraints of settlement life, she became the most skilled proponent of experiments in friendship and conjugal relationships with non-Aboriginal people. We shall also meet Warlpiri women who converted to Christianity after colourful and risky early lives and who, in their regained sobriety, became matriarchs in town camp households. I will compare one Baptist women's household in Alice Springs and a similar Pentecostal matriarch's household in Bagot in Darwin. Despite the continuing traditionalism of these town camp matriarchs, they had all opted to continue to live in town rather than return to the settlements where there were also like-minded Christians. Analysing what seemed to keep them in town should provide one of the keys to the Warlpiri experience of diaspora and, to anticipate my conclusion somewhat, a new form of Warlpiri traditionalism which explicitly rejects certain aspects of tradition while embracing others.

The Warlpiri encounter with Alice Springs, as their first experience of a European town, began in the 1930s as the town was a destination for medical treatment for Warlpiri people gathered at the mining camps at The Granites and the police ration station at Tanami (Baume 1933: 110; O'Grady 1977: 93–124). Although Alice Springs was initially small and surrounded by the rich mythological landscape and ceremonial life of the Arrernte, most famously portrayed in Spencer and Gillen's *The Native Tribes of Central Australia* (1899), there was also a sense in which Alice Springs was a European enclave in which traditional laws and etiquette about visiting unfamiliar traditional country were in abeyance. This notion was reinforced by the legal regime of the 1930s which outlawed the presence of Aboriginal people in the town except for work purposes (Rowse 1998: 73–79; Rubuntja, Green and Rowse 2002: 73–94). One of the earliest Warlpiri residents in Alice Springs in the 1950s was a gardener for Olive Pink, an eccentric anthropologist and Aboriginal rights campaigner. He had met her during her early fieldwork among the Warlpiri in the 1930s (Marcus 2001: 293–94). Another important Warlpiri man spent some years with his young family at The Bungalow, a former 'half-caste' institution and later government-run Aboriginal settlement north of Alice Springs, in what appeared to be a sanctuary from family revenge at Yuendumu (Nelson 1998).[4] The war years allowed a much larger group of Warlpiri men who joined the Aboriginal Corps the experience of living near Alice Springs, not to mention other places along the Stuart Highway and Darwin. Even before the war, the engagement of Warlpiri people in mining and stock work enabled a high degree of mobility for some.

It is not surprising then that one of the earliest unofficial camps of Warlpiri people just north of Alice Springs consisted of Warlpiri stockmen who had worked with local Arrernte men in the greater Alice Springs region. Using their unofficial camp as their base where their families lived, they would work intermittently at various pastoral stations in the region. It was this group who became one of the obvious contenders for the upgrading of facilities for town campers that occurred in the 1970s and early 1980s and they became the foundational members of what was to become known as Warlpiri Camp (officially 'Ilperle-Tyathe', the Arrernte name of the site). Across the highway was another camp where Collmann based his 1975 fieldwork (Collmann 1979b, 1979a, 1988).

Another Warlpiri man, who took up one of the new houses at Old Timers Camp, another Alice Springs town camp, had a completely different trajectory. His mobility had arisen out of work skills inculcated in the era of tighter administrative control of the settlements, reimagined as educational and training settlements for assimilation. A construction crew of Warlpiri men had been sent to Alice Springs to assist in the building of the new Aboriginal settlement of Amoongana, 10 kilometres south-east of Alice Springs, to replace The Bungalow in 1961. He stayed on in Alice Springs after the building work had been completed and married a local Arrernte woman. These two were the foundational couple mentioned in the previous chapter. Later, in the 1980s it seems that a number of Warlpiri people had secured positions in town camps through marriage to local Arrernte people.

The 1980s was a propitious time for Warlpiri women to arrive in Alice Springs. I have already mentioned in a previous chapter how the combination of foundational couples and serial migration resulted in a critical mass of Warlpiri people being present in Alice Springs so that the experience of later arrivals was never one of fraught negotiation with strangers, but rather one of seeking out already established kin. I estimated that in 2009–2012 there were about 370 Warlpiri people living more or less permanently in Alice Springs. About 27% of these were the involuntary diaspora (12 in age care facilities, 6 fostered children, 41 in Alice Springs jail, mostly young men, 2 in alcohol rehabilitation and 40 in town for dialysis). Of those not in purpose-built facilities, about three quarters (232) lived in the official town camps; one quarter (77) lived in suburban public housing; and only one in private housing. These figures do not include the large number of Warlpiri people who might be visiting Alice Springs at any one time for a variety of reasons (hospital treatment, court attendance, following the football competition, attending NGO meetings, transiting to other more distant places, drinking binges, and so on). The average number of Warlpiri visitors was difficult to estimate but based on my frequent encounters I would say conservatively that there may have been 30 to 40 Warlpiri visitors in Alice Springs at any one time. Even without allowing for my probable undercounting of the Warlpiri permanently residing in Alice Springs, the numbers I was able to verify represented about 12% of the total Warlpiri population (approximately 3,120) and about 15% of the town camp population of Alice Springs (approximately 1,500). These numbers and pre-existing Warlpiri interrelatedness meant that all Warlpiri people had some relations living in Alice Springs and this had

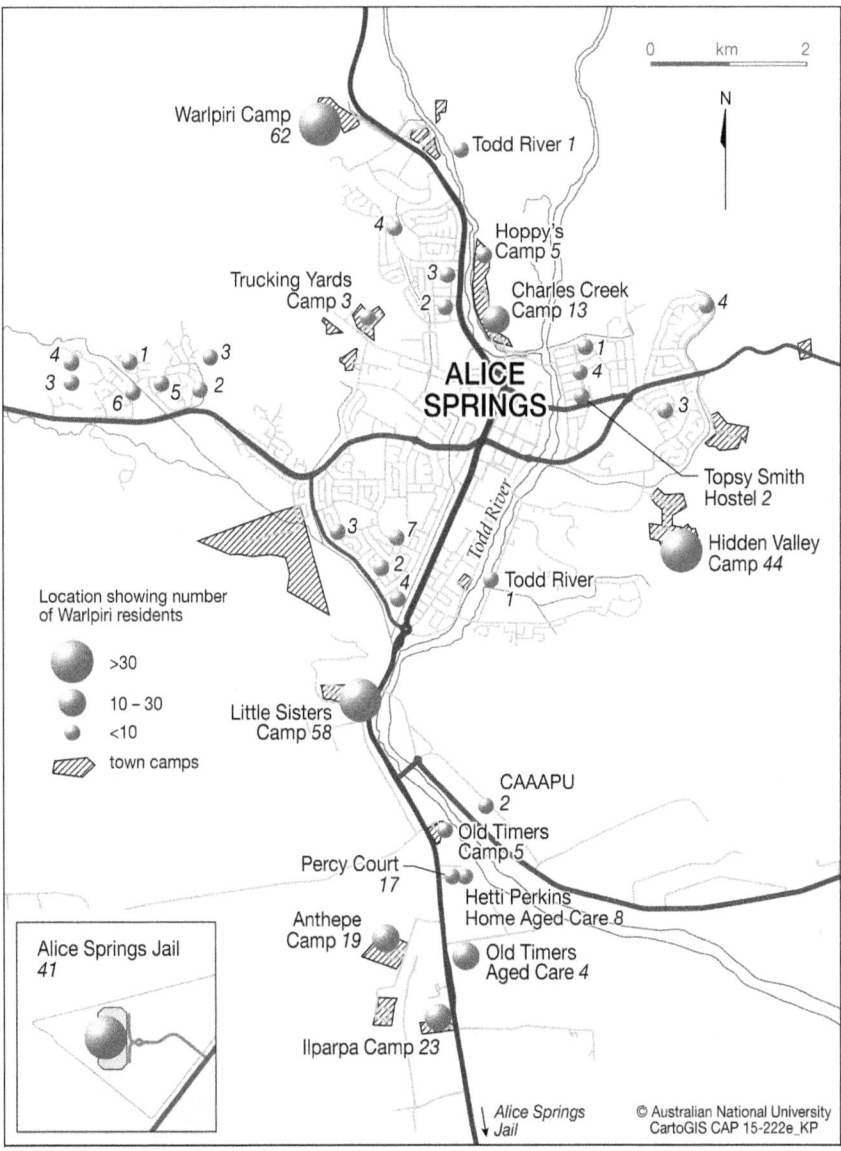

Map 3.1 Distribution of Warlpiri residents in Alice Springs, 2009–2013

profound consequences for the ease of visitation and the gradual naturalisation of Alice Springs as a Warlpiri destination and, increasingly, as a place of Warlpiri cultural assertion.

The other sense in which the 1980s may have been a propitious time to arrive was that Alice Springs was a key site of the flowering of the new government policy of self-determination which had encouraged the proliferation of Aboriginal NGOs: the legal service, the medical service, the town camp organisation, the land council, the adult education centre, the bi-cultural primary school, the arts centre and so on, in other words, the emerging Indigenous sector (see Rowse 2005a, 2002 on the diversity and contradictions of the sector). These NGOs provided opportunities for the Warlpiri migrants to become members, clients, employees and board members. Thus, the Warlpiri women of this chapter, who already had significant contacts with the Baptist Church in Alice Springs, also gathered at an adult literacy course at the Institute for Aboriginal Development and at its arts centre offshoot, Jukurrpa Artists, and Yipirinya School, an Aboriginal controlled primary school pursuing 'two way' education, where the Warlpiri women provided cultural input. It was not just about participation as clients. Their intact traditional language competence, hunting skills and traditional knowledge allowed them additional recognition and status within these organisations. One of the women who took advantage of the multifarious opportunities was my long-term friend and informant, a middle-aged Warlpiri woman 'Dulcie'. When I re-established contact with her in 2009 she had been living in Alice Springs for twenty years. Although she was exceptional in her adventurousness and networking skills and in her commitment to living in Alice Springs as opposed to the remote settlements, she was representative of a number of Warlpiri matriarchs who were pivotal figures in developing Alice Springs as an important node in their own Warlpiri kinship networks. By examining something of her life and relationship with other Warlpiri matriarchs in Alice Springs, we can begin to chart the dynamics of the tension between the reproduction of traditional settlement norms and the transforming opportunities afforded by Alice Springs.

'Dulcie' – *Joie de Vivre* in a Town Camp

Except for her abiding pursuit of fun and her personal adventures, 'Dulcie' (born circa 1955, died 2010) was like a number of the middle-aged Warlpiri women of Alice Springs whose increasing sense of personal autonomy resulted in a geographical demarcation in their life stories: their early constrained lives as young wives and mothers on the home settlements and their relative freedom and exuberance in town after their separation from Warlpiri husbands. After a brief and unsuccessful foray into welfare housing in the suburbs of Alice Springs, 'Dulcie' was able to secure a house in Hidden Valley Town Camp having received the support of an influential Arrernte family in the camp, one of whom had married 'Dulcie's' eldest daughter. 'Dulcie's' son-in-law was an athletic man who was always in work. He brooked no nonsense from drunken people and it was the strength and the security provided by his household that was one of the stable foundations of 'Dulcie's' own adventurousness which expressed itself in various ways. While personal assertion and brinksmanship in personal relationships are common features of Warlpiri women of her age, it seemed to me that 'Dulcie' would delight in testing the risky outer limits of such self-assertion. For example, she would override the sensitivities of grieving relatives and threaten not to attend the funeral of a close relation if those organising it held it on the home settlement where she thought the deceased had been neglected. She made wisecracking refusals to drunken male relations seeking food from her, before relenting. I saw her teasing an already wild and disruptive drunken man about the likely extramarital affairs of his wife. She pulled funny faces at her grandchildren during a break in the sorry business. Moreover, she pointedly refused to ask permission of local Arrernte traditional owners about hunting around Alice Springs and, in private, was dismissive of their traditional prowess.

Another aspect of her adventurousness was the variety of non-Aboriginal people whom she befriended and with whom she maintained relationships: members of the Baptist Church congregation, schoolteachers, legal aid lawyers, welfare workers, art advisers, taxi drivers, policemen and political activists. In fact, she and her ex-husband both excelled at this kind of networking with non-Aboriginal people whom they judged to be well-disposed to having some sort of relationship with them and who would appreciate the conferring of a skin (subsection) name. Through the conferring of skin names, she had created a number of 'sisters' among the white congregation of the Baptist Church and two of these developed a close relationship with her. Sustaining her various friendships required of her a degree of energy and confidence, of which she had plenty, but also a more subtle ability to interpret differing moods and expectations and to calibrate the scale of her requests for assistance to individual circumstances. Associated with this networking ability was her openness to new experiences and travel. She was readily co-opted by political activists to protests against the Intervention and enjoyed travelling to two protest camps in Canberra. With my assistance she would make side trips to sell a painting or raid the bountiful metropolitan op shops (charitable thrift stores) before returning to her official protest duties. These included a meeting with the local member of parliament, Warren Snowdon, where she upbraided him for 'doing the wrong thing'. She delighted in the role and in the telling of the story.

It seemed to me that one of the other foundations of her adventurousness was the tacit support she received from other Warlpiri women in Alice Springs who had a similar life trajectory to her. They all in their own way had become matriarchs of their own households in the town camps and some in the suburbs, with needy kin and drinking relations gathering around them. A number were Warlpiri leaders in the Baptist Church and a number, like 'Dulcie', had moved on to relationships with white men. In this respect, some of them overlapped with the younger Warlpiri sorority I described in the previous chapter. These networks of like-minded women would coalesce on certain occasions into a viable group of mourners at mortuary rituals held in Alice Springs and sometimes for overtly political actions like the Aboriginal women's march against grog. Subsets of them could be found at the Baptist Sunday services dressed in their distinctive brightly coloured bandannas and floral skirts, praying over sick Warlpiri members of the congregation. Mostly, however, the Warlpiri women were engaged with their own immediate family affairs, and their own contacts and art dealers. The network of Warlpiri women was not a straightforward support group. There were significant social divisions among them between the drinkers and the non-drinkers. There was also the usual run of personal feuding, sometimes over the bad behaviour of their children and grandchildren or a perceived slight to themselves. In arenas like traditional hunting, painting and ritual performance, there was a strong competitiveness and assertion of hierarchy (so well described by Dussart [2000: 85–138] in relation to competition between two ritual bosses at Yuendumu). 'Dulcie' was drawn into these divisions and competitiveness on occasion but also seemed to be able to distance herself and assert a kind of leadership through her personal adventurousness and irrepressible fun-seeking in all her diverse engagements.

Where she went too far, especially in the eyes of her close family and her Warlpiri friends in the Baptist Church, was in her last relationship with a much younger white man who also happened to be an alcoholic and schizophrenic. It began during a period in which 'Dulcie' was 'backsliding' and had started to drink. She eventually gave up drinking but he could not, despite some desultory short stays at the local rehabilitation centre. When his money ran out and he began drinking methylated spirits, he would sometimes violently attack 'Dulcie', although later he would not remember it. Thus, her family's tolerance of the relationship, as yet another of her bold eccentricities, was also tinged with anger and alarm. It was in 'Dulcie's' attempt to assert the normality of her relationship with the schizophrenic alcoholic boyfriend that she misjudged the limits of my generosity when she suggested that he would be good company for me on the research trips I had been planning with her.

'Dulcie's' experiments in conjugal relationships with white men and friendships with white people could be seen as a variant expression of a traditional female life-cycle with its increase in personal autonomy with increasing age or widowhood. That progression was common on the remote settlements but there the scope for activating non-kin friendship networks and relationships was quite limited because of the small numbers of non-Aboriginal people and their predominantly short stays. Alice Springs provided 'Dulcie' with opportunities to develop modes of relating to non-kin that had no exact precedent in the kin-saturated world of the settlements of which she was still a putative member, but to which she had added a highly developed bi-cultural skill of befriending. To be clear, it was her exceptional skill at extending her personal networks beyond kin, rather than her relatively limited formal education, that placed her squarely within the class of the Warlpiri bi-cultural adepts.

The skills I am referring to include attentiveness to opportunities for transforming contacts into stronger social ties, the methodical application to retaining contact details, the establishment of common ground and the moderation of requests for assistance to conform to the arc of the relationship and the kind of assistance that the contact was willing to provide in the past. When some anti-Intervention protesters visiting Alice Springs took an interest in her, she invited them all to visit her house in Hidden Valley Camp where, to the amazement of 'Dulcie's' daughters, their large bus (dubbed by them 'the hippy bus') arrived and disgorged 'Dulcie' leading the protestors into her yard where they sat around in a circle listening to her. Despite her limited literacy 'Dulcie' was good at retaining contact details, a considerable feat in the rather chaotic comings and goings of most Warlpiri households. This enabled her, for example, to follow up, a year after the event, an offer of free painting materials made to her by a protester who lived in Canberra. Over the years it enabled her to arrange holidays to see white friends in Melbourne and Canberra. In Alice Springs, she worked hard at retaining the friendships with white welfare workers that had been formed jointly with her Warlpiri ex-husband, also a formidable networker. Some of the white contacts had private swimming pools and allowed 'Dulcie's' grandchildren to use them. With me, I noticed 'Dulcie' was careful to use only as much Warlpiri language as she knew I already understood. She rarely asked me for money. I appreciated her considerable restraint given that, like most Warlpiri grandmothers, 'Dulcie' was chronically short of funds due to the many kin demands upon her that she acceded to. She also knew from past experience that I could be more easily persuaded to provide other services for her such as a ferrying her around in my research vehicle. Merlan also noted in relations of Aboriginal people with non-Aboriginal people the reckoning of a likely fit between the demand and its satisfaction but suggested that these kinds of calibrated demands may have a traditional precedent in avoidance relationships (1997: 109–14). According to this view, 'Dulcie's' moderation in her demands may still be viewed as part of a traditional repertoire rather than a completely new social technology.

'Dulcie's' personal social network was so large and diverse that managing it was sometimes a stretch for her. For the radical activists she had to be the person who 'spoke out', someone who had mastered to some extent the rights discourse of oppositional dissent. For the art advisers she had to demonstrate authentic knowledge of traditional iconography and Dreamings. For the Baptists she had to be the clean-living Christian. For potential white suitors she had to be sexually available and sometimes tolerant of their alcoholism and drug taking. For her close kin there were expectations of all kinds of help, hunting expertise and willingness to assist with mortuary rituals. Mostly the different networks could be dealt with separately and few of the Baptists made it beyond her front door, where they would have found the questionable boyfriend. The collision of these worlds would have been problematic because of the clear Christian expectations (at least as interpreted by the Warlpiri) of non-drinking, non-gambling, personal neatness and non-conflictual relationships.

'Dulcie' was able to draw strength from and rely upon her eldest daughter and son-in-law both of whom had jobs and household routines that included consistent provisioning and their children attending school. Other middle-aged Warlpiri women in Alice Springs had to rely on their own resources. Some of them, drawing upon settlement norms of homosociality and the recognised institution of the widows'/single women's camp (*jilimi*), banded together to create a Warlpiri women's space in one of the town camps of Alice Springs.[5] This *jilimi* also had a strong Christian ethos that could be viewed as the emergence of a hybrid cultural form in Alice Springs.

The Christian *Jilimi* and the Leveraging of Traditional Expertise

'Sarah' was the leader of the *jilimi* household in the southernmost town camp of Alice Springs, the one nearest the airport. She was a friend and admirer of 'Dulcie' whom she once took with her for company on a two-week artists' residency in Tasmania. They both regularly attended the Baptist Church and prayed over the sick, but it was 'Sarah' who had more fully embraced Christianity and the work of the church, and who was officially listed as one of the Church elders. She had been a nominal Baptist when she was growing up and raising a family at Yuendumu, but her reconversion happened much later in life. It was prompted by her involvement in a serious motor vehicle accident in which her young son was severely injured and, according to 'Sarah', only recovered through the power of prayer and divine intervention: 'I been change my life to *wapirra* [Father-God]'. This involved a commitment to Sunday services, attending prayer meetings, participating in organised good works such as visiting the sick in hospital and visiting the prisoners in jail, yearly Bible study camps and the Easter *purlapa* held at different Warlpiri settlements each year. In addition, 'Sarah' had inveigled the Baptist congregation into sharing her love of hunting and it had become an established routine for some of them to take 'Sarah' and the other Warlpiri women on hunting trips to the north-west of Alice Springs after the Sunday morning service.

For 'Sarah' and the other middle-aged Warlpiri women who regularly attended the Baptist services, the Baptist Church represented the most certain welcome for Warlpiri people among all the non-Aboriginal organisations in Alice Springs. The Sunday service attracted about 300 non-Aboriginal Baptists and varying numbers of Warlpiri people (10 to 20), mostly older women. There was a long, shared history and some deep and long-standing personal associations between the white Baptists and the Warlpiri. In one case one of the white members of the congregation had been involved with Warlpiri people in the long-term project of translating the Bible into Warlpiri. Another older white couple who had been married at Yuendumu by the long-term missionary Tom Fleming had over the years fostered many Warlpiri babies. The Warlpiri were familiar with the order of the service, quite similar to settlement services, and there was a generally positive attitude on the part of many white people in the congregation to pursue friendships with the Warlpiri women. Other white people in the congregation had become a little wary of the frequency of family crises among the Warlpiri and the seemingly endless requests for assistance that would inevitably flow from such friendships. The deep and broad links between the Baptist congregation and the Warlpiri meant that the congregation were always up to date with regard to the latest deaths and family vicissitudes, such as the unfolding events of the violent family feuding from 2010 to 2012, and could construct, with 'Sarah's' help, appropriately specific prayers to share with the wider congregation at the Sunday service.

Back at her house in the town camp 'Sarah' was assisted by 'Camilla', her Warlpiri kinswoman and long-term co-resident, who was of a similar age and temperament. They were the core of the household which included aged mothers, one who was becoming quite senile, two women in town for dialysis, young children being fostered by 'Sarah' and 'Camilla', and occasional visiting kin who would sometimes camp outside the fence at a distance. Part aged care facility, part painting workshop, part children's nursery, part dialysis hostel, part bush camp, there was always a line of beds and swags outside the house, after the Warlpiri fashion (Musharbash 2008b: 26–45), and an outside wood fire. On one of the fences a large metal cross had been erected and it was near this cross that weekly Tuesday prayer services were held, curiously led not by the Baptists but by adherents of the Pentecostal Assemblies of God church in which 'Camilla's' brother was intimately involved. Explaining this denominational openness, both 'Sarah' and 'Camilla' would assert 'it's the same God'. One of 'Camilla's' other contributions to the yard, one pregnant with diasporic symbolism, was several seedlings of bean trees (*yininti*) which she had transplanted from her father's traditional country at Mikanji on Mount Doreen Station west of Yuendumu (cf. Boym 2000).

Male relations did sometimes visit the *jilimi* and would occasionally cause consternation through their drinking habits and consequent violence. In the face of my scepticism, 'Sarah' persisted in her assertion of the power of her prayers to prevent the drinkers camping outside their fence becoming violent during the night. Maybe that was just for the benefit of the anthropologist who had the look of a missionary about him, although it is also consistent with Merlan's account of the lack of censoriousness about drinkers and the efforts, of variable effectiveness, to institute micro 'dry' areas around their dwellings (1991: 273, 1998: 203–205). In any event, despite the occasional infraction from a close male relative, the integrity of the household as a women's space seemed to be generally respected. This allowed them to pursue a new kind of Warlpiri project: to live out the greater autonomy bequeathed by their mature age in Alice Springs rather than on the home settlements or some remote outstation. Emblematic of this project was their cultivation of a friendly Indian taxi driver who would take them out to their favourite

Illustration 3.1 The yard of the Christian *jilimi*, Alice Springs (photograph by the author)

hunting grounds just south of Alice Springs. There, they could escape the immediate pressures of the town camp, boil a billy and cook a frozen kangaroo tail in peace, go hunting for goanna and collect bush medicine which was still familiar to them from their own traditional country hundreds of kilometres to the north-west.

In the normal run of things, however, they were very busy interacting with needy kin and other visitors, performing their church duties and coping with the perennial problems of provisioning in the lean week of their fortnightly welfare payments.[6] The volume and range of such visitors gives an indication of the widespread presumption by officials of the accessibility of the town camps, at least in daylight hours, and the various ways their inhabitants were sought out to be the recipients of charity or to be engaged as clients, as a political constituency and as partners in welfare projects. Interruptions to my interviews of the matriarchs in the town camps became such a constant and striking feature of my research that I began to record them.[7] In the space of one and a half hours, an interview with 'Sarah' was interrupted by her having to deal with five visitors. The first was an art dealer from Queensland seeking his artist within the house, followed shortly after by an employee of the old people's programme run by Tangentyere Council (the town camp NGO) delivering meals. Next was a field worker from Central Australian Aboriginal Congress (the Aboriginal medical service NGO) delivering pills to some residents; then a taxi driver responding to a call; and finally, a bus driver from an old people's home in Alice Springs offering them transport to a free barbecue at the nursing home where 'Sarah's' mother was a resident.

The ability of the Warlpiri matriarchs of the Christian *jilimi* to cope with and even thrive in such circumstances had a number of consequences that seemed to me to increase the pressures on them. Warlpiri female visitors to Alice Springs looking for a relatively safe place to camp until their town business was transacted were drawn to the Christian *jilimi*. One senior Warlpiri man had placed his increasingly senile mother with them because he thought she had not been adequately protected from extortionate demand sharing by her grandchildren while at the Old People's Program facility at Yuendumu. With the assistance of a daughter, who was also a long-time resident of the town camp, he eventually moved into the adjacent house where they could monitor the old lady. Another consequence was that 'Sarah' and the other fully functioning members of the *jilimi* became reliable contact points for the town camp NGO, medical and legal services and government welfare agencies, particularly child welfare, who all approached the matriarchs for help. This is the other side of the Warlpiri matriarchs' active networking: they were also actively recruited into other activities and networks that were far more numerous in Alice Springs than on the settlements.

The intensity of being the centre of such networks seemed to enliven 'Sarah' as long as she was physically capable of responding to the multifarious demands. At the peak of her holding this centre together, she seemed to be everywhere: holding her arms aloft in praise during the final hymn at the Sunday Baptist service, leading the hunting trip after the service, praying over the sick at the hospital, visiting the Warlpiri in jail (she and 'Camilla' knew the names of every Warlpiri person confined there), arranging a hunting trip, arranging for one of the congregation to help them gather some firewood, liaising with the town camp NGO to help them clean up the yard, monitoring family communication networks for news of the sick and dying, and arranging visitation, prayers and attending sorry camps in Alice Springs. On occasion, her location near the airport was helpful in her monitoring activities since she was able to recognise the Royal Flying Doctor Service plane landing following an evacuation from one of the Warlpiri settlements. Such strategic positioning is perhaps emblematic of the possibilities of developing an intense network of connections and activities that only Alice Springs as a regional centre could provide. I suspect it was this pivotal position of service that bound 'Sarah' to Alice Springs.

Lest it be thought that the example of 'Sarah' is simply the transposition to Alice Springs of the traditional expectations of grandmothers in the service mode (Merlan 1991), her reputation as someone who would respond to demands for generosity and help was mediated by her Christian beliefs. Those beliefs had the effect of broadening the targets of her help beyond the usual categories of close kin to include all Warlpiri people, other Aboriginal people and, occasionally, white people who they prayed over at Sunday services and at the hospital. Christian beliefs also enabled her to refuse some requests to help. Her most steadfast and pointed refusal was in not becoming involved in the violent altercations of the family feuding when its locus moved to Alice Springs during the combatants' various court appearances. Instead, she and her fellow Warlpiri Christians conducted a prayer service outside the courthouse and advised other women not to engage in violence, citing their non-violent response to their own similar family tragedies. Gender, age and the social capital of 'Sarah's' good works may have facilitated the acceptance of her pacifist position. Other mature Christian Warlpiri men who absented themselves from the fighting were widely criticised for what was seen as their cowardly refusal to defend their close kin from attack, and they came under intense pressure to join in.

The Warlpiri women's prowess in traditional hunting and gathering took on new dimensions in Alice Springs. I have already mentioned the way in which it enabled them to provide cultural input into the bi-cultural programme of Yipirinya School and to offer something unique to the mostly non-Aboriginal Baptist congregation. It seems their reputation as good hunters also got them occasional paid work as hunting guides for visiting school groups and Aboriginal nursing home groups. In carrying out these tasks and in their own private hunting expeditions, the Warlpiri women paid scant regard to the prerogatives of the local Arrernte traditional owners. 'Why should we ask them', they argued, 'they only buy food from the shop'. Implied in this argument, and in pitying explanations of how the Arrernte lost their traditional dancing skills due to early missionary prohibitions, was a degree of cultural chauvinism and self-assertion that the Warlpiri had become renowned for.

Before pursuing some of the implications of Warlpiri cultural assertion, it is convenient at this point to compare some of the similarities and differences between the Baptist *jilimi* in Alice Springs and a quite similar assemblage of Warlpiri women in Bagot in Darwin who instead became involved in the Assemblies of God Pentecostal Church and took an overtly negative position on aspects of traditional law. Although this comparison is something of a detour in the trajectory of this chapter, it will help in some way to flesh out the Alice Springs scene because some Warlpiri people had become involved in a Pentecostal church in Alice Springs as well. Unfortunately, the central Warlpiri figure in that church, who I had seen leading the singing and falling down to the ground after being possessed by the spirit, did not want to participate in the research.

The Pentecostal Warlpiri Women of Bagot, Darwin

The fact that there was an almost identically structured Warlpiri household in Bagot in Darwin with Christian matriarchs at its core suggests a more widespread pattern of response to the circumstances of a town: the functioning household around which needy kin and visitors congregate, sustained by the Christian matriarch who receives support from her church and other diverse contacts in the non-Aboriginal population. Notwithstanding the matriarchs sustaining the household in Darwin, it did not have the same feeling of a women's space as the Christian *jilimi* in Alice Springs. There were more Warlpiri men permanently camped at the Darwin household. One was the brother of the matriarch, another the husband of one of the female dialysis patients, and occasionally some demanding and troublesome young Warlpiri men would stay there. One of the women explained their conundrum with their young male relations who wanted to drink. They knew if they allowed the men to drink in their houses that other drinkers would then arrive and the inevitable mayhem would follow. But, they reasoned, if they insisted on the drinkers going away to a long-grass camp the women would fear for the safety of their male relations. It was also possible, in the event of the serious injury or death of one of their drinking relations, that there would be reprisals against the matriarchs. The reprisals would be couched in well-worn traditionalist terms, indicating that the women had not looked after them properly. At least having the drinkers close by allowed for monitoring and the possibility of a last-minute intervention to prevent a serious injury.[8] The 'Gurindji shed', a large dilapidated barn-like structure, provided something of a half-way house between these options.

The middle-aged Warlpiri women I found at Bagot in 2009–2012 were the survivors of the precarious life of the long-grassers I described in the previous chapter. Through emotional exhaustion or health crises or religious conversion, they had regained their sobriety and some control over their lives and now ran functioning households in the camps (cf. Brady 1995 for further accounts of Aboriginal people giving up drinking). A few had joined forces with two white Assemblies of God missionaries and had become elders in the local Pentecostal church in the camp that had years before been a Baptist stronghold. They became partners in the project of sustaining the Pentecostal church against all the odds. The congregation was relatively small (I would say less than 100), putting pressure on the same core group, and the pace of conversions seemed to be fairly sedate. Moreover, their functioning households at Bagot required much of their time and energy because they continued to be a destination for hard-core drinkers and a reception centre for kin visiting Darwin for business or pleasure or those just passing through. I estimated the core group of the church to comprise about five Aboriginal and five non-Aboriginal people. During the week they would organise Bible study groups, band and choir practice, informal prayer meetings at people's houses, and good works such as prison visits, a youth group and, occasionally, practical assistance for the long-grass people. The climax of the week was the Sunday service at the meeting centre at Bagot.

It was during the testimonials at the Sunday service that I heard the most dramatic and forthright challenge to Aboriginal traditions. The three middle-aged Warlpiri women I saw at the service had belonged to the Baptist Church back on the Warlpiri settlements; that church had generally taken a non-confrontational attitude to traditional rituals and had taken on some indigenised modes of evangelisation (see, for example, Jordan 2003). Two of the women had been on a long journey since then. One, on becoming a widow in Lajamanu, had taken up the drinking life first in Top Springs, then Katherine and then at Bagot in Darwin, before being 'saved'. The dramatic change in her life – becoming a sober elder in the church and head of a functioning household – still seemed something of a surprise to her. Another had left Ali Curung after the unsettling premature death of her adult daughter and had taken some of the grandchildren with her to put them through school in suburban Darwin. She had first attended a Baptist church in Darwin but was shocked when no one in the unfamiliar congregation spoke to her. She then joined the more intimate and welcoming Assemblies of God congregation at Bagot where she found other settlement women like her. One of these women in her testimony specifically denounced the male Aboriginal witchdoctor: 'he did not heal me. He is a liar and a thief. I got out of that system, praise the Lord'.

This denunciation was not an aberration, but reflected the doctrinal approach of all Pentecostal churches including the Assemblies of God (McDonald 2001: 66; Robbins 2004: 127–30; Ono 2007). Occasionally, a drunken Aboriginal man wandering past the open service would briefly remonstrate with the women for expressing such views. In that moment the women, with the support of each other and of their congregation and church, were undeterred. In one sense, the form of their challenge to traditional law represented the most radical statement of rejection of traditional male authority (in favour of the authority of the Lord). As one of the Warlpiri matriarchs explained, in response to what I have written above: 'When we turn our lives around, we want to start a life that is freely given, instead of falling into the same trap. It is something that touches our minds and hearts instead of having a male to rule over us all the time'. In other respects, however, the Warlpiri women involved in the church retained aspects of home settlement traditionalism. They maintained their Warlpiri language and participated in demand sharing networks of kin. They retained traditional knowledge of their own traditional country beyond the home settlements and they organised traditional mortuary rituals in the town camps. The matriarchs did seem to revel in their superior position of being able to provide assistance to their kin, rather than having to continually ask them for help. When I tried to enquire about the degree of reciprocity from kin, one of the Pentecostal matriarchs actually stated that she preferred not to be in a position where she had to ask for help from them. That seemed to me to go beyond the norms of demand sharing (a sort of stepping outside while appearing to remain inside) and I wondered whether it was a novel development inspired by her Christian beliefs. Whatever may have been the pathway to this position, it entailed a degree of frustration which my sympathetic ear would sometimes elicit: 'they can't listen. Old people have to do everything for the young people. Stop watching video all the time. [They have] no education'. When voiced in the camp, typically to all present rather than directed towards an individual, such complaints rarely had any noticeable effect.

Their defiance of the power of the traditional healer, though, placed them well outside the vast majority of contemporary Warlpiri people who continued to believe in the ubiquity and efficacy of sorcery and the need for such healers. Their denunciations marked a dramatic challenge to well-entrenched

Warlpiri social norms and a defiance of the powerful interests of senior male ritual leaders. I suspect that the Warlpiri people involved in the Pentecostal church in Alice Springs took a similar position.

The Warlpiri Matriarchs in Context

The Baptist matriarchs of the town camps of Alice Springs, while indicative of some common tendencies of the Warlpiri in town, were not necessarily representative of a broader group of Warlpiri permanent residents of Alice Springs, who were quite diverse. My focus on the matriarchs is as much to do with their relative accessibility as their commitment to remaining in town. Other long-term Warlpiri residents were relatively inaccessible to me because of their continual heavy drinking. One such woman lived quite close to 'Dulcie' in her town camp, but in an old humpy made out of scrap materials, which in 2009 was a conspicuous anachronism among the other large, solid houses. She quietly went about her routines, devoting all welfare income and the proceeds of the sale of her paintings to the purchase of liquor to be consumed in the humpy with like-minded visiting Warlpiri relations who were known to the Warlpiri people in the nearby houses. Among the Warlpiri in town, the distinction between the drinkers and the non-drinkers, and the largely overlapping distinction between the Christians and the drinkers, had a much more immediate social import than on the home settlements. On the remote settlements, state agencies like the police maintained the overall non-drinking character of the settlements even though their enforcement activities met with mixed success. For the non-drinkers in town it was a matter of fairly constant vigilance and negotiation with close relations who could not easily be refused. The town camps were the most socially and physically porous to visiting relations whose drinking parties would gather pace at night and sometimes invade the houses of their relations. Confronted with such a situation once, 'Dulcie' called her detective friend from the Baptist Church and he dispatched a police vehicle to help her. Most did not have such useful contacts and had to find other means of forbearance or avoidance and catching up on sleep the next day when the drinkers were exhausted. Another matriarch had originally tried to convince her younger relations to stop drinking but eventually tired of the inevitable assertions of personal autonomy: 'they say "This is not your body, this is my body", like that, smart people'.

Warlpiri non-drinkers in suburban public housing in Alice Springs had even more cause to be concerned about visiting drinking relations putting their tenancy at risk. Many of these households had applied to the government to have their premises declared alcohol free under the Northern

Territory Liquor Act and displayed prominent official signs to that effect on their front gates. It was, however, sometimes difficult to get the police to respond quickly to a crisis situation and it was difficult for the Warlpiri tenants to be seen to inform on their relations. One elderly first-time tenant hid herself in the toilet while calling the police so that she could more effectively deny her role in the arrival of the police to her partying relations. As in Darwin, the Alice Springs matriarchs sometimes had ambivalent feelings about sending their young relations away, fearing that harm could come to them more easily in more dangerous public spaces. Compromises were inevitably made. The elderly first-time tenant returned to her humpy in the creek, much to the disappointment of the NGO supporting her tenancy, after finding the inevitable confrontations with her relations too stressful.

In addition to differences in sobriety and religiosity, the general social trajectory of non-Warlpiri partners also provided another avenue of social differentiation among the Warlpiri diaspora in Alice Springs. 'Dulcie's' daughter and Arrernte son-in-law, the working couple mentioned earlier, provided an example of a social trajectory that was quite different to the Warlpiri matriarchs. Although economically tied to more affordable housing in the town camps and continuing to have deep connections with their respective kin, in many ways they belonged to an emerging and distinct section of Alice Springs society fostered by the growing Indigenous sector. Among other things, 'Dulcie's' daughter's on-going connection to kin meant that she was particularly useful in her Aboriginal liaison role at the hospital. For example, she knew in advance that relations of a recently deceased Warlpiri person would be seeking access to the deceased's body (for a lock of hair) to enable the completion of the sorry business. She was able to use her position within the hospital to facilitate access to the mortuary. While very much tied into their kinship networks, their friendship networks expanded to embrace their Aboriginal work colleagues who had similar values about raising a family and limiting their drinking so as not to disrupt school and work routines. It was from 'Dulcie's' son-in-law that I heard something unique in the annals of Warlpiri child rearing which has been universally characterised by indulgence and freedom from direction. Berating his children for their boisterous play inside the house, he firmly stated 'if you want to play like that take it outside. I have paid for everything in this house and I don't want you to break it'. 'Dulcie's' daughter and son-in-law were not involved in the Baptist church like her, instead enjoying secular activities like sporting events and friendly social gatherings like a fancy dress birthday party based on famous movie stars. While being acutely aware of pervasive racism within the town and in the schools their children attended, they were also critical of other Warlpiri people. They saw some of the settlement Aboriginal people who had taken up the drinking life in Alice Springs as lazy and were well aware that they neglected their children. They were fostering one of them. 'Dulcie's' daughter was also critical of those who behaved in other self-destructive ways, such as absconding from hospital before their treatment was finished.

The social networks developed by Bess Price in Alice Springs overlapped with 'Dulcie's' family but also extended far beyond them. An important early network seems to have involved other similar inter-racial couples described briefly by Bess's friend and distant relation, Ngaatjatjarra woman Lizzie Marrkilyi Ellis, in her autobiography (2016: 68, 76-77). There were seven such couples. Four of the white partners were teachers and all of the Aboriginal partners were from different Aboriginal settlements. They spent time together, helped each other out with short-term accommodation and childminding, and presumably supported each other through their mutual recognition of their relatively unusual partnerships. This friendship network was somewhat separate from the freewheeling Warlpiri sorority described in the previous chapter, although it did overlap. Bess and her husband had eventually set up their own consulting firm to provide cross-cultural training, including to the mining company employees on Warlpiri land; initially quite gradually, and with the encouragement of her husband, she began to comment on Aboriginal issues in the political arena. This brought her to the attention of Northern Territory political elites and, through some bruising nationally reported political encounters, to national attention and ultimately a ministerial position in the Northern Territory government (2012–2016). Despite this and other trappings of their relative social mobility, such as financing their grandchildren's attendance at a private secondary school in Alice Springs, it was also clear that they had not cut their family ties and transferred to a new class (cf. Lahn 2012 on Aboriginal sensitivities about the label 'middle class').[9] Rather, they had expanded their personal social network into a unique configuration that included the broad sweep of Northern Territory society. The network included Bess's immediate Warlpiri family, with their requests for assistance, their crises and tragedies as well as their own friends in similar inter-racial relationships and similar educational backgrounds. It included work friends, Indigenous leaders in the Indigenous sector, their daughter's school friends and through her the music scene in Alice Springs. For Bess it included her own Aboriginal girlfriends with whom she could relax and celebrate. Following their direct involvement in party politics, it extended to local Alice Springs and Northern Territory political elites. Their location in Alice Springs and Bess's continued involvement in family communication networks meant that the various networks continually overlapped and impinged on any private life they wished to sustain in suburban Alice Springs.

Bess had already noticed how the initial social distance from Yuendumu in 1983 had begun to collapse in the 1990s as more Warlpiri people moved to Alice Springs or found visiting easier to achieve: 'Yuendumu came to us'. This drastically increased the frequency of demand sharing and having to deal with drunken relations. From her husband's perspective it was a continual struggle to maintain his 'island of sanity' from the continual pressures that would have turned their house into a Warlpiri camp. Such a transformation was happening in the town camps and in other Warlpiri suburban houses where white partners did not have the same stamina and fortitude to insist upon certain boundaries.

Second-Generation Diaspora

There was a similarly wide spread of experiences and trajectories among the second-generation Warlpiri diaspora in Alice Springs who had been born and/or raised there from a young age.[10] As would be anticipated from the literature on diaspora and migration, there were sometimes dramatic differences between the Warlpiri growing up in Alice Springs and those who had grown up on the settlements in a previous era.[11] Critically, some children of inter-racial parents and intertribal parents did not gain fluency in speaking Warlpiri. Although close kin were accepting and would generously stretch the concept of speaking Warlpiri to include those who had a few words and could understand some of the spoken language, this occurred against a background of a more unforgiving and broad brush identification of Warlpiri identity with language competency. Both language and other cultural mores did seem to survive among the Alice Springs born generation because of widespread endosociality, particularly in the town camps and their relative social marginalisation. Moreover, many of the youngest children were being cared for by their grandmothers who spoke to them in Warlpiri. Two Warlpiri teenage boys from Alice Springs town camps had also spent time at Yuendumu where their fathers had remained, and they appeared to be able to integrate themselves well enough into settlement life, in one case through his involvement in the Yuendumu AFL football team.

Their mothers, who had grown up in Yuendumu, considered Alice Springs to be their home now. Typically, they were not expansive in their reasons, instead making the global judgement that 'Yuendumu is boring' (cf. Musharbash 2007). At one level, it was easy to see their point. In town, even the most prosaic of activities, like walking to the centre of town and sitting on the council lawns, had the air of possibility that was mostly absent in the much smaller and quieter settlements. And, indeed, the convergence of Warlpiri people on the town centre from all parts of Alice Springs was one of the rhythms of daily life in the town. The heightened ambience of possibility that something exciting would happen could be attributed to the availability of liquor and the knowledge that this town was the destination of so many known Warlpiri people who wanted to shake off their ordinary lives on the settlements and engage in some form of extreme behaviour. Ganja (marijuana) was easier to obtain and one did not have to worry about embarrassing settlement relations who might be employed as a police aide or on the night patrol. There was also a vast array of diversions unavailable on the settlement: the casino, nightclubs (one favoured haunt unsubtly named 'The Juicy Rump'), a range of retail outlets, varieties of takeaway food, and the yearly round of public entertainments and tourist spectacles (see also Povinelli 2006: 117–18 for a similar emphasis on excitement and the range of services by one of her informants who relocated to Darwin). Moreover, for the unattached women (the majority) there was a greater variety of possible sexual partners and possible meeting places which were (marginally) less likely to be under surveillance by relations.

While the 'Yuendumu is boring' judgement seemed to imply an active choice for a more exciting life, most of the closely related women I am considering, all first cousins, would, I think, have found it difficult to base their lives at Yuendumu. Had one of them returned to Yuendumu, they would be bereft of company and without their mother's or sister's functioning households. Since most of their close relations (their actual or genealogically very close 'mothers' and 'sisters') were in town, a return to Yuendumu would present the dreaded prospect of being alone. In town they could also support each other as a kind of personal security strategy in the sometimes dangerous town camps. The functioning households run by the matriarchs also provided aspects of stability and security and the ability to care for young children when their mothers were preoccupied with partying.

Solidarity of the Town Warlpiri?

To what extent could these overlapping networks, different social trajectories and different generational perspectives be considered to function as a social group – the Warlpiri diaspora of Alice Springs – and to what extent were traditional settlement modes of solidarity, affiliation and identity being transformed? What has been presented so far are the fragmented Warlpiri places within Alice Springs: the officially designated Warlpiri Camp; the Warlpiri households congregated together in other town camps; and the gathering of the Warlpiri Baptists at the Sunday service. To this could be added the royalty associations' office, whose clientele were predominantly Warlpiri; favoured drinking haunts and liquor outlets; and the casino. What is also apparent in residential arrangements and patterns of visitation is the persistence of the significance of close kin and networks of demand sharing and the informal sharing of information. The kinship networks follow their own configuration, typically spread out over Australia, but concentrated in nodes in the settlements and in towns like Alice Springs. One consequence of this was the relatively weak forms of pan-Warlpiri solidarity in Alice Springs. This was reflected in the most basic level in the incomplete knowledge of each other's presence. Even those in official intermediary positions whose work involved monitoring the Warlpiri comings and goings had some blind spots in the Warlpiri census I constructed with them. The blind spots were usually those to whom they were only distantly related. Understandably perhaps, as their own families grew, their focus narrowed somewhat. One of the weak, although temporarily fervent, forms of broad-based Warlpiri solidarity expressed itself through barracking for the Warlpiri AFL football team when they played in Alice Springs.

A stronger form of solidarity and acknowledgement of common traditions arose in the performance of mortuary rituals upon the death of close kin of Warlpiri permanent residents in Alice Springs. These events galvanised both the drinkers and the sober matriarchs I have been describing. In one case, one of the middle-aged drinkers rather dramatically gave up her drinking for a number of weeks to ensure that the requirements of a traditional sorry business for a 'brother' were complied with. In the normal course of things, the matriarchs helped the bereaved family to set up a sorry camp, typically at one of the town camps, and assisted the grieving family in receiving other Warlpiri people in town, since all of them would feel obliged to attend and grieve with the family at some stage.

Deaths also raised the question of compliance with the traditional obligation on close relations to move house. Such an obligation was still evident among the Warlpiri matriarchs of Alice Springs but was subject to modification. Among the modifications, my general impression was that, for deaths which occurred back on the home settlements, the Alice Springs residents did not expect each other to permanently move house, provided that a certain period was spent at a separately established sorry camp. When the death occurred in the households of Alice Springs, however, the pressure to move house was more intense. I witnessed such an occurrence when the 'brother' of one of the Warlpiri matriarchs in one of the town camps died in her house. She and her family immediately left to live with another Warlpiri family in a different town camp ('Dulcie's' house). She did not abandon her own house altogether, having locked the door and retained the key. The sorry camp was set up on vacant land outside 'Dulcie's' house. After three weeks, 'Dulcie's' temporary visitor decided to return to her own house. The sorry business had finished but the funeral service was still being planned. Prior to settling back into the house where the death had occurred, the Warlpiri matriarch marshalled all of her resources (including me) to thoroughly cleanse the house. This involved scrubbing its floors and installing a white crucifix on a wall in the house close to where the body had been found. As far as I know, there were no social repercussions for her return to the house in such a fashion and she remains in that house to this day.

Another Warlpiri woman took a more confrontational stance to the expectations of her settlement relations. The case was not clear cut because she lived in her private suburban house with her white husband who could more easily deflect expectations that they would move, even temporarily, because of the death of a close relation. In any event, over several decades she resisted the temporary abandonment of the house as the deaths occurred and argued that the Warlpiri people who might criticise her should take into account her many happy memories of the house in which they had raised their daughter and created a garden.

Some instances of sorry business being held in Alice Springs, such as that for 'Dulcie' in 2010, seemed to be more than a matter of convenience. Instead, it was an assertion by her closest relations of the proper place of burial taking into account 'Dulcie's' explicit wishes during her lifetime. In another instance, three competitive sorry camps were set up: one in an Alice Springs town camp, one in a remote settlement where the deceased's in-laws lived, and another in a more distant remote settlement where his father lived. The three sorry camps were spread out over a distance of approximately 800 kilometres. While this reflected contemporary demography and internal family tensions, part of the argumentation was conducted in the terms of an emerging home and away politics of identity in which the Warlpiri migrants were critical of life on the settlements and those remaining on the settlements were critical of the migrants, often implying that they led a less culturally authentic life. Some of the Warlpiri mourners, for example, thought that Alice Springs was an inappropriate place to hold such an important traditional ritual. The theme of the emerging home and away politics will be taken up in more detail in Chapter 5 (Ambivalent Homecomings).

Another aspect of the emerging home and away politics is relevant to the internal differentiation among the permanent Warlpiri residents of Alice Springs: the relationship between the voluntary and involuntary diaspora. Dialysis patients, a significant proportion of the involuntary diaspora, sometimes lived in town camps or Aboriginal hostels. In the town camps, the middle-aged Warlpiri female patients would find common cause or an easy *modus vivendi* with the Warlpiri matriarchs I have been describing. These patients would provide welcome ballast and support for the matriarchs. The hostels were cleaner, well serviced with regular meals and less accessible to relations intent upon drinking. Even so, their relatively superior accommodation sometimes became another destination for visiting kin who would be surreptitiously hidden from the staff of the hostel. The vast majority of the dialysis patients seemed more orientated towards the home settlements and some did not easily integrate themselves with the voluntary Warlpiri diaspora who had made the break with home settlements years before. Most of the dialysis patients looked forward to the time when dialysis services would be established on the settlements and to their return. In the meantime, they became more intimately confronted with their kin in the towns, whose lifestyle they had previously been able to avoid – a sort of unexpected internal culture clash. One Warlpiri woman from Yuendumu, a non-drinker and Baptist who had worked at the school at Yuendumu as a cleaner for much of her working life, found herself as a dialysis patient in an Aboriginal hostel in Alice Springs. She was partly dependent upon her relations in the town camps where the drinking lifestyle of some of them appalled her. She felt no hesitation in expressing her views directly to them in her characteristically blunt way. It was her adult son, however, who felt most keenly her reluctant presence in Alice Springs because she threatened to refuse her own dialysis treatment unless he gave up his drinking and attended the Baptist church services with her. I saw the miserable man at a few of the services with his temporarily victorious mother.

Inter-group Politics

The internal diversity among the Warlpiri people of Alice Springs, described above, tended not to be recognised by white authorities and recently emboldened Arrernte leaders. Instead, there was a tendency to describe the Warlpiri in terms of cultural traits and stereotypes: the loud and assertive bush people who were also good at dealing with non-Aboriginal people.

In Alice Springs, there had been some long-standing and recent marriages between Warlpiri and Arrernte people, which, it will be recalled, were the basis for a number of Warlpiri families gaining a foothold in other town camps that had not been officially designated as Warlpiri camps. One private Arrernte commentary on such a development was to approve the Warlpiri spouse but then to disapprove the large number of Warlpiri relations that then followed them to their new Alice Springs base.

The reassertion of Arrernte ownership of Alice Springs following the successful native title claim occurred through the NGO set up in 2002 to administer the newly recognised rights of native title holders, Lhere Aretepe Aboriginal Corporation. While similar in some ways to the accumulation of state-like functions by the resurgent Larrakia in Darwin (Fisher 2012,

2013), Lhere Aretepe had to contend with entrenched Aboriginal NGOs like Tangentyere which was already providing services to town campers including the local Arrernte. The Arrernte reassertion in Alice Springs took a number of forms, including the purchase of local businesses, separate representation on the board of the Aboriginal medical service, the withdrawal of two of the Arrernte town camps from under the Tangentyere umbrella, and the adoption of a more aggressive stance in the public arena about the misbehaviour of visiting Aboriginal people. One example of the new stance was the public statement by a representative of the Lhere Aretepe: 'We don't see a lot of that behaviour as antisocial, we see it as anti-cultural. If you don't think it's okay to urinate and defecate and sleep on sacred sites in your own country, why is it okay to come to Alice Springs and scream and rant and carry on'.[12] In a very similar vein, Lhere Aretepe filmed a public service announcement which was broadcast on local Imparja TV during 2009. The announcement called on Aboriginal visitors to Alice Springs to behave properly or to return to their own country, and similar sentiments were reported in the local press. There were three versions of the announcement and one of them included a mention of the Warlpiri during the Arrernte language part of the announcement.[13] Perhaps not surprisingly, many Warlpiri people took the whole campaign to be directed at them and this precipitated a moment of increased Warlpiri solidarity in Alice Springs. Some Warlpiri became quite enraged by what they saw as the blanket accusations made against them and resolved to target the Arrernte people who appeared in the announcements for the perceived insult to the Warlpiri. I do not know whether these threats were followed through. The long-term Warlpiri residents predictably thought it was hypocritical to infer that all the problems of drunken violence and littering in Alice Springs were completely attributable to visitors. They were well aware of the problems of the local Arrernte people.

Years before this public escalation of underlying tensions, Tangentyere Council had actively pursued a campaign to repatriate visitors, but in that case it was more subtly and cleverly named as a 'Return to Country' programme for people who had become 'stranded in town'.[14] It operated in a similar way to the Bush Bus (reimbursement from Centrelink welfare payments) and was linked into the Tangentyere's individual case management team.[15] The subtlety of the Tangentyere nomenclature and its packaging as help fitted nicely within the bounds of intertribal shared etiquette of not criticising individuals or groups. That subtlety demonstrates Lhere Aretepre's faux pas of naming the Warlpiri in its televised public service announcements. Such problems also attend the building of multi-language group political coalitions of permanent residents against visitors.

Conclusion: Cultural Reproduction and Transformation in Town

While having different social trajectories and different personal proclivities, the Warlpiri matriarchs described in this chapter shared their commitment to living out their lives in Alice Springs rather than the remote settlements or outstations. A number would mysteriously say they no longer had family on the settlements, confounding anthropological orthodoxy about their world where everyone was kin of some kind. It soon emerged, however, that they were talking about an inner circle of key relationships, particularly parents and siblings (in the extended sense of those terms), from whom they felt most support.[16] Life stories also revealed other reasons. Some associated their home settlement with their subservience to dominating and sometimes violent husbands or with family tragedies such as a gang rape or murder of a relation. Others were still unsure about their likely reception from the family of jilted promised husbands. Some rationales were more deeply hidden. One of the matriarchs would regularly state that she stayed in town because of her job. In fact, she had also become addicted to poker machines which consumed most of her wages. It was only after 'Dulcie's' death that I found out that her strongly held view of Yuendumu as an irredeemably bad place was based on her experience of illness on some return visits. She took those illnesses as proof of sorcery against her by Warlpiri people at Yuendumu.

But it should be apparent from this chapter that a major reason for them not returning to their home settlements was that Alice Springs offered them greater opportunities to assert their personal autonomy, to construct their own lives and to use their expanded personal networks to deliver help for their families and to amaze them. Personal autonomy, both in the sense of the skilful enactment of traditional social relations and the rupturing of constraining relationships, was evident, for example, in 'Dulcie's' care for her family (skilful enactment) and her adventurous relationships with white men (resisting constraints). In a similar way, 'Sarah's' establishment of a service-providing Christian *jilimi* could be seen as a skilful enactment, while resisting involvement in the family feud had the potential to rupture her traditional social relations. More dramatically, the direct challenge to traditional sorcery was a deliberate rupturing of relationships by the Bagot matriarchs, who were nonetheless enacting other forms of traditionalism, particularly the service mode expected of grandmothers. In framing these achievements as extensions of personal autonomy, differing degrees of vulnerability also have to be acknowledged. Households in the socially porous town camps could be more easily overrun by drunken partying and the inevitable mayhem that ensued. In the suburbs, white husbands, depending on their own personal resources and attitudes, could act as something of a buffer.

Since the observation of the increasing autonomy of women with age is a commonplace in settlement ethnographies, the question arises as to what is different about locating this increased autonomy in Alice Springs. In essence, the answer seems to be one of increased scale and complexity. For the high level cultural entrepreneurs, there were more audiences and contacts to be made. The same was true for the women of the Christian *jilimi*. They found the various audiences that enabled them to leverage their practical traditional skills by providing cultural services to the new audiences. For those seeking a sexual adventure, there were more unattached men (both in the sense of single and unrelated).

The effect of Alice Springs was much more profound on the second-generation diaspora who were raised in Alice Springs in such a different environment to the settlements. Because of enduring social marginalisation and endosociality, the effects on the second generation were not uniform. For the settlement-born generation cultural transformations were not so dramatic, although the probable trajectory of such transformations was indicated by the supplementation of kinship networks with other personal networks. Numerous new contacts were made in the course of satisfying the demand for exotic objects like Aboriginal paintings, the tourist demand for an Aboriginal experience (the leveraging of traditional hunting skills), and the need for cultural brokers to explain traditional culture (in Aboriginal liaison jobs in service NGOs, in cultural programmes in bilingual schools and in providing cross-cultural training for miners). These circumstances enabled degrees of cultural entrepreneurship to develop as the Warlpiri people concerned identified themselves as the ones who could best fulfil the various demands.

The relatively intense relationships of some of the Warlpiri Christians with their non-Aboriginal fellow Christians seems to have supported more direct and self-conscious changes to aspects of Warlpiri tradition. These changes ranged from the expansion of the categories of kin who were entitled to help and the moderation of other traditional demands to participate in family feuding, to the more dramatic abandonment of belief in sorcery. Moreover, the nature of the non-kin personal networks seemed different in character to the intensity of the inner circle of kin relationships. The non-kin personal networks included a variety of 'weak ties' which were nonetheless significant, as the case of the Indian taxi driver demonstrates. That case also demonstrates that while new modes of interaction and befriending are being learned, perhaps more ingrained traditional modes of interaction are also apparent in the tendency towards the personalisation and expansion of initially functional relationships.

It was helpful to the assertion of the traditionalism of the Warlpiri matriarchs in Alice Springs that there was only muted competition from other Aboriginal women. In asserting hunting and gathering prerogatives in the immediate hinterland of the town, the Warlpiri were never effectively challenged by the local Arrernte. Once the Warlpiri intermarried with the Arrernte and were accepted as tenants, their increasing presence in the town camps was difficult to challenge. Given the universal sensitivities towards mourners, it is not surprising that others acquiesced when the Warlpiri occasionally asserted their right to hold elaborate mortuary rituals in the Warlpiri enclaves in the town camps. The ability to conduct these rituals was significant in allowing the Warlpiri matriarchs to assert themselves as women who followed traditional law (cf. Povinelli 2006: 117–18 on whether the inability to perform such rituals because of long-distance relocation would threaten the sense of self of such individuals). Unlike the Darwin group studied by Sansom (2010), there was never any suggestion that Warlpiri initiation ceremonies would ever be held near Alice Springs, nor that they could become the traditional custodians of Alice Springs. However, the fact that contemporary Arrernte reassertion had to take place through official channels and public media rather than more personal confrontation was perhaps emblematic of the state of play: the Arrernte had made a belated attempt to re-sacralise the long-standing white enclave of Alice Springs while the Warlpiri kept their own counsel about their superiority in matters traditional and, except for high-level Warlpiri politicians, ignored challenges to their presence and calls for protocols to be followed.

Thence to Adelaide

One particularly telling reflection of the changing demography and perceptions of Alice Springs as a legitimate place for Warlpiri cultural action was the decision in 2010 of approximately 100 Warlpiri refugees from family feuding at Yuendumu to go to Adelaide as Alice Springs could no longer provide sufficient sanctuary. In this regard, Alice Springs had already become too much of a Warlpiri place and not enough of a European enclave.

While this chapter has explored the lives of some of the Warlpiri people who put down permanent roots in Alice Springs, for other Warlpiri people Alice Springs became a stepping stone to a quite different metropolitan experience in Adelaide. One young Warlpiri woman who had stayed in Alice Springs after completing her high school education was jilted by a long-term Warlpiri boyfriend who returned to Yuendumu with a new Warlpiri girlfriend. In her distress she went to live with a Warlpiri relation in Port Pirie in South Australia and commenced a drinking lifestyle which eventually took her to the northern suburbs of Adelaide via the South Australian network of public housing, having been formally accepted into that system in Port Pirie. Another Warlpiri woman had left her Warlpiri husband in

Yuendumu to marry a white man in Alice Springs with whom she had two children. When that relationship ended acrimoniously there was a sense in which the woman felt she had outgrown the possibilities of living an autonomous and adventurous life in Alice Springs and needed the larger canvas that only Adelaide could provide. A few others, including an artist who had established herself in Alice Springs, followed their white partners. As with the reasons for leaving the settlements for Alice Springs, the reasons for leaving Alice Springs for Adelaide were often more multi-layered than these neat summaries suggest. In the case of one of the artists, for example, Alice Springs had become tainted for her by the murder of her son. Her relations with her affines had also been severely tested at a tense sorry business on one of the Warlpiri settlements where some of them, following common modes of response to such tragedies, blamed her for not looking after her son adequately.

It is these Warlpiri people who have used Alice Springs as a stepping stone, along with some who moved directly to Adelaide from the remote settlements, who will be the focus of the next chapter. The escaping Warlpiri refugees in 2010 knew that some of their own relations, including those on the other side of the family feud, had already established themselves in Adelaide. There was therefore no escaping the feud in Adelaide but the refugees had made the accurate judgement that the smaller numbers and the vast geographical spread of Adelaide itself would dramatically lessen its intensity.

Notes

1. Some material in this chapter was previously published in Burke, 2015, 'Rupture and Readjustment of Tradition: Agency and Autonomy in the Feminised Warlpiri Diaspora in Australia', in *Strings of Connectedness: Essays in Honour of Ian Keen*, edited by P. Toner, Canberra: ANU E Press, pp. 215–34; and Burke, 2018, 'Bold Women of the Warlpiri Diaspora who Went too Far', in *People and Change in Indigenous Australia*, edited by D. Austin-Broos and F. Merlan, Honolulu: University of Hawai'i Press, pp. 29–43. Reprinted with permission.
2. Merlan describes the same phenomenon in Katherine in the 1970s (1991: 271).
3. The political struggles of Tangentyere Council in the 1970s and 1980s for secure title for the Alice Springs town camps and improved physical infrastructure are covered in some detail in Heppell and Wigley's *Black Out in Alice* (1981), in Fran Coughlan's MA thesis (1991) and in Rowse's analysis of some of the contradictions in Tangentyere's work (1988). Part of the same period is covered in Wenten Rubuntja's biography *The Town Grew up Dancing* (Rubuntja, Green and Rowse 2002: 107–40). The rise of Aboriginal town campers as a political issue in the policy era of self-determination is reflected

in the House of Representatives Standing Committee on Aboriginal Affairs report 'Strategies to Help Overcome the Problems of Aboriginal Town Camps' (1982). Earlier administrative struggles over the presence of Aboriginal people in Alice Springs are dealt with in Tim Rowse's *White Flour, White Power* (1998), particularly the period of the 1960s (see Chapter 10: Alice Springs and its town camps). The relative scale of the Warlpiri presence in the Alice Springs town camps in the mid-1980s is suggested by a diagram in Khalidi's doctoral dissertation on the Aboriginal population of Alice Springs (1989). It shows Yuendumu as the third largest source of Aboriginal town campers after Santa Teresa and Hermannsburg (Khalidi 1989: 179). Tangentyere Council's response to the initial attempts under the Intervention to transfer ownership of town camp housing to Northern Territory Government instrumentality, Territory Housing, in return for upgrade funding was reported by Tangentyere's William Tilmouth (2007). Some of the legal arguments arising from the attempted Australian Government's restructuring of the town camps as part of the Intervention are outlined by Alison Vivian (2010). The most intimate and uncompromising portrait of the contemporary life of some Arrernte people in the unofficial town camp of Whitegate is Rod Moss's *The Hard Light of Day* (2010).

4. For more on the different iterations of The Bungalow as 'half-caste' institution, army camp and training settlement, see Rowse (1998: 69–70, 95–96, 171–72). Warlpiri presence at The Bungalow in the 1950s was also reported by Meggitt as part of his overview of Warlpiri relations with neighbouring tribes (1962: 41). According to Meggitt, the Warlpiri interaction with the Arrernte people at The Bungalow fuelled their general dislike of the Arrernte as too quarrelsome and unreliable by adding evidence that the long association of the Arrernte with white men had made them 'too sophisticated for their own good'.

5. The existence of the women's camp as part of the typical layout of Warlpiri residential groupings is mentioned briefly by Meggitt (1962: 75–76). Under pre-contact nomadic conditions a separate single women's camp may have only contained a few women. Under settlement conditions the scale of the *jilimi* increased to the extent that they could be seen as 'super-*jilimis*' (Bell 1987: 118). Diane Bell gives an account of the Warlpiri and Kaytej *jilimi* at Ali Curung in the 1970s, emphasising its role as the headquarters of the women ritual leaders of the *yawulyu* (women's ritual) (1983: 81–84, 110–28). Françoise Dussart's description of *jilimi* at Yuendumu in the 1980s contrasts with Bell's description of permanent concentration in one *jilimi*, emphasising instead the changing locations and personnel and the distribution of ritual bosses between different camps at Yuendumu (2000: 43–44; see also Keys 1999). In more recent times, the word *jilimi* has been used as a name for a women's safe house on one of the settlements.

6. The Warlpiri woman I have called 'Camilla' thought that this sentence did not reflect her commitment to and success in managing her finances, or in her words, 'spending slowly'. While I am happy to admit to possible variation within the group, I think the observation about the difficulties of the lean week is valid overall.

7. Åse Ottosson was also struck by the steady stream of visitors and service providers into the town camps and the variable relationships between them and the residents of suburban Alice Springs (2014: 124).

8. These concerns of the matriarchs in 2009–2013 contrast with what now seems to be the exceptional Wallaby Cross mob of the 1970s described by Sansom (1980). Among that mob senior men organised the protection of drinkers who preferred the privacy of their unofficial camps. Now, at least some of the drinkers seemed to be permanently attached to the functioning matriarchs in the official camps and a different cultural dynamic of maternal care was playing out.

9. See also Noel Pearson's 'Through the Class Ceiling' in *The Weekend Australian*, 4–5 August 2007, where he criticises the reluctance of the Aboriginal middle class to acknowledge their objective position as different from other Aboriginal people, for example, their moderation of alcohol consumption to enable careers.
10. Some of the issues canvassed in this section have been explored in the 2004 documentary film *Wirriya: Small Boy* (Director: Beck Cole, Production Company: CAAMA), the story of two days in the life of an eight-year old Warlpiri boy being fostered by an Aboriginal woman in the town camp of Hidden Valley, told from the perspective of the boy.
11. One way into the second-generation literature is via recent debates about the applicability of a model of segmented assimilation to the differing fortunes of second-generation immigrants, most of whom prosper but some of whom decline into an underclass (Portes, Fernandez-Kelly and Haller 2009).
12. Darryl Pearce, then CEO of Lhere Aretepe, quoted in *The Australian* newspaper, 24 May 2009.
13. All three versions were available on YouTube at the time of the research: Lhere Aretepe Respect 1, 2 and 3 TVC by Bellettemedia.
14. A similarly named programme was developed by the local Larrakia in Darwin (see Fisher 2013: 250).
15. Tangentyere Council media release: Tangentyere Council welcomes community support for re-funding of 'Return to Country' programme, 23 April 2007.
16. Other researchers tend to see the development of an inner and outer circle of kin as a relatively recent development. Diane Austin-Broos, for example, reported the elaboration of the Western Arrernte term *tyene* to mean an inner circle of intimates among the totality of one's bilateral kin whom one could rely upon to respond positively to requests for help (2003: 123–24). She interpreted this development partly as a response to the increased opportunities under contemporary settlement conditions to interact with more of one's kin (via improved transport and the proliferation of regional gatherings) and the intensification of settlement demand sharing after the introduction of cash welfare payments. Sercombe suggested that among the Aboriginal people with jobs in the Goldfields area of Western Australia, the adoption of the practise of having an inner and outer circle of kin was a deliberate strategy of compromise to enable material accumulation within a valued network of kin (Sercombe 2008).

Chapter 4

WARLPIRI WOMEN OF ADELAIDE

Introduction

The Warlpiri diaspora I encountered in Adelaide during 2009–2013 provided examples of the extension and intensification of some of the tendencies already identified in Alice Springs and also some unique Warlpiri projects that may only have been possible in a large city of over 1.6 million people a long way from the Warlpiri settlements. At the centre of my story about the Warlpiri diaspora of Adelaide is another matriarch, 'Barbara', a foundational figure with a non-Aboriginal husband and the leader of an expanding family in three close households. After twenty years there, following a remarkable trajectory from her birth at Mount Doreen Station in the 1950s and growing up at Yuendumu speaking Warlpiri as her first language, she now told me 'I feel like Adelaide is my home'. Exploring all the implications of 'Barbara's' statement will be one of the main tasks of this chapter. The theme of escape and experimentation, personified by 'Dulcie' in Alice Springs, was further extended to an extreme in Adelaide in the person of 'Natalie', an exceptionally strong character who dominated the tough drinking scene in the parklands around the city and who seemed to be on a one-woman campaign against shame in all its forms.

The unique projects centred on education and art. There was one household dedicated to putting children from the remote settlement of Ali Curung through school, and another individual who, more than anyone else I encountered in the diaspora, had adopted the education message as her own. These educational projects were supported by a number of non-Aboriginal people who had worked for Warlpiri people on the settlements. Their important supportive and sometimes constitutive role in diaspora locations leads me to theorise another aspect of the Warlpiri diaspora: a parallel diaspora of white friends and acquaintances who were familiar with the remote settlements and who sometimes played a pivotal role. The tendency of the middle-aged women to organise themselves, as exemplified in the Christian *jilimi* in Alice Springs, had something of a counterpart in Adelaide in a loosely organised group of women artists centred on a shared private art wholesaler. It was the leader of this group who, uniquely, told me 'I have to be in Adelaide for my work'. As will be seen in this chapter,[1] there were many other layers to the lives of the women artists in Adelaide in addition to work.

Another clarifying aspect of the Adelaide experience is the significant role played by the eligibility criteria and procedures of public housing authorities and the NGOs they funded to assist struggling tenants. These criteria and procedures tended to shape the location and sometimes the dynamics of diaspora locations by funnelling Warlpiri migrants into areas with short waiting times for houses. Coulehan, in her study of Yolngu women migrants in Darwin, made the even bigger claim that the totality of the extensive welfare network available in the city provided a comprehensive network of care that competed with and undermined traditional kinship networks of care on the remote settlements (Coulehan 1995: 228). I question the radical opposition she proposes, given the saturation of remote settlements by the welfare system for a long time now. But I have also observed in Adelaide how the welfare system enables and moulds diaspora, sometimes in unexpected ways such as when welfare personnel form personal friendships that then exceed their official roles.

Before returning to these issues explicitly, I will give a brief overview of the Warlpiri diaspora as I found it in 2009–2013. This should enable some assessment of the representativeness of the individual stories I have chosen to focus on and to further my exploration of ideas of agency and personal autonomy. As with Alice Springs, the Warlpiri of Adelaide were very diverse and some of them were reclusive. Following the overview and individual stories, I will also address questions of pan-Warlpiri solidarity and relations with local Aboriginal people.

Overview

The administrative, communication and transport links reaching out from Adelaide to central Australia meant that there was a historical and geographical inevitability about central Australian Aboriginal people appearing in Adelaide rather than other capital cities. One informant told me that Pungala Jupurrula was the first Warlpiri person to set up a Warlpiri camp at Port Adelaide in the late 1950s and early 1960s after a career in a travelling boxing troupe attached to a circus.[2] In 1965 the geographer Fay Gale found 300 Aboriginal people from the Northern Territory living in Adelaide, although it is unclear whether any were Warlpiri (Gale 1966, 1972). Approximately two thirds had been brought there for specialised medical treatment, psychiatric hospitalisation or to serve a prison sentence. The remaining third came of their own accord without government assistance and, in a pattern to be repeated in my own research, many had married white partners. The other continuity between my research and Gale's was the large public hospitals which became a destination for many Warlpiri people requiring specialised medical treatment and accompanying Warlpiri persons who would stay in nearby Aboriginal hostels. Coulehan has argued in the Darwin context that such movements to hospitals and the funding of accompanying persons were a major factor in the Yolngu becoming accustomed to Darwin (Coulehan 1995: 88–92; Coulehan 1996). In the period of my research, however, the surest Warlpiri pathway to Adelaide was to visit relations who already lived there.

During 2009–2013 I estimated that there were about 108 Warlpiri people, including 32 children of various ages, permanently living in Adelaide. This represents approximately 3.5 per cent of the total Warlpiri population. Approximately 51 had come from Yuendumu and the nearby predominantly Anmatyerr settlement of Mt Allen, 27 from Ali Curung, 8 from Willowra and 4 were affiliated to Lajamanu. Not counting the exceptional visit of the 100 refugees from the family feuding at Yuendumu during 2010–2011, there were usually about 10 Warlpiri visitors (including some children) at any one time. The visitors included the travelling drinkers, those receiving specialist medical treatment and their accompanying relations and those from Port Pirie on a trip to the Adelaide show.[3] While the scale of the Warlpiri diaspora in Adelaide was relatively small, its existence seemed to have a considerable effect on perceptions of the city among the settlement populations. Back on the settlements, past visitors would tell me with mock irritation and some pride that it was now impossible to walk the streets of Adelaide without being hailed by a Warlpiri relation with an inevitable request for assistance. Knowledge about Adelaide, beyond the medical facilities, was beginning to filter back, such as the source of cheaper second-hand vehicles. Moreover, because of the presence of kin, it became an acceptable destination for impromptu visits.

The location of most of the Warlpiri people in Adelaide, although not all, conforms to a pattern of spatial socio-economic differentiation common to many Australian cities, namely the concentration of welfare housing and the socially underprivileged in outer suburbs and the eventual gentrification of former inner-city working-class suburbs. This geographical stratification has its origins in the so-called Long Boom of the 1950s and 1960s when public housing authorities established broadacre housing estates in the outer suburbs. The establishment of Elizabeth in the late 1950s as a satellite town 30 km north of Adelaide city was unique in Australia for its integration of a State-sponsored manufacturing base, town planning and government-provided worker housing for a largely government-sponsored immigrant population (Peel 1995). The rather tough life of some of the Scottish diaspora in this population is evocatively portrayed in the autobiography of one of its most famous sons (Barnes 2016). Elizabeth's local economic prosperity faltered

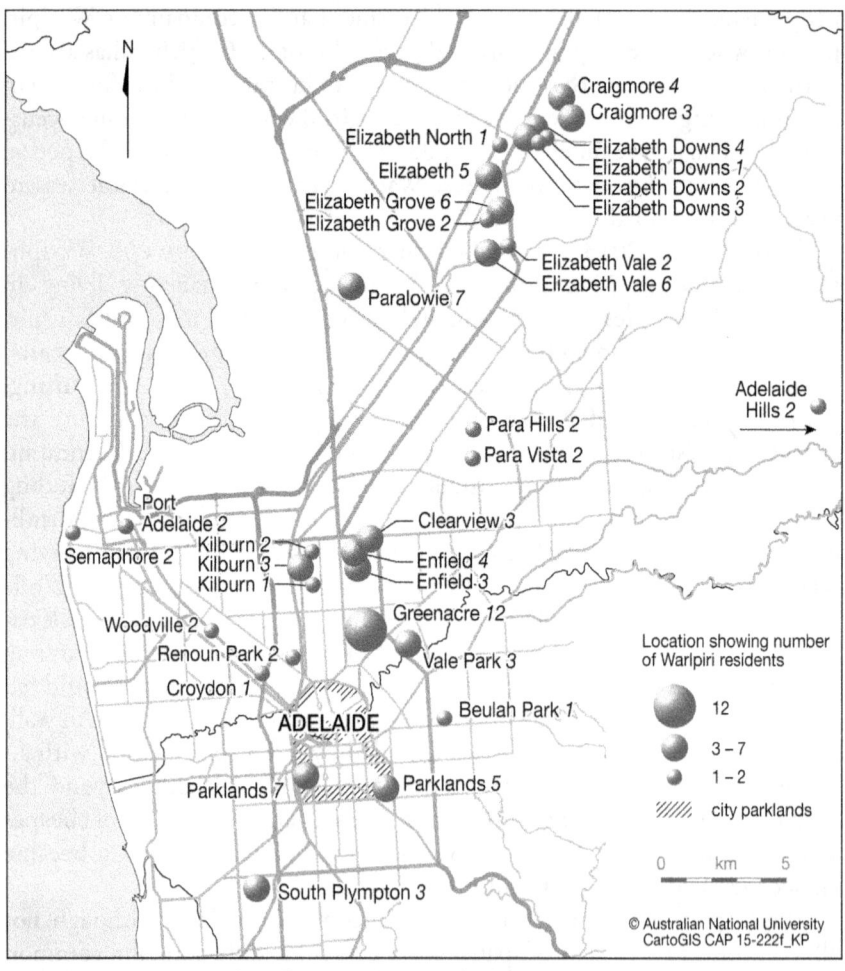

Map 4.1 Distribution of Warlpiri people in Adelaide, 2009–2013

with the recession in the 1970s and the subsequent decline of manufacturing in the restructuring of the Australian economy in the 1980s. Over these years in Elizabeth there occurred a rapid growth in the proportion of welfare-dependent tenants and it was this somewhat dilapidated Elizabeth rather than the new workers' town of the 1960s that the Warlpiri encountered in the 1980s. There were no Warlpiri people living in the wealthy suburbs to the south-east and east of the city, but many lived in the mid-northern suburbs like Enfield, in the far northern suburbs of Elizabeth, in the Port Adelaide area, and the far south-western suburbs. All of these locations now overlap with socio-economic indicators of underprivilege (low household incomes, high unemployment, high proportion of aged people, high proportion of single parent families, high proportion of households without motor vehicles) and the availability of public housing (Forster 1991).[4]

The concentration of Warlpiri people in the northern suburbs generally follows the shorter waiting times for public housing there. As will be explained below, however, a significant number of Warlpiri households in the Elizabeth region were private tenancies. The map also shows two unofficial drinking camps frequented by Warlpiri people, usually in combination with members from other language groups from central Australia (Pitjantjatjara and Arrernte): one in the South Terrace parklands near the Hutt Street soup kitchen; and the other alongside the cemetery in the West Terrace parklands.[5] With the exception of 'Natalie', who had given up drinking because of a health crisis, the group of committed drinkers were difficult to get to know. There was something of a social divide between the sober Warlpiri households and the drinkers, even though individual drinkers would sometimes circulate through the 'dry' households for brief periods and other ostensibly 'dry' households would occasionally relent under pressure from visitors for drinking parties. The broad geographical divide of the drinkers in the parklands near the city and the non-drinkers in the northern suburbs also broke down under a new Commonwealth State funding agreement aimed at housing the homeless.[6] It meant that some of the committed drinkers were transplanted to public housing in Elizabeth, a drinking camp in the shell of a house. There, bleary eyed Aboriginal men and women sat on tatty mattresses in bare rooms drinking cask wine from various makeshift containers and another circle of drinkers sat outside in the backyard which was bare except for a large, silvery pyramid of empty wine cask bladders.

So it is that I now turn to 'Barbara' and 'Emily'. 'Barbara' was the sober matriarch, who with her children was originally welcomed to Adelaide by her white husband's mother and father and siblings. 'Emily', another Warlpiri matriarch from Yuendumu, was welcomed by 'Barbara'. I came to see 'Barbara' and 'Emily' as mutually supporting pillars of overlapping

Warlpiri kin networks being established as the Yuendumu Warlpiri diaspora of the Elizabeth area.

'Barbara' and 'Emily'

'Barbara's' arrival in Adelaide in 1991 came well before the era of mobile phones on the remote settlements and she recalled that early time as one of some personal struggle because of the isolation from her Warlpiri kin. What buoyed her up were the presence of some of her Aboriginal friends from Alice Springs (not Warlpiri) in a nearby suburb and the warm welcome her in-laws extended to her and the blended family, which included two children from her previous relationships. She was also welcomed at the local Baptist Church. She developed a strong relationship with both her parents-in-law, one of whom she cared for in their old age. Moreover, there was a husband to attend to, a household to run and children to settle into schools. Although I never got to know him well (they had been separated for some time when I met 'Barbara'), I gained the impression that the white husband had been a powerful influence, not only because of his large physical presence and the income he generated from his entrepreneurial small businesses, but because of his insistence on discipline and order within the household and on all the children attending school.

After some years the process of serial migration began in earnest with 'Barbara's' offer of refuge to a young female relation with two young children fleeing from domestic violence at Yuendumu. The young woman's mother, 'Emily', was close to 'Barbara' and had already visited her. The plan, to set up a separate household for the fleeing victim and one of 'Barbara's' daughters of a similar age, initially worked satisfactorily. But later concerns were raised about the interest of the young women in the partying lifestyle. 'Emily' left Yuendumu and travelled to Adelaide to take charge of the situation and remove her two young grandchildren. In Adelaide she pondered her options. If she returned to Yuendumu with the grandchildren she would have to deal with the likely claims of the father's family on the children and, being a supporter of education, she had noticed with alarm the declining school attendance at Yuendumu. She made a momentous decision, with the support of her Warlpiri husband and with 'Barbara's' promise of help, to set up a household in Adelaide and send the grandchildren to school there.

'Barbara' helped her with accommodation by introducing her to 'Boris' and 'Svetlana', a Russian couple of her acquaintance, who owned houses in Elizabeth, Port Augusta and Coober Pedy and who were willing to rent to Aboriginal people on welfare. The private rental houses belonging to the Russian couple were a critical part of the expansion of the Warlpiri diaspora in the Elizabeth area. In several instances their houses provided a crucial stop-gap for the typically long waiting period for public housing that could be up to ten years. My initial inclination, to view the Russians as slum landlords, was tempered by 'Barbara's' more even-handed assessment and I began to see the *quid pro quo*. The Russians got a government subsidy for the bond ($900), guaranteed rental income via authorised deductions from Centrelink welfare payments, and got tenants with relatively low expectations that their landlords would maintain the house in good repair. The Warlpiri tenants got a foothold in a suburb where there were other Warlpiri people, the prospects of cheaper welfare housing in the same area becoming available upon the expiry of waiting times, and all without the intrusiveness and unrealistic standards of care required by the mainstream private rental market and public housing authorities.

When I began working with 'Barbara' as an informant and guide in 2010, she had been in Adelaide for twenty years. I found a confident, outgoing and energetic Warlpiri woman participating in diverse social networks. She was a high-functioning matriarch at the organisational centre of three separate households that constituted her extended family in Adelaide. She had remained in the matrimonial home after the separation and there she continued to raise three of her teenage grandchildren whose mother followed the drinking life in Alice Springs. In another house belonging to the Russians she had installed her adult daughter from her first marriage to a Warlpiri man as well as her daughter's Arrernte boyfriend and sundry other Warlpiri kin. In the third house was another adult daughter, a single parent who had a job in child welfare and, extremely rarely for the Warlpiri diaspora, was paying off the mortgage on the house. There was deftness and vigilance in 'Barbara's' handling of the never-ending demands of maintaining the school routine for her grandchildren and providing an emotional and financial backstop for her daughters in the other households. She was constantly on the telephone making arrangements and checking whereabouts. There was considerable movement of children and other persons between all the co-operating Warlpiri households, including 'Emily's', that reminded me a little of the micro-mobility and continually recombining households of Yuendumu (Musharbash 2008b, 2000: 57–59). While the Christian *jilimi* of Alice Springs was a deliberately created women's space, 'Barbara's' three households seemed more like the model of a matrifocal household that arose out of Caribbean ethnography. The household routine revolved around the care and education of children and grandchildren. The fathers of the children were mostly absent and the affective bonds seemed to be focused on the female heads of the households. 'Barbara's' sense of achievement was also apparent: 'I like living here. I really miss my homeland but I have a good home here. My grandkids go to school and my kids finished year 10 and 12.

At Yuendumu there is a lot of family fighting and I feel sorry for my family. I want to do something for them'. At her grandchildren's primary school she had developed a positive relationship with the principal who had commissioned some traditional artworks from her and displayed them prominently in the school. Also on the school's staff was an Aboriginal liaison officer whose professional involvement with both 'Barbara's' and 'Emily's' grandchildren grew into friendship with them and a closer involvement with both families. In 'Emily's' case the officer involved was given a Warlpiri skin name and 'Emily's' grandchildren referred to her as 'Nanna'. The officer was also able to help the Warlpiri women deal with public housing and welfare authorities.

More generally, 'Barbara's' knowledge of the opportunities presented by the city and how to negotiate its vastness had accumulated over time. After so many years, she had developed a mastery of the public transport system which, among other things, enabled her to visit Warlpiri patients who had been flown to the major hospitals for the treatment of acute or complicated conditions. The hospital visits seemed to be a constant feature of her life in Adelaide and a means of providing support for her kin at a critical time. She knew where one could sell a painting, the location of the best op shops (charitable thrift stores) and the most affordable retail outlets. She also knew which second-hand car yards had creative ways of financing purchases through the barter of a painting or the illegal handing over of welfare debit cards with confidential pin numbers.[7] It seemed to me that the accumulation of this kind of knowledge and its transmission to other Warlpiri matriarchs and their relations, who were curious about the possibilities of living in Adelaide, constituted them as the Masterful Warlpiri Matriarchs of Adelaide (cf. Sansom's Masterful Men of the Darwin fringe camp in the 1970s [1980: 63–67]). For the curious relations who may have seen Adelaide as dauntingly impenetrable, these Masterful Matriarchs possessed arcane knowledge that could, improbably, materialise into rental accommodation, cars and supplementary income from selling paintings.

'Barbara's' time in Adelaide overlapped with the general rise in the availability of mobile phones and more particularly the extension of the mobile network to Yuendumu in the early 2000s.[8] The technology and 'Barbara's' diligence in keeping in touch with her kin enabled her virtual participation in settlement life. Her intimate knowledge of unfolding events on the settlement in very close to real time sometimes confounded her more technologically savvy daughters who maintained contact with their age-mates via Facebook and chat rooms. It was through her virtual participation that 'Barbara' and all the Warlpiri people in Adelaide quickly became aware of the terrible manslaughter at Warlpiri Camp in Alice Springs in September 2010 that sparked riotous retaliation and an ongoing and pervasive family feud that lasted for more than two years. 'Barbara' and 'Emily', mutually supportive for so long in Adelaide, found themselves on opposite sides of the feud and its various flare-ups which would be repeated in the suburbs of Adelaide. How they and the other Warlpiri people in Adelaide responded to the feud will be dealt with below (Intra-Warlpiri dynamics in Adelaide during the family feud).

Warlpiri Women Artists

At the core of this group were a close triad of Warlpiri women from Mount Allan: two sisters and the daughter of one of them. The leader, who I will call 'Suzanne', was an exceptional woman, in the sense of having been a teacher in a remote settlement school for some time, having moved to Alice Springs and worked there as a semi-professional artist for some years and, finally, having arrived in Adelaide with a white boyfriend. One of her few contacts in Adelaide had been an art adviser for some years in her remote settlement. While not in a position to help her himself, he introduced her to a friend who developed an art wholesaling business which became one of the economic foundations of her life in Adelaide and of the other Aboriginal artists in the group who eventually joined her in Adelaide. The first was her sister with her own white husband and the son they had together, and the second was her daughter, who among other things was fleeing with her children from a violent relationship in Alice Springs. The fourth member of the group was a more distantly related woman from Willowra who had been prompted to leave that settlement when her Warlpiri husband had insisted upon taking a second, younger wife.

The artists received a few hundred dollars for each canvas they completed, typically one or two a week, thereby doubling their welfare income. This allowed them to buy the food and clothes they liked, even during the lean week after the fortnightly welfare payments. It also enabled them to purchase motor vehicles, send money to relations and, for at least one of them, attend a local club to pursue her favoured diversion of playing the poker machines. The geographical distance from most of their relations enabled some circumvention of opportunistic demand sharing, although the increasing incidence of mobile phone ownership was encroaching upon that. The moderation of the continual demand sharing on the settlements was also mentioned by Povinelli in her description of one of her informants who had relocated to Darwin, along with 'the relief of stranger sociality' (2006: 117–18). It seemed to me that the circumstances of the Warlpiri matriarchs in Adelaide enabled unprecedented personal autonomy which I observed first-hand when one of the four artists arrived in Adelaide with literally no possessions, having recently broken up with her white partner. Ill and penniless and without access to welfare payments, which she had diverted to paying off a car (long since broken down), she commenced painting in a small spare bedroom of a Warlpiri relation in Adelaide ('Barbara's' daughter's place). By the end of the week she had replenished her wardrobe with the proceeds of one painting and purchased another second-hand car with another painting.

The relationship with the art wholesaler endured primarily because their project of relative economic independence coincided with their art wholesaler's own project of economic independence.[9] Both were reliant upon the fickle flows of changing tastes in the international and national art market and cyclical fluctuations in the disposable income of art buyers. Critically, the wholesaler had chosen to deal only with artists whose work he thought he could sell and had developed a niche of affordable Aboriginal art that was to some extent insulated from the wilder fluctuations of the high-end fine art market. His relationship with the leader of the Warlpiri women artists sometimes came under strain when she tried to encroach on it by appealing to him to advance loans and assist her with sundry everyday problems and family crises. He resisted these pressures and relied instead upon his consistent payment, his honest dealings and a much appreciated annual artist residency he had organised for some of them that allowed them to spend time in an art gallery at Yulara (near Uluru/Ayers Rock), a major tourist destination in the south-east corner of the Northern Territory. From Yulara they could more easily visit their relations in Alice Springs and back at Mount Allan. For their part, the Warlpiri artists were broadly loyal to the art wholesaler, but to varying degrees. 'Suzanne' had in fact developed multiple relationships with gallery owners in the greater Adelaide region and was occasionally able to receive an advance from them when money was tight. But she realised that because of the volume of artworks she delivered to the wholesaler and the consistency of payment, he would remain her economic mainstay in Adelaide.

Supplementing her economic mainstay were 'Suzanne's' other useful contacts. She knew the Russian landlords and the second-hand car dealer mentioned above and had regular interactions with them. She also seemed to collect admirers along the way such as a previous white neighbour of hers with whom she had an ongoing arrangement whereby the neighbour would give 'Suzanne' her old furniture and bedding when she was upgrading.

'Natalie'

'Natalie' (born 1967) was even more adventurous than 'Dulcie' in remaking her life. As the previous chapter demonstrated, in Alice Springs 'Dulcie' continually tried to hold together the various strands of her life that were pulling in different directions: the dangerous sexual adventures, the caring grandmother who would teach her grandchildren traditional painting, the mother attempting to deal with the problem drinking of some of her own children, the intrepid traveller, the occasional political activist and the respectable Baptist church woman. 'Natalie', on the other hand, had been willing to shed her former selves to embrace the drinking life of the Adelaide underclass and to scorn shame in all its forms. Her journey to become one of the indomitable characters among the tough men of the Adelaide parklands had commenced long before at Yuendumu in the 1960s where she had been born into a talented Warlpiri family. Her father, who was the first Warlpiri person to learn to drive a truck while serving in the army in the Second World War, was a prominent intermediary figure in post-war missionary and government projects on the settlement. From my interactions with her I judged that she had done well at school. Looking through the old photographs of Yuendumu from that era, she saw an old man who had been given the name Romeo and she recalled how he had playfully chased her as a young school girl saying that she had the right skin (subsection) to be his wife. She now quipped 'I suppose that made me Juliet'. Her first marriage was to a Warlpiri man and subsequently she married a white man in Alice Springs where they had two children prior to the relationship ending and her embrace of life in the Adelaide parklands. Although she was not there to assist in their secondary schooling, her son became the second student of Warlpiri descent to matriculate to university.

In the parklands she developed a wide circle of friends, acquaintances and drinking partners and she had a number of different relationships with white men she met there. Some of these relationships ended violently but it was also clear that she was never the helpless victim. As well as having a strong personality, she was physically strong and had a reputation for smashing up the houses of ex-boyfriends. The man she had the most intense relationship with took out a restraining order against her after being threatened with a knife. Rather than being afraid of such situations, she seemed enlivened by their dangerous intensity and extremity. She had become irritated with the company of Warlpiri women, especially their criticism of her behaviour and their gossip about her. This did not stop her from taking on the role of self-appointed matchmaker and urging the single among them to consider her male acquaintances from the parklands as prospective boyfriends.

Her focus on asserting herself and her personal freedom (she described herself as being 'free as a bird') were also reflected in her stylish and sometimes outrageous clothing. She was no longer a young woman yet another Warlpiri acquaintance described in amazement one of her outfits: tight miniskirt, fluorescent pink leggings and ponytail with pink headband to match. Mixed with incredulity, there seemed to be among the other Warlpiri people in Adelaide a certain vicarious pleasure in her defiance of social conventions, even if the loud declaratory monologue, for which she was well-known, was very wearying and they became apprehensive about their chance encounters with her. Her style and her articulate forthrightness made her a figure of renown, 'a character', among the staff of the soup kitchens and NGOs dealing with homeless people in the city. She seemed adept at dealing with all the governmental authorities she required to sustain her life and was also unusually successful in quickly converting to her cause any strangers she happened upon in the course of her day.

Over the course of the research project her life went through a remarkable transition because of a cancer scare and subsequent chemotherapy. She was forced to give up drinking and this allowed her to change her life, to accept permanent welfare housing and to vow to return to Christian practices. But these possibilities placed her in conflict with her previous life and her many friends who continued to live rough and drink. She surreptitiously shared her new accommodation with them, allowing them to have their breakfast of sherry, cigarettes and vitamin pills in the flat and encouraging the despondent and self-critical among them ('no, don't say that about yourself, you are a beautiful person'). The most disturbing of these conflicts, however, was her continued love for and obsession with her previous boyfriend, who had apparently forgiven the knife incident.

Because of the health crisis, 'Natalie's' reign as the Warlpiri queen of the parklands did not last. But while it did, she seemed to have achieved a unique and total inversion of the gender relations on the home settlements as demonstrated by her physical aggression and intimidation, her assertive promiscuity, her preference for the company of the opposite sex, and the organisation of sexual partners for her female Warlpiri friends. Even more fundamental, however, was the self-selection of her circle of friends and partners who formed the core of her life in Adelaide. This new circle of friends in many ways replaced her kinship network.

The Ali Curung Children's House

In contrast to the theme of escape and the inversion of gender relations so evident in 'Natalie's' diasporic trajectory, what I have called the Ali Curung children's house represents a more deliberate and moderated attempt to maintain links with the home settlement and to find some accommodation between the norms of settlement life and the possibilities offered by distant education. Central to the project was 'Valmae', born of Warlpiri parents at Ali Curung in the 1960s. Growing up there in the 1970s and 1980s, she absorbed the traditionalism of her father and other renowned cultural leaders like Topsy Nelson and Engineer Jack, who were non-drinkers at the forefront of land claims, the outstation movement and the continued performance of Warlpiri rituals. Her family, more than others, had grasped the opportunity of education on the settlement. In the wider context of deteriorating social conditions, largely attributable to alcohol abuse, her father, critically, supported her postponement of promised marriage to further her education, first at boarding schools, then at an Aboriginal college in Adelaide with some of her close relations from Tennant Creek. In Adelaide some of them had already reunited with their old school principal who had retired there and now took an active and extraordinarily generous interest in supporting their further education by directing their familiarisation with the city and purchasing accommodation for them.

The idea of hosting children from Ali Curung and putting them through school in Adelaide commenced in a small and somewhat accidental way when 'Valmae' found herself the guardian of some younger siblings when her parents died. She joined forces with a white man, a friend of the ex-principal, who was also hosting children from Ali Curung, and they eventually married. They did not have any children of their own. With the support of the ex-principal and 'Valmae's' stepmother, an Aboriginal police aide back at Ali Curung, their work of hosting settlement children grew. Over a period of twenty years they hosted 65 Aboriginal children from Ali Curung for varying periods of time. This remarkable project was conceived of and operated outside any targeted government programme. It was partially financed unofficially by virtue of generally available welfare payments for carers for looking after the children concerned. But the bulk of the financial support came from the husband's job as a technician at a TV station, and a bank loan which funded the purchase of a minibus.

There was no written manifesto of the school education project but it was expressed in the 'two laws talk' contrasting Warlpiri culture with European culture (cf. Austin-Broos 1996; Harris 1990) and it was clear that they aspired to produce bi-cultural individuals (cf. Pearson 2009b: 292–300). It was always envisaged that following the completion of their school education the visiting children would return permanently to Ali Curung. They all visited Ali Curung on a yearly basis; sometimes that visit would include spending time at the deceased father's outstation where they received some instruction in traditional culture from his widow. The non-Aboriginal husband had been increasingly drawn into the ceremonial life of the settlement over the course of these return visits. Emblematic of this group was its small bus. Its purchase strained their already stretched financial resources but it was essential for their frequent orbiting back to the settlement (a distance of 1,900 km one way) and ferrying children to school.

'Rosie'

'Rosie' is an Aboriginal woman from Ali Curung who had been living in Adelaide for thirty years. I was keen to meet her, especially since I had been discouraged from seeking her out because she was thought to no longer associate with Aboriginal people (a gross exaggeration I found out) and had joined a Pentecostal church (true). Her initial journey to Adelaide in 1983 was via a well-trodden route to Adelaide Hospital[10] where her mother was being treated for a chronic illness.

After some hesitation and prolonged negotiation, I finally met 'Rosie' at a mutual friend's house. The mutual friend was a white woman who had worked for Aboriginal NGOs in Alice Springs for a long time in the 1980s and had returned to teaching in Adelaide at an Aboriginal college where 'Rosie' was a student. They got to know each other at the college and eventually the friendship expanded beyond their respective roles at the college. The three of us met a number of times over the course of the research project and I was eventually able, following detailed negotiations, to secure 'Rosie's' approval for the following account.

I found 'Rosie' to be a self-possessed and articulate woman who had become a cross-cultural educator involved in many community organisations and a person who ran her own well-maintained household. What she wanted to impress upon me was her career in education. Following her initial course at an Aboriginal community college, she gained her certificate in cultural awareness training and was registered for part-time work with the State Department of Education's children's services. In addition to her work with school children telling Aboriginal stories through her paintings, she provided cross-cultural input into the training of police and community centre coordinators. When I met her she had completed a further course at the Aboriginal college in business studies and was planning to enrol in an adult entry matriculation course. Of all the Aboriginal people I met in the Warlpiri diaspora, she seemed the person who had most strongly internalised the education message. She explained to me sincerely: 'education gives you more opportunity and self-esteem'.

Her cross-cultural teaching typically involved some demonstration and explanation of her dot painting and she had learnt to adjust the presentation to the level of the intended audience. The subjects of her paintings were deliberately innocuous, such as designs representing various kinds of seeds. Like the semi-professional artists already mentioned, she was well aware of the settlement norms surrounding the ownership of different traditional designs. Her choice of subject matter was meant to avoid any potential antipathy should her paintings stray into designs associated with Dreamings owned by others or otherwise cause offence back on the settlement. As well as cross-cultural education, she was interested in art. She saw her painting as being part of who she was. On the strength of her interest in art, she was able to secure a position in an elite, government-sponsored artists' workshop where she had completed a certificate in visual arts and was now studying ceramics. The other strand of her cross-cultural training was a critique of stereotyping and prejudice.

Her personal support network in Adelaide included her sister who lived nearby and who, according to 'Rosie', was an even more private person than herself.[11] She also had supportive contact with the Warlpiri woman from Ali Curung who, with her white husband, ran the Ali Curung children's house. 'Rosie' herself seemed to make fewer return trips to the settlement and was more cautious about visiting kin disrupting her household, her educational career and her painting. When I raised the problems that other Warlpiri households in Adelaide were having with visiting kin disrupting school routines and not contributing to household expenses, she was explicit in her attitude: she found the idea of mixing mainly with kin extremely limiting and wrong in principle. Perhaps reflecting her strong Christian beliefs, she stated her alternative view: 'I don't care who they are as long as they are good people'. As an illustration, she spoke of her involvement with the Pitjantjatjara women in Adelaide who were all artists, not relations and 'non-alcoholic'. She also seemed proud of having the ability to gradually get to know people at her local community centre which she initially approached as a stranger. The centre brought back childhood memories of the early days of Ali Curung when the Country Women's Association had established a centre and taught Aboriginal women to sew. She found the atmosphere at the community centre inviting and soon made some friends there. Eventually she became a project officer responsible for reaching out to the local Aboriginal people and this work counted as her placement for her business studies course. Moreover, in response to our discussion about demand sharing, she asserted her own Aboriginal family tradition of the need to ask for things and the possibility of being refused. She rejected the taking of possessions from close kin without asking as lacking in respect and trust that their requests would be responded to with generosity. As to visitors, she had her own rules: they had to respect her things.

Parallel Diaspora of White Friends

Having just described something of the extraordinary role of the retired school principal in supporting the Ali Curung diaspora and the regular orbiting back to the settlement and the friendship of the college teacher exceeding her official role, it is convenient now to consider this category of white person more thoroughly. These are non-Aboriginal people who have worked in Warlpiri settlements or Aboriginal NGOs in Alice Springs over a lengthy period of time, long enough to form personal friendships with Aboriginal people and to understand the degree of cultural difference between the settlement-raised Warlpiri and the non-Aboriginal city dwellers. Although they came from all over Australia, a number of them returned or moved to Adelaide. Apart from those already mentioned, they included an early Baptist missionary at Ali Curung; another ex-school principal from Lajamanu; teachers who had worked at Yirara College (the Aboriginal secondary boarding school in Alice Springs); a young man who had worked in adult education at Yuendumu; one young lady who had gone to school at Yuendumu, where her father was a teacher and later principal; and her husband, who had worked with her at a mediation NGO at Yuendumu. Such work experiences in relatively exotic places like the remote settlements tend to have a powerful emotional effect on the people concerned. The number of white staff who churn through the jobs on the settlements and the relatively small scale of Australia compared to global diasporas meant that seemingly extraordinary coincidences of meeting known non-Aboriginal people at local schools and local shopping malls in Adelaide were not that unusual.[12]

Not all those in the parallel diaspora had the same reaction to their erstwhile Warlpiri friends moving to Adelaide. Some blended into the background as it is so easy to do in the suburbs of a city, let contact details lapse and became invisible to the Warlpiri. Another person, a former adult educator on a Warlpiri settlement, had the chastening experience of seeing a few hundred dollars that was cadged off him by visiting Warlpiri 'brothers', ostensibly to feed hungry children, being used for a drinking party. Henceforth he was inclined to blend into the background like the other invisible ex-settlement workers. The couple who had worked for the mediation organisation unexpectedly found themselves called back into service when the 100 refugees from the family feud arrived in Elizabeth in 2010. But it was the ex-principal from Ali Curung who had taken the most extreme steps to support and extend the Ali Curung diaspora in Adelaide by diverting his own financial resources, his own house and the remaining years of his retirement to the projects of diaspora and orbiting that seemed to have become the centre of his life.

To be clear, this category of white person does not necessarily form its own social network. The academics, such as the linguists and anthropologists who have studied Warlpiri language and culture, could be considered part of the parallel diaspora. They may form a sparse network which consists of knowing of each other's existence, reading each other's work, meeting at conferences and seminars, and occasionally co-operating on research projects. The stronger personal links, however, remain with their Warlpiri informants.

When considering the totality of the parallel diaspora, the academics are significantly outnumbered by all the white people who have worked in a wide variety of jobs on settlements and they tend not to know each other.

Some of the white people of the parallel diaspora overlap with the 'White anti-racists' analysed by Emma Kowal in *Trapped in the Gap* (2015). Kowal analysed the contradictions in the way of thinking of white, middle-class professionals employed to assist Aboriginal people improve their health. The original commitment of the white health professionals tended to unravel when confronted with deep and unsettling connections between their advocacy for necessary lifestyle change and processes of assimilation that they assumed had been supplanted by the era of self-determination. The differences between this category of people and the group I have called the parallel diaspora is instructive. The range of class positions represented by the various jobs on a typical settlement is much broader than the tertiary-educated, health professionals that were the focus of Kowal's study. As well as the tertiary educated settlement doctors, teachers, nurses and researchers (and, in a previous era, missionaries), the ranks of the parallel diaspora would also include administrators and employees of settlement NGOs, tradesmen, store managers, and office workers in various government services, not to mention their spouses. Accordingly, the overwrought self-doubt that tended to characterise the professional practice of Kowal's 'White anti-racist' health professionals was not so marked among most of the parallel diaspora of ex-settlement workers. In addition, except for the few instances mentioned, their continuing relationships with Warlpiri people in the diaspora were not a continuation of their work roles on the settlement and therefore potentially less problematic.

Those Without a Project – a Balancing Comment

In the interests of comprehensiveness, I want to make some attempt to overcome the methodological bias towards the stable, accessible Warlpiri matriarchs I have been describing thus far, even if the result is necessarily more impressionistic. For as well as those women who had taken positive action in various projects of personal autonomy and self-direction, there were also others who were drifting or stuck or who had entered into such controlling relationships or drug dependency as to severely limit their capacity for personal autonomy and active and constructive agency. Emblematic of these women was one middle-aged Warlpiri woman who had taken up with a much younger white man, who was also dependent upon the drugs purchased out of the proceeds of the sale of her paintings. She seemed to be defeated by the sadness of the murder of her son in Alice

Springs and she had moved to Adelaide because she could not bear to see those she thought responsible for her son's death walking free around Alice Springs. She looked thin and vacant when I met her and I got the impression that the basis of the relationship with the young man was a shared commitment to oblivion. I heard that she died shortly after the completion of my fieldwork. It was unclear whether her remaining relations would be able to organise a funeral for her.

One of the Warlpiri women, who was in fact the named tenant of the drinking household with the silvery pyramid in the backyard, met 'Barbara' and I a year later and we were shocked by the deterioration in her appearance. She had discharged herself from hospital and was trying to warm herself in front of a single bar heater in her bare house while talking to us in a strange and rambling stream of consciousness. She and her sister had left Yuendumu years before for the long-grass life in Darwin where they met a white alcoholic ex-biker with whom she formed a relationship and who she followed to Sydney and the Adelaide parklands. During that time she was badly injured when a car ran into her as she was crossing a street. After a long period of hospitalisation, public housing was provided for her lengthy rehabilitation and a young relation sent from Yuendumu to be her carer (and, as it turned out, her fellow drinker). During this time the ex-biker boyfriend returned to the long grass in Darwin and she complained bitterly of being 'dumped'. Now, in her deteriorating mental state, she accused him of taking all her compensation money from the accident and buying himself a flash car in which he was 'running around' (having affairs).

Her deterioration continued over the course of the research, as did the state of her housing. Her vulnerability to predatory members of the white underclass increased and even though she became more delirious and immobile, there always seemed to be some shabby white partner on the scene looking hungover. From conversations with one of them I gained the impression that there was a small network of such men who knew each other and, at various times, had relationships with similarly vulnerable Aboriginal women.

The silvery pyramid house was not the only drinking household. A Warlpiri man who had transferred to Adelaide after the dissolution of the large Warlpiri outpost in Murray Bridge also lived in public housing. Because he was never sober, however, I was unable to ascertain how he maintained the tenancy. His house became the destination for travelling Warlpiri drinkers and his own network of kin. He also died in the course of the fieldwork. It may have been that his poor health had put him in a higher category of need under the guidelines of the public housing authority. This was the case with another Warlpiri woman whose recent drastic surgery (a liver operation) had precipitated successful advocacy on her behalf by the Aboriginal Health Service notwithstanding a succession of wrecked welfare houses in her past.

The drinker/non-drinker identification continued to be a significant social cleavage among the Warlpiri diaspora in Adelaide. The most successful defenders of their non-drinking households were those who could point to their schoolchildren as the rationale for their abstemiousness and who had the support of their white partners. Others who would normally prefer a 'dry' household would relent on occasion and allow selected individuals to drink in their houses. But they were wary of the consequences of such occasional relenting. News of the possibility of establishing a new drinking camp would spread quickly and a number of the Warlpiri matriarchs had bad experiences of finding their temporarily vacated homes (when they returned to the settlements for funeral trips) filled with partying homeless people on their return. For their part, the drinkers complained about their relations who would not drink with them, sometimes accusing them of ignoring their own kin and of being racist. The non-drinkers tended to see alcoholism as an inherent personality trait that was difficult if not impossible to moderate. Their preferred strategy for dealing with the drinkers and the demands and mayhem that accompanied them was simply to politely avoid them.

Those who, like 'Natalie', were forced to give up drinking because of health crises, had a more benign attitude to mixing with the drinkers. I witnessed her operating fearlessly among them and even extracting money from one of her drunken ex-partners. There were also Warlpiri women who seemed to occupy an intermediate position like the Warlpiri woman in Darwin who lived in the suburbs with her non-drinking partner and school-attending son. She still enjoyed the occasional drinking session with her long-grass friends but always had her path of retreat planned in case the partying turned violent.

Other more subtle, subterranean differences seemed to be emerging among the non-drinkers over household budgeting and the issue of visiting kin. Some of the matriarchs ran financially viable households that depended upon the careful application of scarce funds to second-hand clothes, cheap foodstuffs and their successful application of demand sharing to their own networks when bills fell due. They were amazed that other matriarchs would spend a financial windfall from the sale of a painting by splurging on poker machines at a club rather than paying off a pressing overdue utility bill. The finances of all the households were vulnerable to visiting kin, but to varying degrees. 'Rosie's' rather strict approach to limiting visitors has already been mentioned. At the other end of the continuum, I witnessed one of the women artists and her white partner shivering in their cold house. Their gas had been cut off for non-payment of a

$600 bill incurred when visiting kin insisted upon the continuous heating of the house during their stay in what they found to be an unusually cold city. Another household had even more trouble with two young male visiting kin who became involved in a gang rape which was widely reported in the mass media. One was acquitted and returned to Yuendumu. The other is still serving his sentence in a jail in Adelaide.

Pan-Warlpiri Dynamics in Adelaide

If anything, pan-Warlpiri solidarity and cohesion was even weaker in Adelaide than in Alice Springs. As far as I could gather, there had never been a sorry camp set up in Adelaide as there had been on numerous occasions in Alice Springs. The Warlpiri in Adelaide were more orientated towards their own kin networks which typically emphasised one particular settlement where most of their kin resided. Thus it was that 'Barbara', orientated towards Yuendumu, and 'Valmae', orientated towards Ali Curung, did not know each other despite both having lived in Adelaide for twenty years. Similarly, the occupants of two Warlpiri households in neighbouring suburbs but from different home settlements did not know of each other's existence. There was no pan-Warlpiri meeting place or movement emerging, nothing like the Indian bars or organised cultural events in large American cities that became the focal point for tribal diasporas (see Ablon 1964; Hoikkala 1998; Janovicek 2003; Krouse 2001; Lobo and Peters 1998; Ramirez 2007; Straus and Valentino 1998; Weibel-Orlando 1998, 1999). The Warlpiri people tended to know where the Arrernte and the Pitjantjatjara people lived and some friendships with them had been formed. One of the Warlpiri women lived with a Pitjantjatjara boyfriend. But there was no pan-Central Australian Aboriginal meeting place or organisation emerging. The Warlpiri people in Adelaide did become regular clients of the local Aboriginal medical service and Aboriginal legal aid service but those services were firmly in the control of the local Aboriginal people.

In contrast to the fragmentation of the Warlpiri, the Pitjantjatjara and Yankunytjatjara were a much more established diaspora. Since the Anangu Pitjantjatjara Yankunytjatjara (APY) lands lie within South Australia, State responsibilities towards them made them more of an official diaspora. This resulted in there being a residential secondary school for them in Adelaide and a government-funded programme of assisted return to the remote settlements. As mentioned in the story of 'Rosie', they also have their own artists' centre and retail art gallery. In addition, the history of missionisation linked the APY settlements to the Uniting Church in Adelaide, particularly through the continuing involvement of a long-term missionary, Bill

Edwards. His deep knowledge of the Pitjantjatjara migrants, his command of the Pitjantjatjara language and his service as an interpreter in Adelaide hospitals and courts made him and the Uniting Church a unique unifying presence. He was able to provide the church with an insider's overview of the many social problems facing the Pitjantjatjara diaspora in Adelaide (Edwards 2010, 2012, n.d.). Like the Warlpiri, the Pitjantjatjara migrants tended to congregate in the northern suburbs. So many of them began to attend services at one of the Uniting Churches that it became feasible to appoint a Pitjantjatjara minister. In theory, the Baptist church in Elizabeth could have become a similar focal point. However, Warlpiri attendance at Baptist services had waned everywhere including in Adelaide and a number of Warlpiri Christians in Adelaide had become involved in other denominations. Consequently, there did not appear to be any critical mass of Warlpiri Baptists to develop some attractive dynamism as had happened in Alice Springs.

Relations with Local Aboriginal People

I formed the impression from piecemeal evidence that there was not the same intensity of competition between the Warlpiri and the local Aboriginal people of Adelaide that had been such a feature of the Warlpiri diaspora in Alice Springs. This is consistent with the relatively small-scale of the Warlpiri diaspora, the lack of centralised organisation and the more prominent Pitjantjatjara presence. The Warlpiri women of Adelaide never volunteered stories of a negative response by locals to Warlpiri cultural assertion, although there was a recognition of difference. 'Valmae' came to know many of the local Kaurna and Ngarrindjeri families through the Aboriginal college she had attended. But she would not send her hosted school children to a local Aboriginal dance class because she thought the children should learn their own traditional dancing first and she did not expect the locals to understand her reasoning. One of the Warlpiri women had partnered with a local Aboriginal man in what appeared to be an amicable union. Among other things, he used his local contacts to help her gain access to a major Aboriginal art gallery run by the local Aboriginal people. His patience was tested when, in defence of his Warlpiri partner, he became embroiled in the family feud when it flared up in Adelaide. Although he complained that such violent feuding should not take place on other people's traditional country, he seemed powerless to enforce such a view. The issue did not seem to register with the Warlpiri combatants who were preoccupied with more immediate concerns of defending themselves.

Intra-Warlpiri Dynamics in Adelaide during the Family Feud

The family feud and the arrival of the 100 Warlpiri refugees disrupted a number of the matriarchs' projects and temporarily distorted the shape of the Warlpiri diaspora in Adelaide. The strain on the foundational and mutually supportive relationship between 'Barbara' and 'Emily' has already been mentioned. As in Alice Springs, the Warlpiri Christians felt both internal and external pressure to abandon their commitment to peaceful, non-combative relationships and they did so to varying degrees. 'Barbara' verbally confronted the refugees as soon as they arrived in Adelaide, not far from where she lived, suggesting they should return to Yuendumu to face her aggrieved relations. She also made a return trip to be with her relations and participate in the violent contretemps that began to dominate settlement life at Yuendumu. Another long-term Warlpiri resident of Adelaide also faced conflict due to his strongly held Christianity. He had specifically embarked upon migration, first to Murray Bridge then Adelaide, to 'change his life' through involvement in a succession of Christian denominations and finally a Pentecostal church in Adelaide. He stated with some regret that during the feud he had 'turned away from the church'. Both he and 'Barbara' were at pains to explain to the anthropologist, who gave off missionary vibes, that they were only involved in blocking actions, interposing themselves to protect their relations from aggression, and did not lead any violent attacks on the other side. 'Barbara' also discouraged her children in Adelaide from becoming involved and argued that exceptions should be made for 'good people', like her long-term friend 'Emily', when choosing targets for retaliation. And indeed, actual co-operation between the two women over the care of grandchildren in Adelaide was resumed well before the end of hostilities.

Although other things were happening in 'Emily's' household, it was the aftermath of the 100 refugees that undermined its economic sustainability. As she was a close relation of the refugee group, her household became the destination for visitors even after the majority of refugees had returned to Yuendumu. In a pattern I had already observed in Alice Springs (of incomplete return after fleeing a family feud), some of the refugee group stayed on in Adelaide at her house. While 'Emily' was on a return trip to Yuendumu, they held a loud drunken party in the front yard and damaged various parts of the house. While the housing authorities were sympathetic, given her previous good record, she was lumbered with additional fortnightly payments to cover the cost of repairs. She despaired of trying to impress upon her Warlpiri guests that unlike at Yuendumu she was personally liable for such things. The stark economics of the situation confronted her: it would be cheaper to return to Yuendumu to live.

Conclusion: Cultural Reproduction and Transformations in the City

The surprising isolation of different Warlpiri settlement groups in Adelaide helps to clarify the overall shape of the Warlpiri diaspora Australia wide. It consists of overlapping networks of kin spread out over Australia in nodes of various concentrations. The remote settlements remain the biggest nodes for all kin networks which extend to significant nodes in the city where exceptional matriarchs, who have gained support through various non-kin networks, pursue a variety of projects of schooling and art that are also vulnerable, to varying degrees. Yet again, the maintaining of inter-racial marriages has been important but so has the maintaining of friendships in a parallel diaspora, turning educational and welfare personnel into friends, maintaining key economic relationships such as the one with the art wholesaler, and generally maintaining supportive networks of people outside of their existing kinship networks. It will be recalled from the previous chapter on Alice Springs that 'Dulcie' was perhaps the most relentless networker of non-kin. Now we can see that such networking and the non-traditional social technologies it requires are a more general feature of the Warlpiri matriarchs who can sustain themselves in the diaspora. The social technologies I am thinking of involved the finding of common ground. In 'Dulcie's' case there was shared commitment to fun-seeking and shared Christian values, beliefs and ritual practices. In Adelaide there were also shared projects of household routines in support of children's education, shared economic projects in the art market, and, in the case of 'Rosie' and her long-term white teacher friend, a shared project of women's autonomy and self-actualisation. The contemporary networking with non-kin seems to have a completely different basis to demand-sharing networks of kin or the extension of ritual networks by older men. In those cases, the participation in networks was predicated upon shared beliefs about obligations to certain categories of kin and shared beliefs about the value of the rituals. It should be made clear, though, that the Warlpiri matriarchs had not abandoned their kin networks. They have moderated their impacts to varying degrees, principally through sheer physical distance from most of their kin, and they have enlarged their personal social networks in significant ways beyond their kin.

The exceptional character of 'Natalie' also clarifies some of the more general aspects of the feminised Warlpiri diaspora and its relationship to the home settlements. She represents an apogee of boldness, of the assertion of personal autonomy in the mode of severing constraining relationships and of the inversion of the typical gender order on the settlements. Yet her vulnerability to romantic love also recalls the feminist critique of romantic love as antithetical to personal autonomy (Friedman 2003: 115–39). Put more positively, she could be seen as the exemplification of a grand transformation that could be extrapolated from the ubiquity of love in contemporary desiderata (see, for example, May 2011): from spiritually emplaced and socially embedded personhood on the settlements to diasporic personhood grounded in de-territorialised love and self-created social networks of non-kin.

Notes

1. Some material in this chapter was previously published in Burke, 2015, 'Rupture and Readjustment of Tradition: Agency and Autonomy in the Feminised Warlpiri Diaspora in Australia', in *Strings of Connectedness: Essays in Honour of Ian Keen*, edited by P. Toner, Canberra: ANU E Press, pp. 215–34; and Burke, 2017, 'Bold Women of the Warlpiri Diaspora who Went too Far', in *People and Change in Indigenous Australia*, edited by D. Austin-Broos and F. Merlan, Honolulu: University of Hawai'i Press, pp. 29–43. Reprinted with permission.
2. Interview with Neville Japangardi Poulson, 9 November 2011.
3. Originally an agricultural fair involving the competitive display of animals, plants and produce in a dedicated field or stadium, its city version has now been transformed into a venue for spectacle and mass entertainment, sideshows and increasingly elaborate mechanical rides.
4. Ameliorative policies seem to have stabilised what could have been an ever-increasing residential divide. But the basic structures of residential income inequality are still entrenched and subject to intensification with the continued decline of manufacturing and general restructuring of the Australian economy in the 1980s (Beer and Forster 2002; Baum and Hassan 1993).
5. Because the parklands of the city of Adelaide are a seemingly unlikely location for a skid row, some explanation is in order. Adelaide, founded in 1836 as the capital city of the colony of South Australia, was unusual in Australian history in that it did not originate as a penal settlement but was a planned settlement of free immigrants. The parklands around the city were a very early version of a green belt around the planned administrative and business centre of the city, giving Adelaide its distinctive appearance (Gamaut 2008). Beyond the parklands stretch the suburbs of Adelaide. The closest suburbs to the parklands have undergone significant gentrification in recent years due to their convenient location near to the city centre and the amenity of the parklands which consist of well-tended lawns, formal gardens, water features and walkways (Badcock 2001). Thus to be an itinerant alcoholic in the parklands is to be shockingly out of place in this most civilised of Australian cities and to be exposed in a way that would never happen in an inner-city slum of any other city. It lends the Aboriginal campers there an air of bold defiance which may be surprising given the precariousness of their position on the doorstep of the neat respectability of the city centre.
6. See Department of Families, Housing, Community Services and Indigenous Affairs (2008).
7. With the cards and pin numbers in their possession, the wily second-hand car dealers would usually be assured of repayment and the new owner of the second-hand car would risk penury if their relations did not support them or if their income stream from

painting was interrupted. The car dealers were not the only wily party. One trick after the transaction had been completed was to cancel the debit card using the pretext that it had been lost and be issued with a new one.
8. By 2006 the Warlpiri settlement of Lajamanu had mobile phone reception as did Ali Curung, a settlement with a large Warlpiri minority. The Warlpiri settlements of Willowra and Nyirrpi are still without mobile phone reception (Broadband for the Bush Alliance 2013; Tangentyere Council and Central Land Council 2007).
9. In describing himself as a wholesaler, I think the person concerned wanted to distinguish his role from that of gallery owner and dealer who may not have any contact with the artist. This wholesaler had a direct relationship with the artists, supplied canvases and artists' materials to the artists, and purchased all of the resulting finished canvases. He then sold them to gallery owners around Australia.
10. Coulehan, in her study of Yolngu women living in Darwin, had already noticed how town medical treatment and government support for accompanying persons had become an important means of naturalising the unfamiliar urban environment for remote settlement dwellers (1995: 88–92).
11. Since Sansom has written on the idea of 'private fella' (Sansom 2009), it may be informative to contrast what I see as the different connotations and contexts of his use of the phrase and 'Rosie's' self-description as 'a private person'. Among the labile drinking mobs of hinterland Aboriginal people in Darwin in the late 1970s, the Aboriginal man who described himself as 'the very private fella, me' was exceptional, somewhat incomprehensible and typically in an interstitial period between mobs, which were the usual mode of everyday life. In order to be effective in this milieu, the intention to be detached from a mob, however briefly, had to conform to other shared practices such as widely broadcasting such an intention to members of the mob. It is somewhat unclear whether the temporary achievement of being a 'private fella' was open to all members of a mob or whether it was an infrequent consequence of the bravado of those members of a mob who already possessed a degree of status and respect. In Adelaide in 2011 when 'Rosie' described herself (and her sister) as a private person, it was in the context of not wanting to potentially expose her private life to a visiting anthropologist but also private in the sense of living at a considerable distance from other kin who might disturb her hard-won household and educational routines with excessive demands and unpredictable behaviour. Her kind of solitude was not liminal and not necessarily licensed. It was more like a career choice that would be defended indefinitely.
12. For some data on the turnover of various white staff at Yuendumu in the late 1990s, see Musharbash (2001). As for the concerns about the rising tempo of teacher turnover in remote settlement schools and efforts to overcome it, see Brasche and Harrington (2012).

Chapter 5

AMBIVALENT HOMECOMINGS AND THE POLITICS OF HOME AND AWAY

Introduction

As explained in Chapter 1 of this book, more recent theorising about diaspora tends to underplay the desire to return to the homeland as a constituting element of the field of study. Instead, there is the more inclusive idea that the diasporic identity is significantly defined by an ongoing relationship to the homeland rather than an ongoing desire to physically return. That is certainly the case with the Warlpiri matriarchs of the diaspora who did not seek a permanent return. The significance of the Warlpiri homeland to them is further exemplified by their short-term visits to the homeland for various reasons. This chapter seeks to systematically examine the kind of homeland visitation that occurred, including for initiation ceremonies, mortuary rituals and funerals, mining royalty meetings and participation in the family feud. The result of this examination reinforces the limited social distancing of the first-generation migrants I anticipated in Chapter 1, in other words, that there are certain minimum commitments for any self-respecting Warlpiri person. These temporary return visits of those committed to their diaspora locations are generally unproblematic, as was the permanent return, in their old age, of two of the foundational figures in the Darwin and Alice Springs Warlpiri diaspora. Their return again raises the relevance of the stage in the individual life-cycle in structuring the diaspora.

In contrast, for those who were born or raised in the diaspora, their ability to reconnect with and re-embed themselves into the home settlement culture varied enormously. Various degrees of attenuation of connection are examined in this chapter, ranging from those who were removed at birth and raised by white foster families, to an exceptional example of a young Warlpiri woman who was raised in Adelaide but retained sufficient connections to re-establish herself as an adult at Yuendumu. In between these extremes were those who retained some connections which were difficult to activate in a meaningful way. There were also some who were rebuffed or disappointed in their efforts to reconnect.

An important context for the return visits was the emergence of a politics of identity between those who remained in the homeland and those who migrated to diaspora locations. This kind of politics was anticipated by Jeremy Beckett's work on the Torres Strait Islander diaspora on the Australian mainland, which accounts for 80 per cent of the Torres Strait Islander population (Arthur and Taylor 1995). Differences emerged, for example, when those who remained on the islands took responsibility for land management decisions without reference to the majority diaspora on the mainland (Beckett 1983). While the Warlpiri diaspora is a small minority (23 per cent), differences did start to emerge between the Warlpiri of the homeland and the diaspora. I explore these differences via the mutual stereotyping between the two groups. In two instances these stereotypes had developed into different kinds of mythologising stories about the dangers of being far from one's homeland. The differences were also reflected in disputes over preferred burial sites and differing assumptions about the geographical reach of sorcery.

The emerging home and away politics gave the return visits an ambivalent quality, hence the title of this chapter. That ambivalent quality could have been anticipated from the literature on global return migration (Markowitz and Stefansson 2004; Long and Oxfeld 2004; Tsuda 2009).[1] In that literature, the essence of the ambivalence is the contradictory feelings of identification with the former homeland yet estrangement from it. Migrants in the diaspora, especially their children born there, become somewhat naturalised into their new cultural surroundings, while in the homelands the culture there also continues to transform. Thus, upon return there is an almost inevitable disappointment as nostalgic images of the past homeland and expectations of welcome are confronted with an unromantic present. The returnees realise for the first time how much they themselves have changed and have to contend with the ambivalent or even negative reception by those who have stayed behind. Sometimes what were previously seen as a relaxed lifestyle and traditional cultural practices seem on return narrow-minded and old-fashioned.

Constable's study of Filipina contract domestic workers in Hong Kong is also suggestive of the particular ambivalence of a feminised diaspora (Constable 2004). Separated for long periods from their husbands and children, many of the contract workers had to reconcile their longings for return with their actual experiences of return when they began to realise how much they appreciated their escape from domestic drudgery at home, increasingly fraught relationships with husbands and children, and the surveillance by relations and neighbours. While they were quite lonely sometimes in Hong Kong, their paid domestic drudgery enabled a degree of self-direction, responsibility and a pleasing inversion of the typical gender order at home where men were usually the wage earners.

The Emerging Home and Away Politics of Indigenous Diaspora

The formation of general presuppositions about the differences between the settlements and diaspora locations can be exemplified by the attitude of the Warlpiri of Yuendumu to Alice Springs and the views of the Warlpiri permanently residing in Alice Springs about the settlements. Despite the increasing circulation of Warlpiri people between Alice Springs and the home settlements and the increasing integration of the Warlpiri diaspora and home settlements through better transport and communications, there persist broad polarities in the characterisation of town versus settlement among many of the Warlpiri in the settlements, but particularly in the older generation. The settlement was seen as a place of traditional culture, no grog and of order, and the town was seen as the opposite: no culture, grog and disorder (cf. Merlan 1998: 205 on Aboriginal spatial modes of social ordering). Aspects of these broad polarities have already been mentioned in Chapter 3 in relation to the awkward relationship between the settlement-orientated dialysis patients who do not see the same benefits of town life that the voluntary migrants do. Arguably, the prominence of community studies in the anthropological archive of the Warlpiri has reinforced this perception of the remote settlements as the 'idealised locus of Warlpiri-ness' (Rowse 1990: 176).

These broad oppositions did represent something of the social reality of the people in the current study. Liquor restrictions in the hinterland, although sometime porous, meant that it was generally difficult to get alcohol on the settlements. It is hard to imagine that the broad ideological polarities around settlement versus town among the older Warlpiri could have arisen if alcohol sales had been allowed on the settlements as happened in the same era in remote Queensland settlements. 'Wet' canteens were established there, thus bringing the immediacy and destructiveness of drunken behaviour directly into the settlements (Martin 1998; McKnight 2002).[2]

The location of Warlpiri initiation ceremonies was always in the hinterland and never in town, unlike the mixed Darwin group described by Sansom (2010, 1980: 60, 169, 200). Sansom's Wallaby Cross mob managed to hold initiation ceremonies at their Darwin camp in the 1970s. This comparison enables us to see more clearly the peculiar innovative (and doomed?) nature of the Wallaby Cross mob's project of combining continuing traditionalism in ritual with 'livin' longa grog'. Given the devastating effects of drinking rights on ritual in other parts of Australia (see, for example, McKnight 2002; Sackett 1977), the prospects of such a project would appear to be dismal and its promotion as a distinctive part of the 'Darwin style we got' a sign of naive self-delusion. That Sansom provides no hint of such a perspective may be a tribute to his pursuit of an emic perspective, but it is also a result of his exclusive focus on the Wallaby Cross mob and the Masterful Men who explicitly pursued this unlikely project. What those who remained in the hinterland thought of the Wallaby Cross mob's initiation ceremonies is left rather shadowy. Some hints are given that there may have been a hinterland critique, for example, in the perceived need of the Wallaby Cross mob to demonstrate to their apparently sceptical hinterland kin that they could still muster the resources necessary to perform a traditional ceremony back on the settlement (1980: 219). As pointed out in Chapter 1, however, Sansom does not fully develop a regional perspective (town camp plus hinterland). Instead, he seems intent upon demonstrating the regular, law-like characteristics of the practices developed in response to the unique circumstances of Darwin and on challenging the stereotype of the Darwin camps as a place of orgiastic anarchy (Sansom 1977: 59).[3]

The blunt global judgements of the sober senior Warlpiri settlement dwellers equating town with *pamajanka* (drunken people) and *warungka* (mad people, people who do not listen) also represented exasperation at the accumulation over the decades of individual examples that had a well-worn predictability. Young Warlpiri men would go to town to drink and would get into fatal fights. Warlpiri people of all ages would leave their family responsibilities behind to take up the drinking life in Alice Springs, relying on others to put their sons through initiation ceremonies. Moreover, there would be instances of Warlpiri people of all ages doing things in town under the influence of grog completely out of character compared to their lives on the settlement.[4] The constant mobile phone chatter ensured that all the excesses of behaviour in town were transmitted tabloid-like to those remaining behind in the settlements. This meant that worried parents could follow the progress of the binges of their adult children on an hour-by-hour basis, although they were generally powerless to influence its inevitable course. Some of the more notorious town camps, including Warlpiri Camp, were given nicknames like 'Vietnam' and 'Cambodia' by the non-drinkers of the older generation of bi-cultural adepts back in the settlements to indicate their war-torn character ('Iraq' and 'Afghanistan' might be more contemporary references). When these non-drinkers had to travel to town for some purpose, they exhausted every possible alternative place of accommodation, especially white friends with relatively secluded back yards (see, for example, San Roque 2011), before choosing to stay in a town camp with relations. They knew that in the town camps they would be importuned by drunks, probably not get much sleep and would be anxious about their safety. One story doing the rounds on the settlement was of a drunken man entering a house in the town camp at night with an axe so that he could access food in a locked fridge. Of course, those bent on a spree would head directly to the town camp houses of known relations, or at least camp within walking distance of such houses.

One manifestation of the polarising discourse on settlements was the characterisation of the settlements as refuges from the chaos and disorder of town – Alice Springs as Babylon, Yuendumu as Jerusalem. Usually the liquor restrictions on the settlements did enable a less violent and more orderly existence there. However, in the era of the last petrol-sniffing epidemic at Yuendumu in the 1990s, it was the isolation and more manageable scale of the outstation that was mobilised against the destructive possibilities of the settlement (Stojanovski 2010; Preuss and Brown 2006). In the last years of my fieldwork, settlement-as-refuge talk also had an anachronistic feeling since the family feuding, which started with a death in town. The feuding had spread to every aspect of life on the home settlement, interrupting sleep, making trips to the shop problematic, disrupting school and causing the temporary abandonment of participation in the regional football competition.

Predictably, the permanent Warlpiri residents of Alice Springs did not see things in such black-and-white terms. 'Dulcie', for example, delighted in pointing out how much some of the leading Warlpiri figures of the settlements enjoyed aspects of town life, like the casino, and were frequently to be seen in town. More generally, though, through the life stories of the matriarchs it was apparent that they associated the settlements with humiliating domestic violence, the sadness associated with the loss of close relations, family feuding, fighting over royalties, and sorcery. Through their actions they also implicitly rejected the characterisation of town-dwellers as those who had turned away from traditional culture. They continued to assert themselves as traditional people by continuing to use their Warlpiri language, conducting sorry business, going hunting and painting their traditional designs. All these factors allowed them to overlook some of the difficulties of life in Alice Springs and to see it as a respite from some of the difficulties of settlement life. Thus, the stage was set for a struggle over the meaning of respite and, for the less permanently entrenched travellers, a circular movement of respite from settlement in town, then respite from town in the settlement, and back again (cf. Povinelli 2006: 117–18 on respite in Darwin for a woman from Belyuen; Taylor 1989 for 'circular mobility' especially of the Warlpiri between Lajamanu and Katherine).

The bi-cultural adepts, including those who remained on the settlements, also tended to have a more nuanced view of towns and cities. One of them, Neville Japangardi Poulson (now deceased), a long-term Warlpiri teacher and briefly my research assistant in Darwin, associated his own education in Darwin and his travels to other countries positively with an expanding Warlpiri consciousness of the wider world. Particularly impressive to him was seeing in Papua New Guinea the indigenous people performing roles in administration and technical professions that were still the preserve of whitefellas back in Australia. He was also well aware of the sordid fate of many of his relations in Darwin and it was interesting to witness his confrontation with one of them at a long-grass camp near Palmerston. Breaching general Warlpiri etiquette of not publicly criticising individuals, he singled out a middle-aged 'nephew' of his and berated him for spending so much time drinking in Darwin. He forcefully suggested that it was time for him to return home. The situation was made even more awkward by my presence, a white stranger who appeared to be a missionary. It was not the first time I have been used as a convenient prop in a transgressive confrontation. The heightened embarrassment was met with defiant nonchalance from the 'nephew' who simply stated 'no, I think I'll stay in Darwin a bit longer'.

Over the years Alice Springs has been a destination for those who want to escape the strictures of promised marriage arrangements in the hinterland settlements and those seeking to conduct illicit affairs away from the heightened suspicion and comprehensive mutual surveillance on the settlements. The idea of Alice Springs as a destination for dalliance may hark back to the era before mobile phones since they now enable mutual surveillance by family members in all corners of Alice Springs. Indiscretions can be communicated in real time on multiple gossip networks and it is not long before codes of silence around the affected wives or husbands back in the settlement are breached.

In the era before mobile phones and ready access to transport, Alice Springs was a serviceable destination for an eloping couple. In one case from the 1980s, the eloping man left a wife and children behind in Yuendumu and the eloping woman left an old promised husband behind in Yuendumu. They felt reasonably safe in Alice Springs since the family of the promised husband did not have a car. In any event, when they heard the news that the family was coming to town to take reprisals against her, the Alice Springs couple would hide in the bush nearby Alice Springs and, in that terrain which was unfamiliar to their Warlpiri relations, she felt safe. I heard similar stories from that era in which those eloping had to make similarly complex calculations of various factors to decide whether Alice Springs was a sufficiently safe location until the immediate threat of anger-fuelling retaliation had receded. In those days, a brief liaison could also be better hidden, especially if one had access to the house of a white friend in the suburbs not often frequented by Warlpiri people.

There was also a degree of disbelief and derision emanating from the settlement dwellers in response to assertions of some in the diaspora about how well they were doing. One long-time Warlpiri resident of Darwin, a drinker and a close relation of my Warlpiri research assistant, given the opportunity to explain her life in Darwin, proceeded to expand upon how many friends she had made in various Top End communities. She had developed a range of quasi-kin connections through her five-year relationship with a Bathurst Island man. These Bathurst Islanders would call her 'sister', share their mining royalties with her and gave her money after a funeral. In Darwin she could count on an old white friend to stay in his flat when it rained. Annoyed by what my research assistant took to be her gross exaggeration ('if she has so many friends where are they now?') and her rather careless slight against the home settlement and himself ('there is no feeling for me at Yuendumu'), my research assistant removed himself from the conversation and waited in the car, fuming.

There was another perceived slight against a Warlpiri settlement by a Warlpiri public figure in Alice Springs that provoked an unusually direct response. In her support of many of the policy measures of the Intervention, Bess Price, an aspiring conservative politician at that time, had placed herself in opposition to other educated Warlpiri women and men who had taken on a high-profile anti-Intervention political stance. Some white anti-Intervention activists rather crassly made the point on social media that because the aspiring politician was living in Alice Springs and had a job she would not be subject to the measures of the Intervention. They questioned her right to speak on the issue, also referring to her relatively long residential absence from the home settlement. However, one educated Warlpiri woman, who had long since returned to the home settlement, took a different approach when explaining the dispute to her Warlpiri friends. She condensed the issues in the most provocative way, saying 'she [Bess Price] is rubbishing her family' and, unlike herself, was no longer a 'culture woman'. In the context, I took the phrase 'rubbishing her family' to be an incendiary reference to Bess Price's public stance against an anti-Intervention demonstration in Canberra attended by some of her close relations. The reference to Bess Price no longer being a 'culture woman' is more difficult to explicate but seems to be a reference to her different circumstances in suburban Alice Springs, running a successful consultancy business with her white husband, compared to the circumstances of women her age on the settlements. The two Warlpiri women involved in the public disputation in fact had quite a similar upbringing on the home settlement and similar educational achievements. What is interesting for present purposes is how the different residential locations were mobilised in the dispute and given a cultural valence.

Some of the cultural foundations of the emerging home and away politics of identity have already been mentioned in Chapter 1: the emotional link to traditional country, obligations to care for it and pass on traditional knowledge about it and, more practically, the need to continually assert one's interest lest others start encroaching. These factors alone would set the scene for viewing a permanent relocation to a distant city or town as an abandonment of a sacred obligation. The congregation of the Warlpiri in a few settlements has added a further variation on this kind of valorisation of rootedness as the settlements themselves became places of emotional attachment and concentrations of traditional cultural expression (cf. Holcombe 2004 on the emergence of affective attachment to the relatively new community of Mt Liebig). Sometimes the attachment to a particular settlement is revealed in competitive identification with the home settlement in the football competition at sports weekends. Inter-settlement competitiveness sometimes transfers to cultural performances as in the rating of the skill of various *yawulyu* women's dancing troupes (Dussart 2000: 91). Identification with a particular settlement is also indicated by the sensitivity to how the settlement is portrayed in the national media (Hinkson 1999: 14). The relative closeness of Warlpiri traditional country to the settlements, where most of the Warlpiri people still reside, accordingly makes them also a locus of traditionalism and the familiar against which distant locations can be imagined in all their unfamiliarity, danger and cultural degradation. During the research I found this theme to have been objectified in two revealing stories from different historical periods that in their own way mythologised the diaspora. These stories further illustrate the cultural foundations of the emerging home and away politics.

Mythologising the Diaspora 1: Diaspora as a Place of Execution

The first story is about a Warlpiri ancestor named Mussolini (a real person who had lived at Yuendumu and died c.1960) and his miraculous escape from certain death in Darwin. It was told in a genre of Warlpiri story-telling that has not yet been reported in the anthropological literature (as far as I am aware). The essence of the story is that Mussolini had been taken to Darwin for a crime he was alleged to have committed. He was there in Darwin on a scaffold and the authorities were about to hang him when a donkey brayed loudly ('sang out for him'). The authorities took it as a sign the man was innocent and let him go. It is, therefore, quite different to another genre of mythologised historical events, for example, in which miraculous escapes from the Coniston massacre are described in terms of the superior ability of some clever men to make themselves invisible or to 'sing' the bullets that were being fired at them so that they would miss their intended target.[5] The Mussolini story, in contrast, appears to draw upon biblical associations of the donkey.[6] The trope of the vagaries of European justice in Darwin seems to draw upon historical events of early contact history when three Warlpiri men accused of killing a miner at the Granites in 1910 were taken to Darwin and, even though they were acquitted for lack of evidence and released in Darwin, were never seen again (Meggitt 1962: 21).

Mythologising the Diaspora 2: The Prisoner of Queensland

This story concerns 'Abraham', the Warlpiri man mentioned in Chapter 2, who moved to a large coastal town in northern Queensland with his non-Aboriginal wife, whom I shall call 'Lesley'. As often happens, their household in Queensland became the destination for various close kin from the home settlement. First to arrive was 'Abraham's' mother, then the mother's sister (I will call her 'Judith'), then two children who 'Judith' was raising. Some years after 'Abraham's' mother's arrival she died of natural causes and her body was flown back to the remote Warlpiri settlement of Nyirrpi to be buried near her traditional country.

It was following the death of 'Abraham's' biological mother that concerns about 'Judith's' welfare began to be expressed and stories started circulating in the home settlements about 'Lesley' holding 'Judith' in Queensland against her will as a virtual prisoner. My introduction to the story came early while I was consulting Warlpiri people about the proposed research project. Indeed, some came to immediately understand the whole research project as a belated bid to rescue 'Judith'. What intrigued me were the small details that had been built up over the years, such as suggesting that 'Lesley' had a small handgun which she kept in her purse and that she kept 'Judith' in a locked room until she produced a painting which 'Lesley' then sold and kept the proceeds for herself. The trope of the imprisoned artist may have been partly inspired by real life Warlpiri experiences of a practice developed in several art dealers' workshops around Alice Springs. The dealers would lock away the artists, in most cases with their agreement, until they had completed the painting whereupon they would be paid and free to go. It was the detail about the small gun that alerted me to the possibility of the story being elaborated in the retelling. Such elaboration seems to be a relatively widespread process of confabulation and mythologising in Warlpiri story telling (cf. Poirier 2005: 186–8 for an account of story-telling in a neighbouring Aboriginal group).

The fact that some relations had spoken to 'Judith' when they visited the Queensland coastal town for a Pentecostal convention and she had not raised any alarm had no effect on the circulation of the story and the obvious concern with which it was received. One relation, a senior Aboriginal police aide, upon hearing the story had contacted the Queensland police and unsuccessfully requested them to intervene. Concern about 'Judith' reached an even more heightened level when the news came in 2009 of 'Abraham's' death. Without consultation with his Warlpiri family on the settlements and against their expectations of his body being returned to be buried near his traditional country, his white wife 'Lesley' had authorised the cremation of the body and retained his ashes at her home in Queensland. She said she was following 'Abraham's' wishes.

Consequently, when I did take some of 'Judith's' relations to visit her in Queensland the following year, the meeting with 'Lesley' was somewhat fraught. One thing we were able to confirm directly from 'Judith' and indirectly from other sources was that she did not consider herself to be a prisoner. In the first place, she justified her initial departure from the

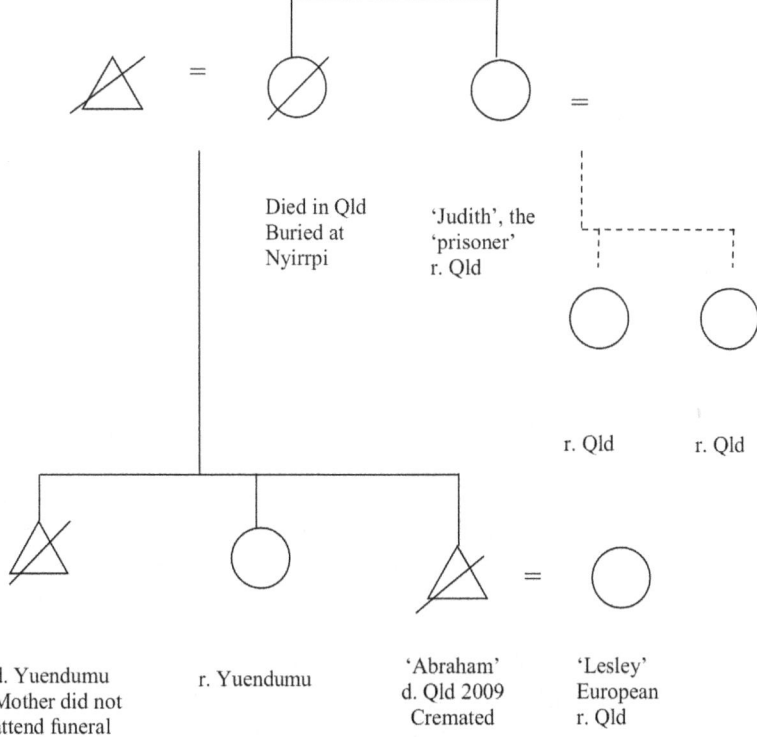

Figure 5.1 Partial genealogy of the 'prisoner' of Queensland (figure by the author)

settlement: 'I bin lose my husband, my father and my son, that's why I bin go away'. Like most mature Warlpiri women, she had a strong sense of her own personal autonomy and was always ready to express her views forthrightly. As proof of her ability to assert herself against 'Lesley', she described heated arguments with her supposed captor when 'I was chasing her with a long stick'. She demanded to know who had been spreading false rumours about her supposed imprisonment.

In fact, there seemed to be many reasons why 'Judith' wanted to remain in Queensland: she had various serious medical conditions and had been receiving specialised treatment in the large regional hospital in the town. In addition, one of her children whom she had taken to Queensland to raise there had unfortunately become an uncontrollable teenage gang member who had her first baby at the age of fifteen and was expecting another baby at the age of sixteen. The baby, who 'Judith' considered to be her own grandchild, had been fostered out via the welfare authorities to a white couple who coincidentally had previously worked in a Warlpiri settlement (more parallel diaspora). 'Judith' was concerned about the welfare of the two babies and what was to become of the wild young Warlpiri gang member roaming the town. Moreover, she had her other quieter daughter to look after and she liked some aspects of living in a town without any other Warlpiri people. She was free to spend her welfare payments on her own priorities, including the methodical and successful completion of various purchase by instalments arrangements, and she stored the purchased goods safely in commercial storage. While her relationship with 'Lesley' was sometimes antagonistic, the household arrangements of sharing food and housing costs and having the benefit of regular meals did have its attractions.

There are obviously many strands to this story and many reasons why the rumours of 'Judith's' 'imprisonment' in Queensland became so surreal: the inter-racial marriage, the suspect partner and the communication difficulties, to name a few. It seems to me that in this story, in the previous execution story and from other expressions of general attitudes, there may be some more pervasive preconceptions at work here. The settlement Warlpiri seemed to find it difficult to comprehend how a Warlpiri person could find such a distant and lonely place preferable to the familiarity of the settlement. Therefore, if someone does not want to return, especially after something as momentous as the death of a 'son' (sister's son), there must be something terribly wrong.

Although I have labelled this process of elaboration as mythologising, it does bear some similarities to the process described by Sansom of developing an agreed 'word' or determination about happenings that then became the essential constituting property of a mob (1980: 22–43). The process involved obtaining all possible details of the happening, whether a death, a beating or a fight at the pub, then from those details fashioning a more compact and appealing narrative of the happening that, through a process of recruitment of individuals to that version of the happening, became the authoritative determination or 'word' about the happening. This had the effect of truncating potentially divisive ongoing arguments about the happening and enhanced the solidarity of the mob. Using Sansom's terminology, the problem with the 'word' about the prisoner of Queensland is that it had developed in isolation from the actual protagonists in the Queensland town. Sansom did report one conflict between the 'word' of the Wallaby Cross mob and their hinterland settlement relations. The conflicting 'words' had to be negotiated at a rather tense meeting between the two groups (1980: 118–36). In the Queensland case, 'Peggy's' rather explosive dismissal of the settlement 'word' about her situation was due to the loss of ownership of her own 'word' about her own situation.

In the end, I did not know what to make of 'Lesley's' assertions about 'Abraham's' wishes about the disposal of his body. At Yuendumu, I was swept along by the outrage of his relations remaining on the settlement and I knew that certain aspects of the traditional mortuary rituals could not now be carried out since they required some of his hair.[7] On the other hand, the more I found out about 'Abraham', in particular his long-standing interest in learning more about white society, the more I wondered whether he would have struck out in a startling new direction by agreeing to cremation as an assertion of his individuality. Such an assertion of individuality against traditional norms of being buried near traditional country was certainly apparent in the case of an Alice Springs Warlpiri woman who had widely broadcast her negative views of the settlement on which she had raised her family. Her daughter, with whom she lived in Alice Springs, shared her views and when her mother did in fact die in Alice Springs Hospital, she made sure that all the traditional mortuary rituals, the funeral and the burial were held in Alice Springs. It is to the family politics of burial that I now turn as the next illustration of the home and away politics of identity.

The Family Politics of Burials and the Geographical Limits of Sorcery

Traditionalist expectations did not, in any case, inevitably lead to a simple calculus of the best place for the burial of the deceased. One Warlpiri family in Alice Springs argued against the burial of one of their relations at Yuendumu. He had spent his last years in Alice Springs and, among other things, they felt that his in-laws at Yuendumu had forfeited the right to decide the issue because of their recent neglect of him. One of their arguments against burial at Yuendumu was that his body would not be safe from interference from the Warlpiri sorcerers who may have caused his death. The Alice Springs family believed that, in an attempt to thwart the avenging spirit of the deceased, the sorcerers who caused his death would dig up the body to obtain various body parts required for their prophylactic rituals aimed at concealing their true role. The family also believed that these rituals were never entirely effective and that the spirit of the deceased would eventually hunt down the sorcerers and exact revenge. Implicit in these concerns was the idea that the public cemetery in Alice Springs would be an obviously safer location. Why this should be so is related to a more general demarcation of the geographical reach of sorcery and dangerous traditional country.

What seems to be happening in this kind of demarcation is something quite subtle and at times contradictory. Continuing belief in the pervasiveness and effectiveness of sorcery is widespread among all Warlpiri people, including those in the diaspora. The traditional orthodoxy about sorcery is that it is geographically inescapable (Elkin 1977; Meggitt 1962: 325). Yet, at the same time, a number of Warlpiri people in the diaspora have included in their list of reasons for leaving their home settlement the excessive amount of sorcery in those places which they compare unfavourably to their present diaspora location where the local Aboriginal people are not supposed to engage in such activities. These statements can be interpreted in a number of ways, including that in diaspora locations Warlpiri people do not have to endure daily encounters with other Warlpiri people who they genuinely believe have killed their relations through sorcery. What also seems to be at play is a degree of cultural chauvinism in relation to Aboriginal people in more settled areas, namely the belief that Warlpiri sorcery is more effective, a view often shared by the Aboriginal people in those diaspora locations. The more subtle element, though, is the idea that a range of traditional spirit beings, methods of sorcery and magical practices are more powerful (perhaps more believable) on country that is more remote from the transforming effects of European settlement and closer to known traditional country. Thus, a genre of stories about the sightings of Aboriginal people still leading a hunter-gatherer lifestyle and of contemporary traditional executions tends to relate to the remotest back roads between settlements. At the other extreme in the towns of south-eastern Australia, Warlpiri mothers are able to convincingly reassure their grandchildren who grew up on the settlements that there are no malevolent spirits or monsters in their new location so far away from the settlements.

The apparently contradictory views about the geographical limits of sorcery can also be mapped onto the emerging home and away politics of identity. When I raised these ideas with a senior Warlpiri person and committed settlement resident, she thought that anyone who believed they were somehow protected from sorcery in a town or city was deluding themselves. This was further evidence, in her view, of their degraded understanding of Warlpiri culture. A comparison could again be drawn with the Wallaby Cross mob in Darwin in the 1970s. Their residence in Darwin seemed to make no difference to their perceived need for vigilance against sorcery especially of the supernatural poisoning or tampering with food intended for the vulnerable young men about to be initiated (Sansom 1980: 62–63). Their protection entailed providing them with European food delivered in sealed containers such as tins of meat and packets of bread.

In other respects, though, the settlement traditionalists reinforced the geographical gradation of spiritual power that was strongest in remote areas and tapered off towards towns and disappeared in cities. As the senior settlement woman succinctly stated: 'there is no *nangkayi* [sorcerer/traditional healer] in the city'. And, indeed, another kind of return visit not previously mentioned is the return to consult a renowned *nangkayi* for illnesses attributed to sorcery: a therapeutic return. The instances I became aware of in fact related to a renowned Pintupi *nangkayi*, who lived far away to the south-west of the Warlpiri settlements.[8] He had become known to Warlpiri residents in one of the Pintupi settlements and one of the prominent Warlpiri men there became a conduit to him for a number of his Warlpiri relations, including two Alice Springs residents. One was suffering from kidney failure and another from undiagnosed weight loss and tiredness. On a more prosaic level, some temporary return visits, particularly from Adelaide, often included the collection of favoured bush medicines that were unavailable outside central Australia, such as *mijilypa*, the red sap of particular gum trees, used in a variety of ways (tonic, lotion, poultice) for aches, pains and sores.

Temporary Homecomings: Kinds of Return Visits

Thus far I have been describing an emerging home and away politics of diaspora at a fairly general level. That description tended to focus upon those who had taken up entrenched positions of commitment to either settlement or town as their permanent residence. This section complicates that sort of stand-off by examining culturally significant return visits of those who still intend to remain permanently in a town or city. The next section will examine the story of those who change their allegiance back to the settlements. Return visits were made for a wide variety of reasons, some to do with purely domestic concerns such as visiting kin or searching for a husband. Others were for rites of passage (initiation ceremonies, sorry business and funerals) and yet others for more public events such as royalty meetings, sporting carnivals such as the Yuendumu Sports Weekend, cultural festivals such as the Milpirri festival at Lajamanu, and Christian religious festivals (especially the Easter *purlapa*). Another strong motivation for return during the period of the research was to participate in the family feuding. I will describe all these various kinds of return visits in turn, commencing with those that seem to represent the very minimal acceptable involvement when non-attendance without a reasonable excuse would cause a severe rupture in many relationships. Like participation in demand sharing and the ability to speak Warlpiri, participation in initiation ceremonies, sorry business and funerals represented potential boundary markers for those who remained Warlpiri and those considered to be no longer Warlpiri (Barth 1969: 15–16 on the boundary making of ethnic groups).

In addition to the benign kinds of temporary return already mentioned, I became aware of instances of what I would call predatory return. These included the return to cheat in high-stakes card games, for example after royalty distributions, and the return to sell illicit drugs, principally marijuana. The shadowy nature of these activities does not lend itself to direct confirmation. Instead, I rely on trustworthy eyewitnesses who observed the mysterious succession of winning hands produced by a visiting Warlpiri man who had been brought up in another state. The evidence of the transit of plastic garbage bags full of marijuana ('hounds') back to the settlements from towns and cities was from Warlpiri people who saw them in transit and were familiar with the slang names for them used by the couriers.

Return for Initiation Ceremonies

Meggitt saw the circumcision initiation ceremony as critical to a Warlpiri boy becoming a social person (1962: 309) so it is perhaps not surprising that while other kinds of rituals have faded in recent decades, initiation ceremonies continue to be regularly performed. It is not clear whether all the social implications in Meggitt's time (1950s) continue in the contemporary scene (Curran 2010, 2011; Peterson 2008; Wild 1977–1978; Bell 1983: 205–26; Dussart 2000: 70, 194–95). Meggitt's account places initiation as the start of a sedate and considered induction into esoteric knowledge of an elaborate traditional repertoire. Today there seems to be more marked intergenerational antagonism and a greater assertion of youthful independence.[9] Whatever the situation, the sons of all the matriarchs I have discussed in this book were initiated. Some of the matriarchs' sons had already been initiated before the matriarchs' move to town and others who were yet to abandon their drinking lifestyle missed their son's initiation, no doubt reinforcing settlement ideas of the cultural degradation of town life. The mother's absence was not critical since it was typically the key men of the patriline and the matriline who decided these things and, provided there was a critical mass of competent personnel among them, the ceremony would go ahead and replacement 'mothers' and 'fathers' would be found to perform the relevant roles (see also Coulehan 1995: 201–202, 208–209 for similar substitution of missing ritual personnel among the Yolngu).

Among other groups there have been reports of medicalised alternatives to initiation ceremonies. Coulehan, for example, reported among the Yolngu in Darwin that some boys whose family could not organise an initiation ceremony had the circumcision operation performed in Darwin Hospital by a white surgeon without any accompanying ceremony (1995: 205–206, 219–22). There are also reports of a certain evangelical pastor at Halls Creek in the past arranging a hospital operation for the sons of members of the congregation specifically to thwart ceremonial initiation but I do not know whether this involved any Warlpiri.[10] One Warlpiri woman involved in the Assemblies of God church at Bagot in Darwin provided a more diplomatic solution that drew on certain traditional mores (sex segregation, certain male-only aspects of traditional knowledge) and extended them. She suggested that the initiation of her grandchildren would be entirely a matter for the grandfather and hence nothing to do with her. Adopting this position allowed her not to sully her general acceptance of the Church's opposition to things traditional, especially initiation, but without directly confronting her male relations back on the settlement.

During the research I did become aware of a few return trips specifically for the initiation of boys who were being brought up in diaspora locations. In all cases, the families back on the settlements were prominent in the continuing ceremonial life of that settlement. One had returned with his Warlpiri mother from Bundaberg in Queensland. Another was in fact the grandson of 'Barbara' in Adelaide but she had raised him from a young child. He and his sisters attended school in Adelaide and all of them had remained in regular contact with his relations who remained at Yuendumu. One of his male relations (his actual mother's mother's brother) insisted upon the initiation and 'Barbara' agreed, returning to Yuendumu with the boy and participating in the ceremony. The boy later returned to his life in Adelaide, completed his schooling, had a number of part-time jobs, enjoyed the Internet and computer games, and found a non-Aboriginal girlfriend. His relative isolation in Adelaide made me wonder whether any significant bonding had been established with his age-mates back on the settlement and particularly with those who had been initiated at the same ceremony.

The story of the initiation of 'Dulcie's' son was perhaps unique because of his initiation into a neighbouring language group (Pintupi) with the support of the boy's father from whom she had been separated for some time. After the separation the boy's father had married a Pintupi woman and had become integrated into the life of a predominantly Pintupi settlement. For various reasons he had become somewhat alienated from the Warlpiri and exercised his prerogative, in the absence of any strong male figure in 'Dulcie's' family, to arrange a Pintupi initiation in which 'Dulcie' and the new wife participated. 'Dulcie' gave me an account of the interesting differences she noted with the Warlpiri initiation ceremony and I gained the impression that she was pleased with the outcome, not least because she herself had developed negative feelings about the Warlpiri on the settlement whom she thought were targeting her with sorcery.

For others, especially those in inter-racial marriages, the issue of the initiation of second-generation and even third-generation diaspora boys raised difficult issues. One of the white fathers had been initiated and he supported the initiation of a son who had grown up away from home settlements but had kept in touch through regular visits. The son, however, wavered in his resolve although he was generally positively disposed towards it. The grandsons of another white father, who had not been initiated, became aware through Aboriginal school friends in Alice Springs that initiation was a possibility. The grandsons seemed positively disposed towards the idea but from a rather naive perspective. The white grandfather worried about what sort of brotherhood they would join, and particularly about the less salubrious aspects of the prevailing norms that accepted heavy drinking, incarceration and violence against women. Moreover, the old Warlpiri men he had respected and would have trusted to do the operation were no longer alive and worrying stories circulated about other tribes in the region allowing drunkenness on the law ground, occasional botched operations and distraught young men being taken to the casualty ward of a hospital. All things considered, it seemed unlikely that the initiation of the grandchildren would ever go ahead.

Return for Mortuary Rituals and Funerals

I have already mentioned the geographical expansion of the politics of the location of mortuary rituals and funerals as a consequence of there being a permanent Warlpiri diaspora, but most sorry business and funerals continue to be held on the remote settlements. For those Warlpiri people in the diaspora, the extra distances involved feed into the usual calculations of genealogical closeness to the deceased, available resources and the consequences of not attending. The current acceleration in the frequency of deaths adds another dimension of strain to such calculations. Unthinkable in the past, now choices are made about which funerals to attend. As a result, there has been an increased frequency of emailed and faxed messages to be read out at funerals expressing condolences and reasons for not attending (typically, lack of transport and money).

One of the difficulties of temporary return for the matriarchs in towns and cities was securing their public housing against the ever present tendency for the homeless drinkers to continually test for weak points among their connections and to converge on empty places. Leaving an apparently responsible relation in charge did not always work as expected. In one extreme case, one of the Warlpiri matriarchs returned from attending a funeral on a Warlpiri settlement to public housing in Adelaide to find a giant hole burnt in the roof. Another time on returning she found her house inundated with relative strangers who had trashed the house.

Disagreement about the attendance at settlement funerals sometime brought into focus more general differing perspectives that seemed to cut across more typical antinomies between settlement and diaspora. One perspective assumed the correctness and feasibility of return of biological kin no matter what the degree of cultural attenuation. This perspective entails a sort of biological essentialism in which the biological relationship trumps all other considerations. The other perspective, perhaps a cultural essentialism, saw lack of knowledge of language, settlement practices and ongoing engagement as prohibitive of the belated inclusion of long-lost kin. One illustrative disagreement concerned the question of whether a young, part-Warlpiri woman should attend the funeral of her Warlpiri father in Yuendumu. The child had been the product of a relatively short-lived relationship between a Warlpiri man and a white writer and historian in Alice Springs in the 1980s. The Warlpiri man had taken up the drinking life in Alice Springs in earnest and the child's mother had little to do with him and raised the girl herself in Alice Springs. The girl eventually became the first child of Warlpiri descent to matriculate to a university in one of the capital cities. The Warlpiri father died an early death in Alice Springs and his older relations, who organised the funeral, were outraged at the suggestion that his daughter would not attend the funeral. They seemed not to appreciate that the child had had virtually nothing to do with her father throughout her life, could not speak any Warlpiri and would not be particularly close to anyone at the funeral. It was as if the knowledge of the child maintained by her Warlpiri 'grandmothers' and their concern for her should have been enough for her to participate. Underlying this mutual miscomprehension seemed to be two quite different approaches to the event: one emphasising the importance of personal authentic emotion ('why should I go if I do not feel anything for him') and the other, the performance of a ritual role and social obligation.

Royalty Meetings

As explained in Chapter 1, the location of gold mines on land successfully claimed by the Warlpiri under federal land rights legislation entitled them to mining royalties in the vicinity of $5 million per year. The meetings to arrange the distribution of mining royalties have a powerful grasp on the imagination of most Warlpiri people and were a constant topic of conversation in informal communication networks. One particular procedure – family meetings to decide the distribution within particular family groups, which were usually held in the home settlements – encouraged a predictable migration of those in the diaspora. The immediate pressures on decision-makers by those family members who were present often led to the discounting of the claims of absent family members for their share. While the procedure resulted in quite different approaches in the various family groups, it was widely believed that the general rule was that if you did not attend the royalty meeting you did not get anything. This rule, relayed to me authoritatively by senior, well-educated Warlpiri people, was never a formal rule adopted by the royalty associations, but it did reflect widespread experience. Some in the diaspora who did not have the time or transport to attend such meetings resigned themselves to their position, adopting the stance that they had stepped back to allow other family members, who lived in the home settlements, to benefit. Many more, however, mustered their resources and made the journey from Darwin, Katherine, Tennant Creek or Alice Springs and sometimes even from Adelaide.

Illustration 5.1 Royalty meeting at Yuendumu, May 2010 (photograph by the author)

There is one exceptional royalty story that is very instructive about the difficulties of the second-generation diaspora. It is the story of a botched return. A Warlpiri woman who married a white man had gone to live in an outback town in Queensland where they raised a family. Their children did well; one became a nurse, another became a social worker and another became a teacher. However, they never visited any of their Warlpiri relations on the home settlements and, it became apparent later, they knew little about Warlpiri language or culture. Their first meeting with the Warlpiri people on the settlements was when they attended a royalty meeting in 2000 where they proceeded to demand the royalties owing to their mother, who had since passed away. They seemed unpersuaded by the increasingly strict patrilineal rules that had been adopted by the royalty committees and threatened to take legal action. A potential homecoming was thus irrevocably tarnished.[11]

Participation in the Feud

At the height of the family feuding some Warlpiri people who had hitherto been committed to their new lives in Adelaide found themselves drawn back to Yuendumu by what they saw as the threats to their families who had remained there. Some of these return visits were described in Chapter 4 (Warlpiri Women of Adelaide). Return to participate in family feuding was not necessarily the universal or automatic response of Warlpiri people in the diaspora and my impression is that earlier feuds were not as all-encompassing as the 2010–2013 one. The Warlpiri man mentioned in Chapter 2 who had married into the local Aboriginal group at Eva Valley near Katherine specifically refused a request from his adult son at Yuendumu to return and help him prosecute an earlier feud. The father had built a new, peaceful life for himself in the Katherine region and the prospect of returning to Yuendumu to help his son, who had a reputation as a hothead, did not move him as much as one might have expected from accounts of the traditional Warlpiri norms of father-son relationships (Meggitt 1962: 115–21).

Before moving on to describe some examples of permanent return to the settlements, it is worth noting the kinds of ambivalence that attended the return trips for the specific purposes of initiation, sorry business and funerals, royalty meetings and participation in family feuds. In theory, such events bound people together in significant demonstrations of their shared cultural heritage and interconnection, at least temporarily bridging divides between settlement and diaspora. Yet in each case there were also instances of such return trips reinforcing the diverging views that were emerging and reinforcing the choice people in the diaspora had made to put themselves at some distance from the intensity of settlement life.

The Return of Some Pioneers and of the First-Generation Diaspora

Some permanent returns were associated with intimate events back on the home settlements. One Warlpiri man who had spent a great deal of his early working life on cattle stations in the Katherine region told me that an old Warlpiri man on the settlement had threatened to kill him. He took the threat seriously and found various jobs away from the settlement until the old man died many years later and he felt free to return. In another case, a Warlpiri woman in her sixties whom I felt sure had settled permanently in a large coastal town in Queensland where she had been living for ten years suddenly returned to Yuendumu upon receiving a call from her old beau who had recently been widowed.

Other returns were more peripatetic and drawn out. In the era of Warlpiri men being sent long distances to work in the 1960s, one had been sent to Darwin and another to Alice Springs. Both married local women and raised families in those locations and both, to varying degrees, had played the role of foundational couples in a diaspora location as outlined in Chapter 2. Their eventual return to Warlpiri settlements in their late middle age after varied working careers brought them back into the settlements with valued skills and expanded networks of kin among the Tiwi of Darwin and the Tiwi Islands and among the Arrernte of Alice Springs. One man who had had jobs as a lay Baptist missionary in Darwin, an army mess hall attendant and a driving instructor, got work on the settlement at the Warlpiri literature production centre and later as a mental health worker. Because of the time he had spent in Darwin, he had long since been given the nickname 'Crocodile Dundee' after the popular movie character, a swashbuckling outback adventurer based in Arnhem Land. The nickname was at least partly ironic, since he was a sober, reliable and steady worker. His skills, including the completion of a course on the care of those with mental health problems, were sought after by a number of the service NGOs at Yuendumu.

This kind of return – to take up leadership roles based on the experience of the wider world – is a recurring motif of Warlpiri history, an early such example being Darby Jampijinpa's post-war return to Yuendumu following adventurous travels and work as a stockman, drover and prospector (Campbell 2006). Then there were the teacher trainees returning from Darwin as planned to take up positions in the school and local council. Åse Ottosson noticed a similar thing happening with some (not all) Aboriginal musicians from central Australia. Their success in music put them in a respected quasi-representative role, giving them a broader experience of other settlements and the wider world and contributing to their own awareness of local social problems that eventually led them to take on responsibilities in service NGOs and local councils (Ottosson 2010: 296–97, 2016: 119–20).

Both Crocodile Dundee and the Warlpiri man who spent so much time in Alice Springs, being from that generation who were born in the bush, were enlisted in various projects undertaken by the school to teach the pupils aspects of traditional Warlpiri culture, such as the manufacture of traditional hunting implements. The Alice Springs man, among others, also sponsored the migration to Yuendumu of nuns belonging to the order of the Little Sisters of Jesus, who he had met while he was living at the Aboriginal township of Amoonguna near Alice Springs.

One woman, who had had an adventurous life in the diaspora with her part-Aboriginal partner in towns in Queensland, New South Wales and Adelaide, only felt the need to return permanently to the home settlements when her own daughters had become relatively independent and her old mother became seriously ill back on the settlement. Independently of their mother, the daughters had returned to Lajamanu and found themselves Warlpiri husbands. This was a further pressure on her to return.

What of the schoolchildren from Ali Curung who had completed some of their secondary school education in Adelaide? I saw some of these young women back in Ali Curung. They had married young Aboriginal men of the settlement and were starting families of their own. I did not get a chance to speak to them. Others, I heard, had not done very well on their return. One boy who had completed his education in Adelaide arrived back in Ali Curung to be taken drinking by friends on his first day back. Apparently, he continued in that vein from then on, much to the disappointment of the house parents in Adelaide.

The Return of Some Second-Generation Diaspora

Thus far those returning had a very good idea of what was awaiting them on the settlements. As could be anticipated from the literature on return migration, however, those who were born and raised in the diaspora sometimes have great difficulty adjusting on their return. This was particularly the case for those who were raised by white people and those who would come under the umbrella of the Stolen Generation. The term 'stolen generations' refers to those indigenous people of Australia whose connection to their natal Indigenous communities was severed by their removal as children by government authorities especially before the 1970s (Haebich 2000; Haebich and Mellor 2002; Manne 2001; Read 1981). The word 'stolen' refers both to the processes by which some, but not all, children were removed by force from non-consenting parents and to the resulting loss of the children's connection to their culture and knowledge of their particular ancestry. The word 'generations' evokes the large scale of these practices, affecting probably around 10 per cent of the Indigenous population, although it is difficult to be precise about the numbers (see Rowse 2012: 80–98 on the politics of enumerating the stolen generations). In 1997 the issue came to national prominence with the publication of the *Bringing Them Home* report of the Australian Government's Human Rights and Equal Opportunities Commission (1997). The question of an apology to the stolen generation became a contentious issue in ensuing national political debate. The then conservative Prime Minister, John Howard, refused to issue the recommended apology and an apology only eventuated in 2008 after a change of government. Recognition of the issue and the apology has become part of the Australian national political landscape with yearly commemorative activities, initially called Sorry Day. The phrase 'stolen generation' has entered into the vernacular language as a shorthand term to describe those who experienced such removals.

Apart from Stolen Generation returns, I am only aware of three young Warlpiri women born and raised in the diaspora who have permanently returned to the home settlements. The issues facing such a group can be adumbrated by considering the case of the return of one exceptional young woman from Adelaide to Yuendumu, namely 'Barbara's' daughter, 'Kimberley'. She had been born in Alice Springs after her mother had moved there from Yuendumu and moved to Adelaide with 'Barbara' and her white stepfather and other sibling when she was seven years old. She completed her schooling in Adelaide. While 'Barbara' continued to speak to her in Warlpiri, her own ability to reply in Warlpiri lapsed, although her passive comprehension continued.

'Kimberley's' move to Yuendumu was not a momentous, single decision. Instead, it involved initial short visits, circuitous wanderings and adventures with her Warlpiri cousin, and a degree of trial and error. After finishing school in Adelaide, she seemed to have led something of a rebellious, partying life. Looking back on it ten years later, she stated, somewhat euphemistically: 'you know what teenagers are like. I had problems with my parents and I ran away and all that … hanging around with wrong friends, just being stupid'. She had lived with her cousin at Murray Bridge when the Warlpiri outpost there was still flourishing and they decided to travel to Alice Springs and eventually to Yuendumu: 'there was never a plan, we just travelled and waited to see what would happen'. Yuendumu was a familiar destination from her early childhood in Alice Springs when there would be frequent school holidays there and returns for sorry business and, while she lived in Adelaide, frequent visits from relations from Yuendumu. She found that she could not understand the version of Warlpiri spoken by her 'grandmothers' at Yuendumu and her initial attempts at speaking Warlpiri were not particularly successful. Her cousin was pregnant to a Warlpiri man. She had the baby while at Yuendumu, the father returned, and the new family eventually went to live in Lajamanu. 'Kimberley' continued to travel between Alice Springs and Adelaide.

At Warlpiri Camp in Alice Springs she met her future partner. She continued her story:

> One time we jumped in a bus with my auntie and came to Yuendumu. It was all drunks there at Warlpiri Camp. We stayed for a month at Yuendumu and it dragged on to two years. That's when I thought I might get a job. It was not like a serious job. I just thought I would get a job to make some money. But, I don't know, I ended up liking it because of the trips we used to go on, conference trips and childcare trips to Adelaide, Melbourne and Perth. Every year we used to go on a trip.

The whole journey back to Yuendumu was overshadowed by the death of a male cousin with whom she had re-established contact and who she was particularly fond of (this was the death that sparked the family feuding of 2010–2011). She was with him and other members of the family at the intensive care unit in Alice Springs Hospital. She had a dream that he had woken up and told other relations about the dream to comfort them. She was part of the discussion of how the family should respond to the death and she was at Yuendumu when the fighting intensified. She appeared in the family photo that was taken when they had contacted the newspapers to make sure their side of the story was put into the public arena, a decision she later regretted when the published story seemed to blame her family for the violence.

At one point during the family feud, she moved to Ali Curung with her boyfriend and found that, compared to Yuendumu, alcohol was too freely available for him despite her vigilance. They found themselves back at Yuendumu when the feud ended and things were falling into place for her. Although some Warlpiri people there were a little surprised at her choice, saying in disbelief 'you're from the city', she saw the benefits. Life there was simpler and less expensive than running a household in Adelaide. Her Warlpiri had been improving through her own attention to pronunciation and the support of her uncle, a significant man in the settlement, who would patiently correct her. She gradually became aware of a much more elaborate and dispersed network of relations than had been apparent to her in Adelaide. The liquor restrictions and the distance to Alice Springs were enough to help her partner avoid the drinking life. Moreover, she received encouragement in various jobs:

> When I meet *kardiya* [white people] here they say 'you have got very good English' and I tell them I went to school in Adelaide and they really encourage me to finish my Certificate Three study as well. They say it would be good to have a *yapa* [Aboriginal person] running the school or running the childcare. That kind of makes me feel good about myself as well. I have experience too and I can speak and read. But I still need learning.

Some aspects of the continuing traditions, like sorry business, remained a challenge:

> You have to go in certain skin groups, which I learned. I get shamed when you have to take your shirt off and get painted up in the white. They say 'it's not about looks' but it's still new to me. For me it's shame. For them, they don't care who looks. They have lost someone, part of them.

As to sorcery, she also had her doubts: 'that's what they say happened to my grandmother when she had the car accident. But I really don't know, I think it was the driver who didn't handle the vehicle properly.'

She had, however, mastered strategies for dealing with excessive demand sharing: 'if people asked me for money I just say I don't have any, even if I do. Sometimes I might give them something. When we go to Alice Springs, people ask us for money. "Money money money", not "how are you?"'

In 'Kimberley's' story there are so many close calls, so many fortuitous events and things falling into place that it should not be surprising to learn how rare her story of return is. Had she allowed her passive understanding of Warlpiri to lapse, had she not persevered with the spoken language through initial mispronunciation, had she not had an uncle who was a senior figure at Yuendumu willing to correct her pronunciation, tell her stories about the old days and the country, had she not found encouraging white bosses and interesting work, had she not found a suitable husband, had any of these elements not been present she may not have found a new life at Yuendumu sustainable. The feud, paradoxically, seemed to have accelerated her re-integration with her stay-at-home relations.

Stolen Generation

Even before the national catharsis that is summarised in the phrase 'The Stolen Generation', there were Warlpiri people returning to the home settlements after being raised in distant institutions. One Warlpiri woman, who had been raised by foster parents in Adelaide, had returned to Yuendumu in the 1980s, had eventually married a local Warlpiri man (one of the bi-cultural adepts) and had two children with him. I saw her a few years later on her return to Adelaide, for things had not turned out that well. Although she was welcomed back, she found it hard to fit in. Other Warlpiri people were somewhat amazed at the bedtime routine she kept up with her children: the daily baths, the clean pyjamas. She tried to learn the language but she found that the old women spoke too fast. She seemed defenceless against relations who took her washing machine.

Others seem to have had a more successful experience of return, although I did not know them personally. One man from a very large Warlpiri family at Yuendumu had been sent to Melville Island as a young child in the 1950s and raised in an institution there. He re-joined his Warlpiri family at Yuendumu as a young man without having learnt any Warlpiri language. However, he married a Warlpiri woman and they had their own large family. In a later era, the 1970s, two young men who had been given up for adoption as babies in Adelaide returned to Lajamanu with the assistance of an Aboriginal Link-Up NGO.[12] One stayed longer than the other, married a local woman and had a family. At the time of my research they had returned to the city and their Warlpiri mother, with whom they had reunited, proudly told me that one was working as a detective and the other in a senior position in hospital administration.

Virtual Return

The extension of mobile phone reception to some Warlpiri home settlements and the increase in mobile phone ownership in the 1990s enabled some in the diaspora, who had the technical skill, the inclination and the contacts, to make a virtual return to their home settlement. All such elements are unevenly spread in the total Warlpiri population. There is still no mobile phone reception at Willowra and Nyirrpi. Some of the older Warlpiri people on the connected settlements continue to have difficulties in saving numbers to the correct folder in their phones. Some found it hard to resist their inclination to give their mobile phone away upon request of a close relation (not so much the younger generation). All the matriarchs described in this book had mastered the technology to varying degrees and it played a significant part in their social lives, subject to the usual fluctuations in their ability to purchase phone credits. But it was 'Barbara' who excelled, both in her conscientiousness of use and her good contacts back in Yuendumu. She provided the best example of the possibilities of virtual return. She received daily reports of events at Yuendumu: deaths, of course, but also those in hospital, including those being sent to Adelaide Hospital and in need of a visit; the location of relations, what they were doing, gossip of the latest affairs and fights; whether new houses were being built, who they were earmarked for; and, during the height of the family feud, a blow by blow description of the contretemps of the day.

It seemed to me that for 'Barbara', this capacity for virtual return strengthened her ability to continue in Adelaide because she no longer had to overcome feelings of loneliness and disconnection from kin that had been a struggle for her in the early years. The equation of geographic distance with social distance had dramatically altered. For others, however, the new compression of social distance that had been previously achieved by long-distance migration put increasing pressure on the sustainability of their lives in the diaspora. Mobile phones and the increasing ease of electronic funds transfer underwrote the extension of long-distance visitation and the geographical extension of demand sharing networks. Paradoxically, the forced engagement with electronic banking and debit cards as part of the implementation of some Intervention measures also extended the infrastructure for demand sharing. Thus, during the height of his football career in Melbourne, Liam Jurrah's fortnightly wages were quickly dispersed to relations back in Yuendumu and other locations within Australia. News of even small windfalls seemed to spread quickly and, for example, I observed Warlpiri women in Canberra for a conference presentation transfer $20 into a relation's account so that back in Willowra they could buy cigarettes for the morning break. Admittedly, denials of having any funds made over the phone were more difficult to verify than in person since wallets and pockets could not be inspected and contrary indications, such as large purchases, would not be apparent at the other end of the phone. In this way, geographical distance did continue to moderate the immediacy of demand sharing.

The Lost

Before bringing this chapter to a conclusion, it is worth noting that in some cases the process of attenuation becomes so extended that the possibility of return becomes negligible, although it can never be absolutely discounted. There are also those who do not want to return and do not want to be found. In both instances they are likely to become lost to the Warlpiri even if this is not the way the older women on the settlements see it. For them it seems that no Warlpiri descendant is ever completely lost while the memory of them is still alive and the possibility of establishing contact is still open.

Many, though not all, of the children of some inter-racial unions represent the clearest cases of attenuation. In addition to the cases already mentioned, I became aware of quite a few others. There are the two young children of a teenage Warlpiri girl in the north Queensland coastal city in the care of the child welfare authorities. There is a single Warlpiri teenage boy in

Muswellbrook being raised by his white mother and stepfather. His Warlpiri father died unexpectedly young, his Warlpiri grandparents have since died and his remaining 'grandmother' (father's mother's sister) is not young. In Sydney somewhere there are two Warlpiri girls, young adults now, who were adopted by a white teacher when he was working in the school at Nyirrpi. After a few years at Nyirrpi he moved to Canberra and then to Sydney. Also in Sydney somewhere with child welfare authorities are two very young Warlpiri children. I crossed paths with their travelling parents, a Warlpiri woman and a white man, in Adelaide where they were already having problems. It seems the relationship dissolved into drunkenness and neglect in Sydney. There was a Warlpiri teenager living in Melbourne, the son of one of the Adelaide artists. His white father had strictly limited his contact with the Warlpiri in-laws and the relationship with his Warlpiri mother ended after some years. The Warlpiri mother became a dialysis patient in a Melbourne hospital where she received visits from her son and, as far as I could tell, that was the only connection he had to things Warlpiri. Also in Melbourne were the grandchildren of a Warlpiri woman who had settled in Katherine with her white husband (the nurse and the union organiser). The school-age grandchildren were becoming involved in fairly common truancy and delinquency among their Aboriginal friends in Katherine and so were sent to complete their schooling in suburban Melbourne with the husband's relations. I wondered what their Warlpiri ancestry would mean to them.

One foster family with three Warlpiri children brought up in Adelaide encompassed the range of problematic returns of Warlpiri children who had been damaged in their early childhood with drunken or absent Warlpiri parents in Alice Springs. For two of them, their last point of contact with their Warlpiri relations was at Alice Springs, a place one of them, now a young adult man, associated with neglect and his continuing phobia about being in a room with a closed door. His negative impressions of the Warlpiri may have been softened as a result of being befriended by 'Barbara's' grandson who, as it turned out, lived only a few suburbs away from him in Adelaide. In any event, he wisely chose to pursue outdoors work as a stockman in a rural area of Western Australia. He eventually did make contact with one of his 'grandmothers', one of the Warlpiri matriarchs of Alice Springs with whom his foster mother had kept in touch. The process of his reconnection with his Warlpiri relations had commenced.

The youngest daughter in the foster family, 'Narelle', seemed to have had a similar life trajectory to the young gang member in a Queensland town: early rebellious behaviour, violent drug-addicted boyfriends, drinking, living rough, teenage pregnancies and the child welfare authority's involvement with the babies. The difference was her complete lack of Warlpiri language and knowledge of her own close relations back in Alice Springs and Yuendumu.

The troubled young girl in the north Queensland town had staged a brief, triumphant return to Yuendumu with her youth workers who were keen to visit the successful Mt Theo anti-petrol sniffing programme (Preuss and Brown 2006; Stojanovski 2010). At Yuendumu they saw their pregnant street kid briefly transform into a Warlpiri speaking community member. There is no way that 'Narelle' could have staged such a visit. She only had vague memories of a Warlpiri foster mother, 'Camilla' from the Christian *jilimi* in Alice Springs, who had looked after her for a short time. My research unexpectedly became a linkup service when, upon hearing the news of 'Narelle', 'Camilla' wanted her to return to Alice Springs where 'Camilla' would look after her, a plan I thought full of emotional outpouring and short on appreciation of 'Narelle's' entanglements. I tried to explain that 'Narelle' had one baby with the child welfare authorities and another with an unsuitable father. Not only was 'Narelle's' support base (her foster mother) in Adelaide, 'Narelle' herself had expressed some trepidation about reconnecting with the Warlpiri. I suggested 'Camilla' make a preliminary visit to 'Narelle' in Adelaide so that she could make her own assessment.

One of the things 'Narelle' had observed was the disastrous reunion between her elder foster sister, 'Tangier', and 'Tangier's' grandmother, one of the Warlpiri drinkers in Adelaide described briefly in Chapter 4. The foster mother worried about 'Tangier's' emotional vulnerability as a teenager who was already coping with some emotional instability and the usual run of teenage concerns about relationships and dealing with new possibilities of alcohol and drugs. Her foster mother counselled her to lower her expectations of the relationship. The initial meeting, for which the grandmother had remained sober, went well and eventually 'Tangier' wanted to move in with her grandmother. The foster mother acquiesced until things began to fall apart with 'Tangier' being used to fund the grandmother's drinking. 'Tangier' returned disillusioned and repeating that nobody loved her. She eventually became estranged from the foster family as well and was last heard of living with an Aboriginal family in the New South Wales outback having become involved with an Aboriginal man in jail for manslaughter. It seemed to me that 'Tangier's trajectory was taking her further away from a Warlpiri identity and further away from continuing involvement with Warlpiri people.

Conclusion

Some of the examples of return already mentioned reveal fundamental motivating factors associated with a particular stage in a person's life-cycle. The return of the two pioneers to Yuendumu in their retirement is consistent with the tradition of feeling the draw of one's traditional country more acutely as one gets older. But there were counter examples as well of several older Warlpiri men viewing the drinking life in the town camps as their retirement option. Among the matriarchs in the diaspora, obligations towards grandchildren and towards their own ageing mothers were important particularly when there were no other competent carers available. In the case of 'Sarah' and the other women of the Christian *jilimi*, there was a cumulative alignment of such obligations that, yet again, reinforced their location in Alice Springs: two of the aged and near senile mothers were being cared for in the *jilimi*, 'Sarah's' own mother was in the aged care facility in Alice Springs and they were able to provide something of a safety net for the most neglected of their grandchildren. In another instance, however, it was the declining health of the aged mother of a veteran traveller of the diaspora (Bundaberg, Wagga Wagga and Adelaide) that finally brought most of her travelling to an end and her return to Yuendumu and Alice Springs for the last years of her mother's life. For some of the diaspora-raised generation of women, there seemed to be yet another life-cycle imperative: return to find a husband. Among the Yolngu, Coulehan found an opposite pattern of young women finding sexual partners in town and returning pregnant to the settlement where the kin support network required for the baby was located (1995: 140–57).

While life-cycle factors do seem to play some part in return migration, the thrust of this chapter has been to explore the theme of ambivalent homecomings which has also been theorised in the international literature on diaspora and return migration. Scaling down such theorising to the level of an indigenous diaspora has enabled an exploration of questions of cultural estrangement, attenuation and ethnic boundary marking rarely thematised in community ethnographies that are more predisposed towards acceptance of the settlement perspective. In this perspective, those who return for important cultural events or to live permanently are coming home, returning to their senses and turning their backs on culturally degraded, dangerous and lonely places. In challenging the universality of such a perspective, the model of ambivalent return has found some direct counterparts in indigenous diaspora, particularly the important distinction between ethnic identity and culture. In the most extreme cases of early adoption or fostering with white people or second-generation migrants brought up in isolation from other Warlpiri people in the diaspora (for example, the Queensland strangers returning for their deceased mother's royalties), their biological connection and their distinctive appearance provided the symbolic markers of their ethnic identity but it was hollowed out of any cultural content which they would have to learn from the beginning. Even the second-generation Warlpiri migrants who had maintained more connections through visitation and familiarity with language faced the realisation on their return of how much they would still have to learn and how different they were, notwithstanding their distinctiveness as Warlpiri people in a predominantly white diaspora. What could not be extrapolated from the international literature on return is the particular configuration of the home and away politics of identity, the emphasis on abstemious, homeland traditionalism and the way in which questions of return are worked out at the level of individual families who are typically very forgiving and inclusive in claiming that their returning kin are still Warlpiri.

Notes

1. For a comprehensive bibliography of the literature about return migration, see Carling, Mortensen and Wu (2011).
2. I do not mean to imply that the 'wet' canteen option was exclusively a Queensland phenomenon. It is just that the best documented examples of the destructive effect of 'wet' canteens happened to be Queensland ones. While the absence of 'wet' canteens is true of all the Warlpiri settlements, the post-1964 situation in other parts of the Northern Territory was mixed. Some Northern Territory settlements did experiment with 'wet' canteens (Brady 2014, 2017).
3. In making this broad comparison between the Warlpiri and the situation described by Sansom, I do not want to homogenise the Warlpiri position. While it seems that the Warlpiri ritual leaders of the 1980s continued to outlaw grog on the ceremony ground, one particular bi-cultural adept and protégé of the ritual leaders once questioned me on the apparent inconsistency in granting full land rights but without what he thought should be an accompanying right to make decisions about grog on an individual basis. I also heard a report of drunken men singing sacred songs and purporting to initiate young men in a town camp in Alice Springs. The report was conveyed to me as a shameful scandal, thus reinforcing the general point about the appropriate location for Warlpiri initiation ceremonies. Sansom's assertion of rule-following among the Wallaby Cross mob does strain credulity on occasion and suggests a parody of structural-functionalist accounts of remote community (cf. Merlan 1995).
4. Merlan provides a dramatic example of contrasting behaviour of a brutalised and abusive drunk in town who was also a highly valued, model stockman out bush (1998: 200–201) as just one of the many manifestations of an underlying socio-spatial logic in traditional life being adapted to town circumstances.
5. Mary Laughren, a linguist with a long-term interest in Warlpiri language and involvement with bilingual education, personal communication.
6. Since the early pastoral era and definitely the early settlement era, donkeys became part of the Warlpiri scene and had entered the local vernacular, for example, to describe the early basic houses of the settlement ('donkey houses'). In the 1980s I became aware that many Aboriginal people in central Australia associated the donkey with Jesus and refused to kill it for meat. I was never able to pinpoint the source of the association, whether it was from knowledge of Bible stories or cruciform markings on the donkeys. Typical of a Warlpiri approach to many genres of stories, there was little interest in the exegesis of the 'Mussolini in Darwin' story so my linking of the donkey with Christianity and/or the

Bible is somewhat speculative. I am, however, indebted to Patsy Napaljarri Rose, one of my Warlpiri collaborators in Darwin, who referred me to the Old Testament story of the talking donkey (Numbers 22: 21–35) that appears to have some overlapping tropes: a critical and magical communication between donkey and person to save that person's life.
7. For an account of contemporary Warlpiri mortuary practice, see Dussart (2000: 72–73) and Musharbash (2008a).
8. The high esteem in which the Warlpiri held distant traditional healers seems to have a long history. Meggitt reported a similar positive Warlpiri attitude to Pitjantjatjara healers (1962: 41).
9. Coulehan also reported social pressure among the Yolngu (1988–1991) for the abbreviation of initiation ceremonies and for the timetabling of the climactic ceremony around holidays and weekends (1995: 199, 219).
10. Personal communication from Dr Heather McDonald who conducted anthropological research among evangelical and Pentecostal churches in Halls Creek, Western Australia, between 1989 and 1991 (see McDonald 2001).
11. Note that the consequences of such decisions about royalty distributions did not have the dramatic legal effects that tribal disenrollment has in the USA where the autonomy of officially recognised tribes to define their own membership criteria is protected from judicial oversight (see Ramirez 2007: 161–65; Reitman 2006; Wilkins 2004). The issue has regained prominence in the USA following the financial pressure to reduce membership lists for the distribution of Indian casino profits.
12. The phrase 'Aboriginal Link-Up NGO' refers to a non-government Aboriginal organisation which provides family tracing and family reunion services to Aboriginal people who were separated from their natural parents. Such organisations were established in most Australian states following the recommendations of the 1997 report of the Human Rights and Equal Opportunity Commission into The Separation of Aboriginal and Torres Strait Islander Children from Their Families (the *Bringing Them Home Report*).

Conclusion

Bold Matriarchs and the Prospects for Cosmopolitan 'Orbiting'

In concluding this book, I will return to some of the questions raised in chapter 1, then address the implications of the Warlpiri diaspora research project for the policy proposal of 'orbiting'. The relationship between geographic distance and social embeddedness is suggested by the very term indigenous diaspora. While various aspects to that relationship will be distinguished, it is the ways in which Warlpiri people of the diaspora extend their personal social networks beyond their kin that has the main effect of loosening the social embeddedness. I will consolidate what has been learned about the various social technologies involved in this extension. Although the personal quality of boldness has been prominent in my account of the Warlpiri matriarchs of the diaspora, I argue that the historical juncture of the 1970s and 1980s entailed numerous points of positive reception for the Warlpiri migrants. I also reflect on whether their settlement upbringing amounted to a school for boldness which predisposed them to taking advantage of the new opportunities. The significance of the Warlpiri matriarchs and their households as the stable nodes of the diaspora encourages me to propose my own take on the anthropological theorising of the matrifocal household. Such households do not figure in the policy discussion of 'orbiting' so I reflect on the limited range of motivations recognised in that discussion. Finally, I address the experimental nature of the diaspora framing of this research.

Social Embeddedness and Geographical Distance

Three kinds of relationship between social embeddedness and geographical distance have been exemplified in various ways in the stories of the Warlpiri diaspora in this book. The first is reasonably straightforward and could be called the attenuation of enforcement at greater distances from the concentrations of Warlpiri people on the settlements. Evading the enforcement of traditional law or punishment by moving a long distance from those who had a direct interest in the matter has a long history, going back to the pre-contact era when fugitives from the consequences of wife stealing or manslaughter would seek temporary asylum with neighbouring tribes. It is a kind of escape from jurisdiction exemplified most obviously in the diaspora material by the escape of young promised wives from the home settlements. The second is what could be called the attenuation of spiritual power as distance from the home settlements increases. It was exemplified by assertions that certain spirits/monsters of the Warlpiri homeland did not exist in the diaspora and that sorcery was less common and less effective in the diaspora. The third is what Merlan summarised as 'spatial modes of social ordering' in which such traditional modes were adapted to new circumstances in the diaspora (1998: 204). These modes are culturally well entrenched and include the designation of different camping areas for married couples, unmarried men and widowed women; the designation of certain places as being for men or women only; and the organisation of some ritual spaces along gender lines. In the diaspora these spatial modes were sometimes extrapolated in a direct way, such as the deliberate creation of a women's space (the Christian *jilimi* of Alice Springs), and sometimes extended to the attempted designation of micro 'dry' areas in the town camps. There was perhaps something similar at work in Adelaide in the de facto 'dry' areas comprising those households who resisted accommodating their drinking relations by asserting the need to preserve household routines for the education of children. Rather than attenuation, the effectiveness of these modes of social organisation depended upon shared understandings and the acceptance of these modes of social ordering. In diaspora conditions the characterisation of spaces was often contested. But the principal means by which the Warlpiri matriarchs of the diaspora distanced themselves from the social intensity of the settlements was by expanding their personal social networks beyond their Warlpiri kin (see below).

In the introductory chapter I noted how the term 'deterritorialised', taken from the literature on global diasporas and transnationalism, had a particularly acute resonance for traditional Warlpiri personhood which assumed a spiritual emplacement in traditional country. Thus, the question arises as to whether the different degrees of distancing from kin networks, especially among the bold Warlpiri women of the diaspora, has been accompanied by a parallel attenuation of spiritual emplacement. For the settlement-born Warlpiri matriarchs, there were contradictory forces at work. The strong sense of spiritual emplacement they had grown up with was part of the relatively unproblematic aspect of the total experience of the settlements and continued to be reinforced in the choice of designs for their paintings and the re-enactment, albeit without the close surveillance of the settlements, of claims to their rightful use of those designs. Even more directly, royalty payments continued to provide additional validation of the importance of those links to country. In some instances, however, even these contemporary reinforcements were becoming attenuated in the diaspora. Among some of the Pentecostal women, although not all, their traditional designs (*kuruwarri*) were part of the life they had to leave behind 'to go cleanly with Jesus leading me'. Others gave up on attending royalty meetings since these typically involved long journeys and, on arrival, fractious confrontations with their own kin about the division of the available funds.

Everywhere in the diaspora, even among the settlement-born generation, knowledge of their traditional country beyond the settlements was becoming attenuated in a similar way to that elaborated by Merlan in relation to the Katherine town campers of the 1970s (1998: 76–113). The use of an outstation for cultural instruction on the return trips organised by the Ali Curung children's house was an exception. The Warlpiri family from Yuendumu whom I had known for a long time was I think more typical of the largely abandoned outstations of Yuendumu. I had seen their outstation flourishing in the 1980s when the old patriarch was still alive. Now it had fallen into disrepair, some of the vital infrastructure had been stolen and the lives of the remaining bi-culturally adept members of the family had taken them to town or to other remote Aboriginal settlements where they were preoccupied with jobs and family commitments. Another person in the diaspora who did return to Yuendumu relatively frequently spoke of driving past the turnoff to her family's outstation but never quite being able to make a visit for all sorts of logistical reasons and the fact that all the people she had come to see were living in the main settlement. Yet another Warlpiri person in Darwin, in reply to my enquiries about her traditional country, was unsure and referred me to the Central Land Council whom she thought would know.

It was in the second-generation diaspora that the possibilities of a more radical attenuation of spiritual emplacement in traditional country became apparent. The most extreme example, outlined in Chapter 5 (Ambivalent Homecomings), was of the siblings arriving at a royalty meeting from a town in rural Queensland where they had grown up in complete isolation from all Warlpiri people apart from their mother. Warlpiri children fostered with white couples were in a similar position. Others had a potential way back to their traditional country, as the extraordinary example of 'Kimberley's' return from Adelaide demonstrates. But some of these connections were becoming tenuous and the knowledgeable old people on the settlements, who could reconnect them in a meaningful way, were becoming fewer.

The Expansion of Personal Social Networks

The various portraits in this book reveal the variable effect of marriage-like relationships with white people on extending personal social networks beyond kin. A key factor has been the social standing of the white partner. Relationships with underclass white men (the unemployable alcoholics, the drug addicted) feature prominently in the diaspora. These relationships rarely involved establishing relationships with the white person's kin, who had often disowned them. Their relative isolation can be contrasted to the stories of the Warlpiri women among the Darwin 'long grassers'. Some of them were treated as the spouse of their long-term Aboriginal drinking partners/ boyfriends by his Aboriginal kin, with all the consequent recognition and assistance. Through the white underclass men, the more usual contacts made by the Warlpiri women were with other underclass men. Typically, it was the Warlpiri women in these relationships who managed relations with welfare and housing authorities, who could occasionally bring in extra money through the sale of a painting, and who maintained relationships with their Warlpiri kin. This higher level of social functioning was rarely acknowledged by the underclass partners who, in effect, 'married up' and joined Warlpiri social networks.

The mid-range of social standing of the non-Warlpiri partners included the owner of the used car sale yard, a bookkeeper and a technician at a TV station. At the top of the social hierarchy of such partners, there were the male schoolteachers. The white men with jobs and prospects tended to partner with Warlpiri women of relatively high educational achievement on the home settlements. The latter combination entailed the possibility of a middle-class experience of family life, even if it was hedged with cultural differences, played out on a daily basis, regarding decisions about household finances, raising children and responding to the demands of Warlpiri kin. Most of the Warlpiri women in such inter-racial marriages developed positive relationships with their in-laws, as did their children. The positive relationships with the white side of the family sometimes lasted beyond the break-up of the relationship. The friends and contacts of the white partners became their own friends and contacts and, moreover, they developed networks of friends and contacts through their own educational and working careers which were at least partly facilitated and encouraged by the white partners.

I suggested in the introduction that the inter-racial marriages would probably be at the intimate cutting edge of intercultural negotiation given the distance between traditional Warlpiri culture and Western ideals of romantic love and companionate marriage. Acknowledging the limits of multi-sited ethnography in pursuing these intimate details (especially of women informants), the pressure of such negotiation is perhaps reflected in the high attrition rate. Of the twenty-six inter-racial relationships I identified, only five of these relationships were ongoing during the period of research. Obviously, all long-term relationships are difficult to sustain and some of the Warlpiri inter-racial relationships seemed to have ended for universal reasons such as the discovery of infidelity. Others seem to have been overwhelmed by illness, by the Warlpiri partner taking up the drinking lifestyle or by violence. The ones that continued or had lasted for a long time typically involved both common projects beyond children and household and the Warlpiri woman having a supportive circle of her own female friends. That is probably true of all long-term relationships. But what I sensed with some of the Warlpiri women in long-term relationships with white men was their need to balance the routine of house and job with the occasional spree with their Warlpiri female age-mates, gambling or carousing or pursuing extramarital affairs. For those in relationships with underclass white men, there was no such balancing.

Befriending non-kin was the other principal way in which the Warlpiri matriarchs extended their personal social networks. As I argued in the introduction, the pursuit of friendship with white people was potentially less familiar than marriage with white people. It involved learning a new social technology. As the example of 'Dulcie' in Alice Springs demonstrated most clearly, the best networkers among the matriarchs had learned skills that reflected an understanding of Western friendship and weaker forms of social ties. They differentiated what was possible with different kinds of contacts and the contexts of meeting them. They understood the likely interest the other person would have in them and were able to moderate their requests for assistance to match the arc of the developing relationship. The least successful would try to turn acquaintanceship into a kin-like demand sharing relationship too quickly, seemingly unaware of the likelihood of being rebuffed and avoided in future.

Some of the more educated matriarchs and other Warlpiri women in the diaspora were adept at speaking in a register that mirrored in many ways typical bourgeois politeness (that I no doubt unconsciously and naturally tended to adopt). It consisted of pleasantries, no swearing, well-formed sentences, the correct enunciation of words and a relatively low volume. Only on occasion did I realise what a conscious effort this required of them. One such occasion was when a pleasant interview with a Warlpiri woman was interrupted by an irritated white partner complaining about having to look after their young children. Turning aside from me, she screamed at the top of her voice 'you're nothing but a fucking old drug addict' and went off to deal with him in a threatening manner. I took this to be an extreme demonstration of a more general skill of the bi-cultural adept of social code-switching.

Religious conversion has provided both the ideological justification for the extension of personal social networks beyond kin and, in theory, a ready-made grouping (the congregation) that could facilitate such an extension. The scale of the enlarged networks depended upon the scale and composition of the congregation. The relatively large, predominantly non-Aboriginal congregation of the Baptist Church in Alice Springs provided manifold opportunities for a variety of social ties with non-Aboriginal people in the weekly services, in special ministries like hospital and jail visitation, and in friendships. Some of these friendships and other weaker social ties also provided useful contacts in the police force, the hospital and Aboriginal NGOs. As explained in Chapter 3 (Making Alice Springs a Warlpiri Place), for some of the Warlpiri matriarchs their Christianity enabled a distancing from some aspects of the operation of their kin networks (drinking, participation in violent family feuding) and the intensification of other aspects. Christianity provided the ideological reinforcement of service to kin as an expression of Christian love, and a broadening of the object of compassion beyond one's own kin, as in the praying over any sick Warlpiri person in the hospital. The much smaller Assemblies of God churches at Bagot and Alice Springs, with their majority Aboriginal membership, offered fewer opportunities for the extension of non-Aboriginal social networks, although the intensity of involvement necessitated by the smaller scale tended to be greater. Opportunities were provided by the church networks which linked the Warlpiri with other Aboriginal people in Assemblies of God congregations in Halls Creek and Coober Pedy, and another opportunity to connect with non-kin arose through national Pentecostal conventions.

As for friends, mentors and business partners, the Christian ideology of the family of God would seem to underwrite and encourage a break from endosociality. This was most clearly expressed in 'Rosie's' declaration: 'I don't care who they are as long as they are good people'. Broader social processes are also implicated in facilitating the formation of non-kin relationships, for example, the general societal revaluation of traditional culture, overlapping with the commencement of the self-determination policy era, and the positive reception of the Western Desert art movement. These processes allowed the matriarchs of the diaspora to be positively situated even by acquaintances in the diaspora. I witnessed the warmth of the reception they received from their regular art suppliers in Adelaide, ex-neighbours and in their favoured retail outlets where they had become known. In trying to understand the positive reception of the Warlpiri matriarchs by their non-Aboriginal contacts, I suggested in Chapter 1 the counterfactual of the suspicion and avoidance of young Aboriginal men in the same situation. While one may extrapolate a general sympathy for the abstemious Aboriginal grandmothers and artists, it is not clear how decisive these general perceptions may be and how widespread they are in the diaspora locations. Quite naturally, the Warlpiri matriarchs tended to extend their personal social networks in directions where they received some initial positive response.

Even with shared projects, the potential for misjudgements, the closure of temporary openings and the collapse of temporary bridges is always present as one would expect given the considerable differences between kin-based interactions and the more central role of non-kin friendship in Western sociality. Among the Baptist congregation in Alice Springs, their common projects of belief, liturgy and service seemed to suppress requests for help, or at least channel them in ways they knew would be acceptable (a lift to Sunday services, transport for a hunting trip) or to members of the congregation with whom they had built up an understanding. Sometimes as these individuals became more aware of the depth of the financial needs of the matriarchs and the seriousness of the inevitable succession of family crises, it made them wary of pursuing open-ended friendship and more willing to negotiate limits. In contrast, it will be recalled from Chapter 4 (Warlpiri Women of Adelaide) that the economic bond between 'Suzanne' and her art wholesaler in Adelaide emboldened her to seek a much broader range of assistance from the wholesaler than simple payment for completed canvases delivered, and such requests became a feature of the ongoing tussle over the limits to the scope of their relationship.

The result of the expansion of social networks by the Warlpiri matriarchs of the diaspora is the continual stretch and negotiation between quite different modes of living. This was most obviously apparent when those who had public housing tenancies had to deal with visiting kin who insisted upon settlement norms of generosity towards kin, non-judgemental acceptance of behaviour, and non-interference in male prerogatives of partying. In the town camps and the unofficial camping areas, the seclusion from white neighbours and the more relaxed approach to tidiness tended to lessen these kinds of conflicts. For the committed Christians, the family feuding made apparent the quite different expectations of the various social groups with which they had become involved. 'Dulcie', perhaps more than anyone else, exemplified the broad range of different social groups she was involved with and the need for deft handling of the various repertoires of behaviour and speech and the active segregation of different social worlds. Bess Price's social worlds, especially after her election and when she became a cabinet minister, were equally diverse, if somewhat differently configured (not so much Baptist Church) and seemed to extend to every level of Northern Territory society.

In answer to the question posed in the introductory chapter, it seems to me that the expansion of personal social networks beyond Warlpiri kin had a direct bearing upon the permanence and sustainability of the diaspora locations. The significance of the white partners having jobs and their own kinship and friendship networks is reflected in the rapid decline of the relatively large Warlpiri outpost at Murray Bridge when the foundational relationship collapsed. But others, like 'Barbara' in Adelaide, weathered a similar dramatic separation, in my view because of the support she received from another of the Warlpiri matriarchs who had similar commitments to household routines and raising and educating children and grandchildren, not to mention the myriad other friendships and contacts that enriched her life.

Matrifocal Households

Through the expansion of personal social networks described above, the Warlpiri matriarchs strengthened their connections to their new diaspora locations so that their households became the stable nodes for their white spouses, friends and contacts as well as for their existing Warlpiri kin, who still mostly lived back on the home settlements. The functioning households in the towns and cities became an asset to the broader kinship network, for example, as a safe place from which to launch a drinking adventure; as a convivial place for visitors forced into town for medical treatment or other business; and, in Adelaide, a possible source of help in buying a cheap second-hand vehicle. There were high-functioning white partners in two of the households, but for the majority of Warlpiri matriarchs in the diaspora, their households could accurately be described as kinds of matrifocal households. Accordingly, I see this research project as a contribution to theorising the matrifocal household in a Fourth World context. In chapter 4 I noted how the three family households coordinated by 'Barbara' in the northern suburbs of Adelaide exhibited some similarities with the matrifocal households described in the Afro-Caribbean literature: mostly absent husbands/fathers, although present sometimes and sending financial support at other times; affective relations focused on the mother/grandmother figure; the house consisting of the matriarch, her daughters and the daughters' children; grandmothers raising their grandchildren in the absence of wayward daughters. Yet there are obvious contextual differences: the Australian welfare net and the special position of the Warlpiri as part of a recognised indigenous minority within a broadly liberal settler state.

Although the Warlpiri matriarchs in their matrifocal households received critical support from similarly minded matriarchs who were typically their close kin, the households were vulnerable to other visiting kin because of their love of travel, demand sharing and easy access to liquor in the diaspora. In the case of the Christian *jilimi* in Alice Springs and the Pentecostal church at Bagot in Darwin, it was a paradoxical vulnerability. The more the Warlpiri matriarchs secured their positions through their white networks of support, the more those households became attractive to needy kin who the matriarchs would want to help. The Warlpiri women of the Christian *jilimi* moderated their vulnerability to some extent using traditional modes of gendering space that made male relations hesitant to join them. In Adelaide, the vulnerability of the matrifocal households to disruptive visitation was moderated to some extent by sheer geographical distance which, in a way, has its traditional antecedents (solving social tensions by geographical relocation).

As mentioned in the introductory chapter, one of the main tendencies of anthropological theorising about Afro-Caribbean matrifocal households has been to suggest that the broader economic and social marginalisation of Afro-Caribbean men is reproduced in family relationships, depressing their role and status as potential heads of households (see, for example, Smith 1996: 1–56). While the absence of the cultural account of masculinity and specifically fatherhood from these kinds of interpretation has also been noted (see, for example, Barrow 1996: 461–62), anthropological theorising about matrifocal households is suggestive of the relevance of broader social hierarchies. This interpretive move is also suggested by the trend in feminist theorising to break up the broad category of women according to other cross-cutting social hierarchies of race, class and sexual orientation.

Boldness in Context

The structure of this book and its portraits of individuals enables the reconstruction of a particular social trajectory of the Warlpiri matriarchs of the diaspora. It seeks to explain how their personal qualities and their experiences on the settlements enabled them to cut across more general racial and gender hierarchies at a particular historical juncture. At its most general level, that juncture was the meeting of the continuation of Warlpiri traditional culture on the settlements with the societal revaluation of traditional culture in the policy era of self-determination. The lives of Warlpiri matriarchs in fact cover the second half of the twentieth century and up to the present. In the trajectory of their lives we see the continuing effects of the investment in education from the assimilation era when the Warlpiri settlements were training institutions. We see the changing social attitudes among some sections of the wider society about inter-racial relationships. We also see locations and spheres of activity where the migrating Warlpiri were likely to receive a warm welcome, such as in the Aboriginal controlled NGO service organisations and in the art market. Going back to the beginning of the overall social trajectory of the Warlpiri matriarchs, however, I want to reflect on the personal quality of boldness and how it relates to their experience of the Warlpiri settlements of the 1970s and 1980s.

'Natalie', with her campaign against shame and her total inversion of the settlement gender order, is the most extreme personification of the quality of boldness among the Warlpiri matriarchs of the diaspora. But other settlement-raised Warlpiri women in the diaspora also exhibited degrees of boldness, for example in disentangling themselves from Warlpiri husbands; marrying non-Warlpiri men; asserting themselves in more fleeting and more difficult conjugal relations; asserting their own educational priorities and independent networking with non-kin; and in myriad other ways in which they asserted their traditional knowledge, particularly through their continued use of the Warlpiri language and in their traditional paintings. I gained the impression from stories about 'Natalie' and from my own observation of others that at least for some Warlpiri women in the diaspora, their boldness was underwritten by their preparedness to meet physical violence with violence and their pride in their fighting abilities. The fact that even the usually fearless and frank 'Natalie' did not volunteer this information about herself, I put down to the skill of the bi-culturally adept who were acutely aware of bourgeois manners and the censoriousness of the broader society regarding recourse to physical violence. Again, I wondered about the relationship of this aspect of boldness to their formative experiences on the settlements.

The no doubt partial view from the diaspora about the settlements in that era emphasises the constraints on women and their relatively subordinate position, at least until they become older widows. The stories of 'getting away' in Chapter 2 provide examples of this: the overriding of personal choice of marriage partners; excessive beatings by drunken husbands; beatings by in-laws on suspicions of infidelity; and the overriding of wishes regarding husbands taking on a second wife. In traditional Warlpiri society wifely submission could not be taken for granted. It seemed to depend on shared understandings about infant betrothal, the superior status of initiated men, and the gradual introduction of the young promised wife to her husband. Even when the rejection of such arrangements was met with violence, occasionally recalcitrant promised wives could wear down the resolve of those wishing to enforce the promise. The traditional balance of forces shifted dramatically in a later period on the settlements as access to alcohol became easier (after the mid-1960s) and new avenues of escape for women opened up. In the case of the young Warlpiri woman at Papunya mentioned in Chapter 2, her separation from her own supportive kin amplified the injustice of the habitual drunken beatings and coloured her view of Warlpiri men for the rest of her life. A similar sense of injustice enabled Bess Price to extract herself from an early relationship, with the support of key members of her family and, much later in life, she used the incident as the foundation of her right to comment in the political sphere about Aboriginal domestic violence.

What the Warlpiri matriarchs of the diaspora shared was their settlement upbringing that in many ways amounted to, no doubt unintentionally, a school for boldness. The elements of this 'school' included the positive valuation and modelling of personal assertion from a very early age and a positive valuation on a degree of interpersonal violence. Among other things, these elements led to an acceptance of some level of domestic violence and a willingness of Warlpiri wives to confront male partners despite the unlikelihood of them ultimately prevailing (derived from Burbank 1994). The school was also constituted by widespread homosociality in many aspects of everyday life and the acceptance of the increasing personal autonomy of women as they matured, particularly older widows (Dussart 1992). Of course, such 'schooling' does not produce uniform results, especially for the shy or mentally frail. Among the cohort of middle-aged Warlpiri women of the home settlement, however, there always seemed to be a group who delighted in their own bravado and scorned the timidity of others and their former selves. Women's separate domains of activity did allow such self-assertion to flourish, if within an overall position of male pre-eminence.

Although this is far from a comprehensive account of gender relations on the home settlements, it may be enough to suggest why the women who grew to maturity there would appear to be so formidable to white men they met in the diaspora and to the white employees of Aboriginal service NGOs of Alice Springs in the 1980s who were obliged to respond to their assertive demands (see, for example, Mackinolty 2011). As explained in chapter 3, the Warlpiri women were able to satisfy the demands of the new NGOs for clients, for board members, for the demonstration of traditional cultural practices, for cross-cultural awareness training and for interpreters. In general, it was an era in which the feisty Aboriginal woman could be lauded and even more so as the bearer of traditional law and culture.

The Refashioning of Tradition

There remains to consider in relation to the Warlpiri matriarchs of the diaspora the general questions I raised in the introduction: whether new forms of Warlpiri personhood have arisen in the diaspora and in what way the Warlpiri matriarchs have refashioned traditional Warlpiri culture. In answering these questions, a comparison will be made with the Warlpiri matriarchs who remained on the settlements yet pursued some similar life projects: a career as an artist, furthering their education and adopting Christian religions. In relation to personhood, part of the answer has already been given via the consideration of the expansion of personal social networks and the attenuation of connections to traditional country. To thrive in the diaspora, the Warlpiri matriarchs who were not married to a white man of high social standing had to become collectors of friends and useful contacts. To varying degrees, these friends and contacts became significant to their sense of self, for example, the Adelaide art wholesaler sustaining 'Suzanne's' identity as a professional artist and 'Rosie's' supportive teacher friend at the Aboriginal College reinforcing 'Rosie's' continuing educational achievements.

Except for the extreme case of the queen of the Adelaide parklands, 'Natalie', friends and contacts supplemented kin networks rather than replacing them. Even in 'Natalie's' case, she did maintain some limited contact with her Warlpiri kin. Considering the broad cultural differences between their Warlpiri kin networks and their white networks, I infer a probable transformation from a unified to a more cosmopolitan sense of self, from a secure self to one that is sometimes put under pressure or is conflicted. This pressure was exemplified in 'Dulcie's' case by the wide variety of roles she adopted and the very different groups in which she became involved.

The complexifying of personal social networks is also relevant to other possible directions for the transformation: from personhood constituted in the immediacy and density of interaction with kin to ideas of a self-conscious individual trajectory and cultivation of the self. As mentioned in the introduction, autobiography – and, indeed, any planning for long-term self-improvement – is not part of traditional Warlpiri concerns. The busyness of the Warlpiri matriarchs in the diaspora would seem to militate against this in any case. Yet some of them were able to develop long-term careers and projects which did require degrees of reflection and planning. However, I did not detect among most of them any grand plan of individual liberation.

Given the experiences of the Warlpiri matriarchs of the diaspora, one might have expected a general critique of the authority of Warlpiri men and traditional Aboriginal law to have arisen in the diaspora. I did not find this to be the universal experience. Instead there was a whole range of responses and different kinds of resolution of contradictory feelings. The most forthright and direct challenge to traditional male authority came in the denunciation of the power of the male sorcerer made in the context of the women's personal testimony in the Pentecostal service in Darwin. Other responses also approximated a generalised critique of traditional male authority. Bess Price controversially left open-ended the degree of reform of traditional law that would be required to assist the resolution of contemporary social problems. 'Camilla' generalised her experience of domestic violence to all potential Warlpiri husbands who she feared would be equally 'quick to anger' and never contemplated remarriage. Yet she revelled in the hunting and gathering skills taught to her by the generation of grandmothers who had grown up in the desert and enthusiastically accepted the opportunity presented to her by the Central Land Council to be one of the knowledgeable elders documenting a newly declared Indigenous Protected Area over traditional country (one of her rare return trips). 'Camilla' and Bess, like many of the matriarchs described in this book, had overwhelmingly positive feelings towards the traditionalism of their fathers and their fathers' generation who they described as stoical, abstemious, hard-working and possessing marvellously encyclopaedic traditional knowledge. Many of the matriarchs then made disparaging comparisons with their would-be Warlpiri promised husbands as relatively feckless, lacking in self-control and prone to drunken violence. Their argument was not with traditional language, the close connection to kin and the continual generosity testing of such relationships, nor with rituals, cosmology, traditional land tenure and their own spiritual emplacement, or even sorcery. It was more about how Aboriginal law was applied to them in the choice of their marriage partners and punishment for perceived misdemeanours.

In this respect, the story of 'Valmae' is instructive (see Chapter 4, Warlpiri Women of Adelaide) since she adopted a positive orientation towards Aboriginal law within the overall aims of two-way education for the settlement children she was hosting. For example, she negotiated with the families of her hosted children to allow compliance with initiation rituals and the fulfilment of their promised marriages. Also, their frequent return trips ideally involved lessons in traditional culture at their outstation and continued involvement in the life of the settlement. It seemed to me that 'Valmae' no longer considered her youthful determination not to marry any man to be the radical challenge I imagined it to be. I thought of the potential disruption to traditional reciprocal obligations and to male authority on the settlement more generally. Now there seemed to be wide support in the settlement for 'Valmae's' work in Adelaide and, with the gradual incorporation of her white husband into the ritual life of the settlement, any idea that there may have been a radical challenge to tradition had disappeared.

As explained in Chapter 5 (Ambivalent Homecomings), some of the matriarchs eventually made peace with their jilted promised husbands after a lengthy period when passions had well and truly cooled and another wife had been found for the man in question. Others, while never contemplating a re-entry into the Warlpiri marriage market, became more philosophical about their early violent experiences of marriage and forgiving of the men involved as products of their limited world. In Adelaide and Darwin I also occasionally heard accepting (pitying?) talk about Warlpiri men and liquor ('they need it') or resignation about it as an inherent personality trait.

All of the projects described in this book had the character of a repositioning with regard to some traditional norms and the creation of a new mix (like choosing from a menu) of elements that make up their contemporary Warlpiri life. Indeed, those repositionings are suggested by commonplace understandings of diaspora as involving a tension between personal/cultural baggage and personal/cultural reinvention. In the case of the Warlpiri artists of Adelaide, the distant location of their project of economic independence and less constrained consumption moderated the immediate impact of demand sharing. The schoolchildren's household followed a 'two laws' or bi-cultural approach but also implicitly acknowledged that the required discipline of the children was easier to maintain in a supportive household in the city. The Alice Springs *jilimi* brought the idiom of Christianity to the operation of a traditionally sanctioned women's space.

The denunciation of some key aspects of tradition and male authority by the Warlpiri Pentecostal women, at least in their testimonies during Sunday services, represents the most extreme version of personal autonomy in rejection mode. In the boldness of their self-assertion, I see them as the diaspora counterpart to some of the separatist elements in Bell's account of the personal autonomy of mature Aboriginal women organising their own lives in the *jilimi* or on the outstation, conducting their own healing ceremonies and rituals and sustaining the sacred local landscape without the mediation of men.

One of the recurring realisations during the research for this book has been that many, although not all, of the transformations of personhood, the expansion of social networks through religion and education, and the pursuit of educational careers and cultural entrepreneurship have their counterparts with Warlpiri people who have remained on the settlements. 'Natalie's' complete reversal of the gender order could not have occurred on the remote settlements and most of the inter-racial relationships would have been more problematic had the women been living in such close proximity to promised husbands. But there were on the settlements middle-aged Warlpiri women who had been long-serving teaching assistants in the settlement schools, some methodically concerned with improving their teaching skills; Warlpiri men and women were involved in leading church services and acting in cultural entrepreneurial/brokerage roles in art and new media; and there were other opportunities for Warlpiri people arising from new government and NGO projects. One of these settlement women, who became one of my principal collaborators on various field trips, noted that the difference between her life trajectory and the similarly well-educated and well-connected Warlpiri women we met in the diaspora was that as a young woman she had been continually retrieved by relations when she had run away from her promised husband.

'Orbiting' as Policy

'Orbiting' has been proposed as an alternative to the permanent migration away from remote Aboriginal settlements. It was part of a suite of controversial policy ideas developed by Aboriginal public intellectual and activist, Noel Pearson, who had grown up in the former Lutheran mission and remote Aboriginal settlement of Hopevale on Cape York Peninsula in Queensland. He was one of the first Aboriginal leaders to obtain a university degree (in law and history) and became an articulate national commentator and activist, most notably in the negotiations over the government's response to the High Court's recognition of native title in its Mabo decision of 1992. While his advocacy for a strong Native Title Act proceeded from an Indigenous rights paradigm, during the long period of conservative rule that followed (1996–2007) he also developed policy positions that might gain bipartisan support. This policy advocacy was directed towards political decision-makers and the wider public, typically via short opinion pieces in national newspapers. The advocacy has been remarkably effective in engaging the conservative side of politics and, one suspects, in facilitating bipartisan support for many of the measures of the Northern Territory Intervention (described in Chapter 1). This effectiveness is despite the simplification that has been necessary for his typical audience (see, for example, Rowse 2012: 143–59 for a more substantive analysis questioning the applicability of some of his historical analyses of the Cape York situation to the rest of Australia).

In his policy writing, Pearson's bipartisan appeal was couched in terms of 'a quest for the radical centre' following the failure of Indigenous affairs policy agendas of both the political left and right. In his sights were the deleterious effects of drinking rights and welfare dependency. He closely, almost ethnographically, analysed the workings of Aboriginal drinking circles, particularly the one-way, gendered funnelling of funds that took precedence over the needs of children and the elderly. He described this as a 'social and cultural pathology' and as a 'corruption' of traditional reciprocity (2009b: 146–50). The decline of traditional reciprocity was also seen as the consequence of unconditional welfare payments which he described as 'welfare poison'. Employing a metaphor derived from a traditional food preparation technique (the leaching of poison from the cycad palm nut), Pearson proposed that the 'poison' of welfare be leached out by making it conditional upon the recipients undertaking some form of work, the proper care of children and self-improvement. These conditions he portrayed as a return to a 'real' economy, which exists outside the welfare system and used to exist in traditional Aboriginal society. This is where 'orbiting' fits in: self-improvement through education and engagement with the 'real' economy. Alongside these policy ideas, Pearson promoted regional economic development which might provide jobs for the returning 'orbiters' and the development of regional Aboriginal organisations. These regional Aboriginal organisations would develop an Aboriginal leadership and negotiate new partnerships with governments so as to implement the required reforms in a coordinated way from a position of greater moral authority. Collectively the various strands of these policies became known as 'the Cape York Reform Agenda'.

The inclusion of orbiting among these ideas was perhaps in response to debates about the future of remote Aboriginal settlements when Senator Vanstone was the relevant Minister in the late Howard government era (2003–2006). That period saw the winding down of Commonwealth support for outstations/homelands in the Northern Territory and the consolidation of services into fewer settlements (see Sanders 2008; Taylor 2009). Pearson rejected any idea of mass forced migration from remote settlements into towns and cities: 'If our people were pressured into relocating to urban centres, then they would just end up joining our counterparts in the dysfunctional (white, black and migrant) underclasses in the cities and regional centres' (Pearson 2009b: 297). Instead, he promoted the ideal of the fully bi-cultural and bilingual Aboriginal person:

> It is about the ability to walk in two worlds. To prosper, Aboriginal Australians will have to be integrated into the national and global economies. But we also want to remain distinctly Aboriginal and to retain our connection with ancestral lands. How can we avoid economic integration becoming a one-way ticket taking the young away from their origins, a prospect many parents and community elders dread? As a solution to this problem, I have introduced the concept of 'orbits'. (Pearson 2009b: 294–95) (see also Pearson 2009a: 60–61)

The more intrusive aspects of the Cape York Reform Agenda, particularly those relating to child welfare, required new Queensland government legislation to set up a Family Responsibilities Commission which had powers to enforce welfare income management as well as offer supportive services to those who were referred to it. Other aspects of the agenda were implemented through the setting up of regional, Aboriginal controlled NGOs: first a land council, then an Aboriginal health service, an economic enterprise organisation and a leadership and policy advocacy organisation. The bi-cultural orbiting aspects of the agenda were most clearly evident in the restoration of more or less abandoned policies on boarding school education and organised labour migration. Links were established with elite boarding high schools in distant cities and towns and money found for scholarships and other support for Aboriginal students sent to these schools. This was supplemented by the establishment of an Aboriginal high school in Cairns, which accepted boarders from the remote settlements, and by a renewed push to improve outcomes in the primary schools on the settlements. The labour migration aspects involved helping settlement artists to make commercial links with agents and galleries in distant cities and overseas, and supporting unemployed young men on the settlements in undertaking seasonal fruit picking in distant locations (Pearson 2005: 16, 22). Pearson's achievement in crafting a set of policies that could engage both sides of politics is also reflected in the bi-cultural ideal. On a global scale, this ideal can be seen as a counterpart to cosmopolitanism, and as such resists being placed within simplified policy dichotomies of self-determination or assimilation. It is a rejection of overt assimilation, while accepting the need for modernisation. But it seeks modernisation on its own terms – namely, that modernisation should not have to entail comprehensive deracination. The early theorists of mobility and modernity, such as Zelinsky (1971), saw personal mobility as an essential feature of the modernisation process. Whereas Pearson was asserting that Aboriginal modernisation did not have to be at the expense of a special sense of rootedness to the home settlements and the traditionalism that they represent (also see Rowse's 2005b review of the recent work of the demographers of Aboriginal Australia).

Returning to Pearson's formulation of orbiting, what is immediately recognisable from my account of the Warlpiri diaspora is the ethnographic realism of his negative prognosis of any sudden closure of remote settlements and the transfer of residents to urban centres. Among the Warlpiri diaspora in cities and towns, I found confirmation of Pearson's prognosis that those from the settlements who had not mastered their addictions were being received into the urban underclass, albeit as a fairly distinctive part of that class, and sometimes graduated to harder drugs. There were the long-grassers of Darwin; the unofficial drinking camps of Katherine and Alice Springs; the Parkland dwellers of Adelaide; the drinking houses of suburban Adelaide; and one Warlpiri member of the street gang in Cairns. Pearson did not anticipate that for some isolated members of the white underclass, joining the Warlpiri underclass, with their relatively intact kinship networks, would be an improvement for them. His preference, that orbiting should be for those bi-cultural adepts who have their addictions under control and would follow an educational or work career, does resonate, in some respects, with the Warlpiri diaspora. Most of those who were flourishing in the Warlpiri diaspora were non-drinkers, although some had moved on to what seemed to be an addiction to poker machines.

While the orbiting plans of the Cape York Reform Agenda focused on formal education and workplace careers, in the Warlpiri diaspora I found other kinds of productive and sustaining activity. All involved the typically feminised work of nurturing relationships and caring for children, perhaps revealing a hidden masculinist bias in the reform agenda. As explained in chapter 2, a number of the Warlpiri diaspora locations were a result of Warlpiri women sustaining relationships with functioning white men and raising families with them. The Warlpiri diaspora as described in this book is also significantly populated by Warlpiri women who had internalised the education message in a similar way to Pearson: the grandmother mentioned in Chapter 2 who moved from Ali Curung to Darwin to put her grandchildren through primary school; 'Emily' of Adelaide who had a similar justification, among others, for remaining in Adelaide; 'Rosie' of Adelaide on her trajectory of greater educational achievement; and, of course, the Ali Curung children's house of Adelaide (all in chapter 4). The project of fostering settlement children while they attended high school in Adelaide arose organically from the propitious meeting and exceptional generosity of like-minded individuals, such as 'Valmae', her white partner and her retired former school principal. Their project could be seen as a small-scale, self-help version of Pearson's multipronged approach to educational orbiting which included partnerships with elite boarding schools.[1] 'Valmae's' project concentrated intimate knowledge of settlement culture and direct support for the students close to their day school. Using their privately acquired minibus, they directly enacted orbiting during the school holidays. This inviting, organic approach was also vulnerable to the health and continuing commitment of the key individuals involved, unlike the grander NGOs established by Pearson for the purpose.

What Pearson's policy advocacy missed was the 'career' of being a matriarch at particular nodes in the diaspora, like 'Barbara' and her three related households in Adelaide (Chapter 4), like 'Sarah' and 'Camilla' of the Christian *jilimi* in an Alice Springs town camp, and like the Pentecostal Warlpiri matriarchs of Bagot camp in Darwin (Chapter 2). They became full-time carers and helpers even though in the town camps the sustainability of their functioning households was under continual pressure from their needy kin who gravitated around them. All the Warlpiri matriarchs of the diaspora described in this book were orbiters in the sense of retaining their cultural links to the home settlements and visiting them for significant events. But their 'careers' in the diaspora did not involve conformity to the usual demands of a conventional workplace of routine, punctual attendance and dedication to tasks other than responding to kin demands.

Given the concerns of elders on the Cape York settlements, already acknowledged by Pearson, about the possible permanent loss of their young people to distant education and jobs, he was also quick to assert that his orbiters would retain their culture. In the background there may also be an awareness that in some parts of Australia, children's dormitories had been used in an earlier period of colonial history as a deliberate attempt to distance Aboriginal children from their parents' culture so that missionary evangelisation could proceed in a more unhindered fashion. Accordingly, reassurance about a definitive break with that history was required. The general assertion of retaining culture, however, tends to obscure the cultural transformations that have already taken place in intercultural history. Intercultural analysis aims to be a corrective to those ahistorical approaches which assert an ongoing, radical separation of Aboriginal and non-Aboriginal domains. In the simplification required by policy advocacy, Pearson tends to conform, at least superficially, to this ongoing radical separation. He uses continuing competence in Aboriginal language as his main example of retaining culture. Coincidentally, among the Warlpiri I found that their tendency was also to equate language competence with continuing Warlpiri identity despite the complexity of what was happening both in the settlements and in the diaspora. As mentioned in chapter 1, the language of the younger generation on the settlements was quite different to the older generation's Warlpiri and, at the Warlpiri settlement of Lajamanu, a new language, Light Warlpiri, had emerged. In the diaspora, the tendency towards endosociality and grandparents raising their grandchildren tended to prolong the use of Warlpiri in the domestic sphere. But the language competence of the diaspora-born Warlpiri was patchy, particularly in racially mixed marriages where the white partner was not fluent in Warlpiri. The attenuation of language competency among the second-generation diaspora was also accompanied by an attenuation of detailed knowledge of their traditional country and traditional rituals. It is likely that similar complexities and attenuation of knowledge would occur on the settlements of Cape York and among its orbiters.

The more fundamental critique is that language, as an objectified artefact of cultural difference, is only one aspect of culture, understood more broadly as a way of life. Among the Warlpiri, language, initiation ceremonies and traditional designs used in paintings are among the objectified aspects of culture that continue to be important both on the home settlements and in the diaspora. But a way of life also includes particular worldviews, beliefs, practices and shared values which may not be so readily identified as distinctive languages, rituals and designs. These less readily objectified, but nevertheless pervasive, aspects of remote settlement culture would include a permissive attitude towards child-rearing; kin solidarity in intra-indigenous disputes; performative kin-relatedness through demand sharing; continuing belief in the efficacy of sorcery; and, more generally, a preference for engaging with the immediate and the local. Both the objectified and less readily objectified aspects of the remote settlement way of life tend to be integrated, if under the transformed conditions of the settlement. While some aspects of the way of life such as language, ritual and traditional designs can be detached from settlement life by the orbiters, the other aspects tend to be inimical to the development of educational and work career orbiting. Such orbiting requires a high degree of self-discipline, self-directedness and personal space that can only be achieved by obtaining some social distance from the frequency and immediacy of kin demands. Perhaps even more problematically, orbiting requires the development of the idea of an individual career trajectory, similar to the modern Western 'project of the self' (Giddens 1991). This project may be quite alien to traditional Aboriginal ideas of the spiritually emplaced and socially embedded person (as outlined in chapter 1). Thus, on analysis, what Pearson's assertion of the retention of culture by orbiters may really amount to is the embrace of certain detachable aspects of objectified culture and a simultaneous distancing from other aspects of culture. Other anthropologists have noticed how Pearson tends to downplay these deeply-engrained cultural constraints in his modernising project or attributes them to the more recent effects of welfare dependency (Martin 2001; Merlan 2009a; cf. Sutton 2009).

Despite his insistence that orbiters would retain their culture, there are some indications that Pearson is aware that a reasonably comprehensive distancing from some pervasive but informal aspects of settlement culture is a prerequisite for high-level education and a subsequent career. He occasionally makes pointed suggestions that Aboriginal families living in town should limit the number of visiting relations living in their households, so that work and school routines are not disrupted. Indeed, one of the themes of my description of the Warlpiri diaspora has been the desire of some Warlpiri to distance themselves from the immediacy of kin demands which they feel obliged to respond to under a shared ethic of generosity to kin. It is this kind of informal aspect of traditional culture that Pearson seems to be content to become attenuated for those from the settlements who have prospects of completing their secondary schooling. In the Warlpiri case, the fact that the settlements are predominantly 'dry' areas would necessitate a slightly different weighing of factors for and against orbiting. As outlined in Chapter 5, although the enforcement of 'dry' areas can be patchy, the relative absence of liquor allows for more productive routines to be followed and for the 'dry' settlements to be a respite from the chaos of towns and cities, especially for the heavy drinkers (see Burke 2013b for a fuller discussion).

The Diaspora Experiment

In the introduction I alluded to the experimental nature of using diaspora as a framing device for this research project. A threshold question was whether Warlpiri migration to towns and cities was permanent enough to consider it a diaspora as opposed to temporary migration, exemplified by the rise and fall of the Warlpiri outpost at Murray Bridge (described in Chapter 2). During the four-year period of the fieldwork, the Warlpiri matriarchs in Darwin, Alice Springs and Adelaide continued to live in those locations as one would expect from their expanded and diversified personal social networks. Notwithstanding the variable degrees of vulnerability of their households, they provided the stability for the diaspora locations. The overall Warlpiri population in the larger diaspora locations was steady over the period of the research, although there was some churn of Warlpiri personnel. The relative steadiness of the overall numbers contradicted the expectations of some critics of the Intervention who had predicted that the harsh measures would lead to a spike in migration away from the home settlements. As to churn, life-cycle factors have already been outlined in Chapter 5: the return of some younger women seeking husbands; the return of some older women to look after their ageing mothers; and the return of older men to retire on the settlements. In the other direction there was the reverse retirement option in town and some temporary refugees from a succession of bitter family feuds deciding not to return to the settlements even after the intensity of the violence subsided. My conclusion is that the permanent Warlpiri migrants to towns and cities will continue to be a significant part of the Warlpiri story, not a temporary phenomenon.

The differences between global diaspora and indigenous diaspora have been evident throughout this book. The small-scale, vulnerable and emergent nature of the Warlpiri diaspora contrasts with the large-scale nature, historical depth and distinctive cultures of many global diasporas. The legal impediments to the permanent migration, which are such a big part of the experience of the transnational diaspora, are absent in the Warlpiri case. Within the limits of recognition by the liberal state, the place of the Warlpiri and all the Indigenous people of Australia is guaranteed. Moreover, the economic drivers of transnational diaspora are much less significant in the Warlpiri case. The issue of remittances is somewhat reversed in the Warlpiri diaspora as mining royalties flow from the homeland to diaspora locations and precipitate return visits for meetings about their distribution. Yet, it is also true that improvements in communication allow for some remittance-like transfers to the home settlements from those with jobs in the diaspora.

Some of the more celebratory accounts of transnational diaspora emphasise the mixing of cultural influences and the creation of distinctive cultural practices (language, music, dance, films and literature). In the Warlpiri case, however, such mixing and cultural creativity seemed to be occurring to a similar degree in both home settlements and the diaspora. The Warlpiri diaspora did provide better opportunities for new life projects even though some of them were also being pursued on the settlements.

The diaspora framing has been apposite to some features of the Warlpiri diaspora beyond the obvious combination of permanent relocation and the continuing significance of the connection to the Warlpiri homeland. The theme of cultural hybridity in the diaspora resonates with the general degree of cultural difference between the Warlpiri and the encapsulating white settler society. Diaspora theorising also entails a politics of home and away that I have found emerging among the Warlpiri. Notwithstanding these apposite features, the Warlpiri diaspora, and perhaps all Fourth World indigenous diasporas, has several distinctive features that set it apart from transnational diaspora. These features include the involuntary diaspora (Chapter 1 and 3) and the parallel diaspora (Chapter 4). While the idea of an involuntary diaspora fits nicely with the active dispersal of Jews from their homeland in the paradigmatic case of diaspora, having a voluntary and an involuntary diaspora side-by-side creates unique dynamics. The existence of a parallel diaspora of ex-settlement staff supporting the diaspora reflects the churn of white staff through the settlements and the relatively small scale of the indigenous diaspora within the nation state.

The other distinctive feature of the Warlpiri diaspora has been the relationship of the Warlpiri migrants to local Aboriginal people in the diaspora locations. This adds an additional indigenous nuance to the theme of uncertain welcome in diaspora theorising. The relationships have ranged from overtly hostile (Katherine), aggressive and competitive (Alice Springs) and minimal engagement (Adelaide). The cultural assertiveness of the Warlpiri against some of the local Aboriginal groups has echoes of the imperial diaspora of a colonising power.

The claim I make about using the concept of diaspora as a framing device is that the theoretical agenda it raises reinforces an intercultural approach. After eighty years of engagement with the encapsulating society, such an approach to Warlpiri ethnography becomes more salient than ever. There have been efforts over the years, particularly by Melinda Hinkson, to explore the intercultural issues.[2] But the understandable tendency when one encounters a group like the Warlpiri, with their relatively short contact history, is to document their rich cultural distinctiveness. My research has built on the settlement ethnographies and, I would argue, has extended them in interesting ways towards a more comprehensive picture of what is happening among the Warlpiri. From the diaspora the stratifying effects of government projects directed towards the Warlpiri are more easily visible. It is also easier to see how changed social circumstances, particularly the tension between endosociality and the extension of personal social networks, can lead to the adoption of new social technologies and the emergence of different ways of being Warlpiri.

Notes

1. To be fair to Pearson and the Cape York Reform Agenda, sending Aboriginal high school students to distant, elite boarding schools is only part of their education reform agenda. Under their current umbrella organisation, Cape York Partnerships, they have set up their own primary school organisation, the Cape York Aboriginal Australian Academy, which operates four local primary schools on remote settlements; Djarragun College, an Aboriginal high school in Cairns which also accepts borders from remote settlements; and the Cape York Girl Academy to help young mothers with babies complete their education.
2. See, for example, Hinkson (1999, 2005, 2014). See also Rowse (1990) and Musharbash (2010). One would have thought that Eric Michael's work on the introduction of the new media of radio and TV to Yuendumu would also have necessitated an intercultural approach (Michaels 1986, 1989). However, his analyses tended towards emphasising the strength of traditional Warlpiri culture to absorb exogenous influences and adapt them along pre-existing lines.

References

Ablon, J. 1964. 'Relocated American Indians in the San Francisco Bay Area: Social Interaction and Indian Identity', *Human Organization* 23: 296–304.
Altman, J., and M. Hinkson (eds). 2007. *Coercive Reconciliation: Stabilise, Normalise, Exit Aboriginal Australia*. Melbourne: Arena Publications Association.
——— (eds). 2010. *Culture Crisis: Anthropology and Politics in Aboriginal Australia*. Sydney: University of New South Wales Press.
Arthur, W.S., and J. Taylor. 1995. 'The Comparative Economic Status of Torres Strait Islanders in Torres Strait and Mainland Australia', *Australian Aboriginals Studies* 1995(1): 18–29.
Austin-Broos, D. 1996. '"Two Laws", Ontologies, Histories: Ways of Being Aranda Today', *The Australian Journal of Anthropology* 7(1): 1–20.
———. 2003. 'Places, Practices, and Things: The Articulation of Arrernte Kinship with Welfare and Work', *American Ethnologist* 30(1): 118–35.
———. 2011. *A Different Inequality: The Politics of Debate about Remote Aboriginal Australia*. Sydney: Allen & Unwin.
Australian Institute of Aboriginal and Torres Strait Islander Studies, and Federation of Aboriginal and Torres Strait Islander Languages. 2005. *National Indigenous Languages Survey Report*. Canberra: Australian Department of Communications, Information Technology and the Arts.
Badcock, B. 2001. 'Thirty Years On: Gentrification and Class Changeover in Adelaide's Inner Suburbs, 1966-96', *Urban Studies* 39(9): 1559–572.
Barnes, J. 2016. *Working Class Boy*. Sydney: HarperCollins Publishers Australia.
Barrett, S.R. 2010. 'Community: The Career of a Concept', *Anthropologica* 51(1): 113–25.
Barrow, C. 1996. *Family in the Caribbean: Themes and Perspectives*. Kingston, Jamaica: Ian Randle Publishers.
Barth, F. 1969. 'Introduction', in F. Barth (ed.), *Ethnic Groups and Boundaries: The Social Organisation of Cultural Difference*. Bergen and Oslo: Universitets Forlaget, pp. 9–38.
Barwick, D.E. 1962. 'Economic Absorption without Assimilation? The Case of Some Melbourne Part-Aboriginal Families', *Oceania* 33(1): 18–23.
———. 1963. 'A Little More Than Kin: Regional Affiliation and Group Identity among Aboriginal Migrants in Melbourne'. Unpublished PhD thesis, Department of Archaeology and Anthropology, Australian National University, Canberra.
———. 1964. 'The Self-conscious People of Melbourne', in M. Reay (ed.), *Aborigines Now: New Perspectives in the Study of Aboriginal Communities*. Sydney: Angus and Robertson, pp. 20–31.
———. 1974. 'And the Lubras are Ladies Now', in F. Gale (ed.), *Woman's Role in Aboriginal Society*. 2nd edn. Canberra: Australian Institute of Aboriginal Studies, pp. 51–63.
Barwick, L., M. Laughren and M. Turpin. 2013. 'Sustaining Women's *Yawulyu/Awelye*: Some Practitioners' and Learners' Perspectives', *Musicology Australia* 35(2): 191–20.
Baum, S., and R. Hassan. 1993. 'Economic Restructuring and Spatial Equity: A Case Study of Adelaide', *Australian and New Zealand Journal of Sociology* 29(2): 151–72.

Bauman, T. 1998. 'No Man's Land and Somebody's Place: Negotiating Aboriginal Identity in Katherine in the Northern Territory of Australia'. Australian Institute of Aboriginal and Torres Strait Islander Studies Library Manuscript MS4176.

———. 2002. 'Test "Im Blood": Subsections and Shame in Katherine', *Anthropological Forum* 12(2): 205–20.

———. 2006. *Aboriginal Darwin: A Guide to Exploring Important Sites of the Past and Present.* Canberra: Aboriginal Studies Press.

Baume, F.E. 1933. *Tragedy Track: The Story of the Granites.* Sydney: Frank C. Johnson.

Beckett, J.R. 1965. 'Kinship, Mobility and Community Among Part-Aborigines in Rural Australia', *International Journal of Comparative Sociology* 6(1): 2–23.

———. 1983. 'Ownership of Land in the Torres Strait Islands', in N. Peterson and M. Langton (eds), *Aborigines, Land and Land Rights.* Canberra: Australian Institute of Aboriginal Studies, pp. 202–10.

———. 1987. *Torres Strait Islanders: Custom and Colonialism.* Cambridge: Cambridge University Press.

———. 2010. 'From Island to Mainland: Torres Strait Islanders in the Australian Labour Force', in I. Keen (ed.), *Indigenous Participation in Australian Economies: Historical and Anthropological Perspectives.* Canberra: ANU E Press, pp. 63–72.

Beer, A., and C. Forster. 2002. 'Global Restructuring, the Welfare State and Urban Programs: Federal Policies and Inequality within Australian Cities', *European Planning Studies* 10(1): 7–25.

Beer, B., and D. Gardner. 2015. 'The Anthropology of Friendship', in J.D. Wright (ed.), *The International Encyclopedia of Social and Behavioural Sciences,* 2nd edn. Amsterdam: Elseveier, pp. 425–31.

Bell, D. 1980. 'Desert Politics: Choices in the "Marriage Market"', in M. Etienne and E. Leacock (eds), *Women and Colonisation: Anthropological Perspectives.* New York: Praeger, pp. 239–69.

———. 1983. *Daughters of the Dreaming.* Sydney: McPhee Gribble/George Allen & Unwin.

———. 1987. 'The Politics of Separation', in M. Strathern (ed.), *Dealing with Inequality: Analysing Gender Relations in Melanesia and Beyond.* Cambridge: Cambridge University Press, pp. 112–29.

———. 1993. *Daughters of the Dreaming.* 2nd edn. St Leonards, NSW: Allen & Unwin.

Bell, D., and P. Ditton. 1980. *Law, the Old and the New: Aboriginal Women in Central Australia Speak Out.* Canberra, ACT: Published for Central Australian Aboriginal Legal Aid Service by Aboriginal History.

Bell, D., and T. Nelson. 1989. 'Speaking about Rape is Everyone's Business'. *Women's Studies International Forum* 12(4): 403–416.

Bell, S., and S. Coleman. 1999. 'The Anthropology of Friendship: Enduring Themes and Future Possibilities', in S. Bell and S. Coleman (eds), *The Anthropology of Friendship.* Oxford: Berg, pp. 1–19.

Berndt, C.H. 1989. 'Retrospect, and Prospect: Looking Back Over 50 Years', in P. Brock (ed.), *Women, Rites and Sites: Aboriginal Women's Cultural Knowledge.* Sydney: Allen & Unwin, pp. 1–20.

Biddle, J.L. 2007. *Breasts, Bodies, Canvas: Central Desert Art As Experience.* Sydney: University of New South Wales Press.

Birdsell, C. 1988. 'All One Family', in I. Keen (ed.), *Being Black: Aboriginal Culture in 'Settled' Australia.* Canberra: Aboriginal Studies Press, pp. 137–58.

Blackwood, E. 2006. 'Marriage, Matrifocality, and "Missing" Men', in P.L. Geller and M.K. Stockett (eds), *Feminist Anthropology: Past, Present, and Future*. Philadelphia: University of Pennsylvania Press, pp. 73–88.

Bourbon, D., S. Saggers and D. Gray. 1999. *Indigenous Australians and Liquor Licensing Legislation*. Perth: National Centre for Research in the Prevention of Drug Abuse.

Bourdieu, P. 1977. *Outline of a Theory of Practice*. Cambridge: Cambridge University Press.

———. 2000. *Pascalian Meditations*. London: Polity Press.

Boym, S. 2000. 'On Diasporic Intimacy: Ilya Kabakov's Installations and Immigrant Homes', in L. Berland (ed.), *Intimacy*. Chicago: University Of Chicago Press, pp. 226–52.

Brady, M. 1988. *Where the Beer Truck Stopped: Drinking in a Northern Australian Town*. Darwin: North Australian Research Unit, Australian National University.

———. 2014. *Lessons from a History of Beer Canteens and Licensed Clubs in Indigenous Australian Communities, CAEPR Discussion Paper No. 290/2014*. Canberra: Centre for Aboriginal Economic Policy Research, Australian National University.

———. 2017. *Teaching 'Proper' Drinking? Clubs and Pubs in Indigenous Australia*. Canberra: Australian National University Press.

——— (ed.). 1995. *Giving Away the Grog: Aboriginal Accounts of Drinking and Not Drinking*. Canberra: Drug Offensive, Commonwealth Department of Human Services and Health.

Brasche, I., and I. Harrington. 2012. 'Promoting Teacher Quality and Continuity: Tackling the Disadvantage of Remote Indigenous Schools in the Northern Territory', *Australian Journal of Education* 56(2): 110–25.

Brettell, C.B. 2000. 'Theorising Migration in Anthropology: The Social Construction of Networks, Identities, Communities, and Globalscapes', in C.B. Brettell and J.F. Hollifield (eds), *Migration Theory: Talking across Disciplines*. New York: Routledge, pp. 97–135.

Broadband for the Bush Alliance. *Extending Remote and Rural Cellular Mobile: A Broadband for the Bush Alliance Discussion Paper* 2013 [cited 6 May 2015].

Brown, J.K. 1992. 'Lives of Middle-Aged Women', in V. Kerns and J.K. Brown (eds), *In Her Prime: New Views of Middle-Aged Women*. Urbana, IL: University of Illinois Press, pp. 17–30.

Brubaker, R. 2005. 'The "Diaspora" Diaspora', *Ethnic and Racial Studies* 28(1): 1–19.

Burbank, V.K. 1988. *Aboriginal Adolescence: Maidenhood in an Aboriginal Community*. New Brunswick: Rutgers University Press.

———. 1994. *Fighting Women: Anger and Aggression in Aboriginal Australia*. Berkeley, CA: University of California Press.

Burke, P. 1998. 'Anthropological Understanding of Warlpiri People'. Unpublished MLitt thesis, School of Archaeology and Anthropology, Australian National University, Canberra.

———. 2011. *Law's Anthropology: From Ethnography to Expert Testimony in Native Title*. Canberra: ANU E Press.

———. 2013a. 'Warlpiri and the Pacific: Ideas for an Intercultural History of the Warlpiri', *Anthropological Forum* 23(4): 414–27.

———. 2013b. 'Indigenous Diaspora and the Prospects for Cosmopolitan "Orbiting": The Warlpiri Case'. *The Asia Pacific Journal of Anthropology* 14(4): 304–322.

———. 2018. 'Bold Women of the Warlpiri Diaspora who Went too far', in D. Austin-Broos and F. Merlan (eds), *People and Change in Indigenous Australia*. Honolulu: University of Hawai'i Press, pp. 29–43.

Butler, J. 1990. *Gender Trouble: Feminism and the Subversion of Identity*. New York: Routledge.

Butler, K.D. 2001. 'Defining Diaspora, Refining a Discourse', *Diaspora* 10(2): 189–219.

Campbell, L. 2006. *Darby: One Hundred Years of Life in a Changing Culture*. Sydney: ABC Books.

Carling, J., E.B. Mortensen and J. Wu. 2011. *A Systematic Bibliography on Return Migration*. Oslo: Peace Research Institute Oslo.
Chesterman, J., and B. Galligan. 1997. *Citizens Without Rights: Aborigines and Australian Citizenship*. Cambridge and Melbourne: Cambridge University Press.
Christen, K. 2009. *Aboriginal Business: Alliances in a Remote Aboriginal Town*. Santa Fe, NM: School of Advanced Research Press.
Clements, N. 2014. *The Black War: Fear, Sex and Resistance in Tasmania*. Brisbane: University of Queensland Press.
Clifford, J. 1994. 'Diasporas', *Cultural Anthropology* 9(3): 302–38.
Cohen, R. 1997. *Global Diasporas: An Introduction*. London and Seattle, WA: University College London and University of Washington Press.
Collmann, J. 1979a. 'Fringe-camps and the Development of Aboriginal Administration in Central Australia', *Social Analysis* 2: 38–57.
———. 1979b. 'Women, Children and the Significance of the Domestic Group to Urban Aborigines in Central Australia', *Ethnology* 18(4): 379–97.
———. 1988. *Fringe-Dwellers and Welfare: the Aboriginal Response to Bureaucracy*. Brisbane: University of Queensland Press.
Connor, J. 2002. *The Australian Frontier Wars 1788-1838*. Sydney: University of New South Wales Press.
Constable, N. 2004. 'Changing Filipina Identities and Ambivalent Returns', in L.D. Long and E. Oxfeld (eds), *Coming Home? Refugees, Migrants, and Those Who Stayed Behind*. Philadelphia, PA: University of Pennsylvania Press, pp. 104–24.
Coombs, H.C., B. Dexter and L.R. Hiatt. 1980. 'The Outstation Movement in Aboriginal Australia', *Australian Institute of Aboriginal Studies Newsletter* 14: 16–23.
Coombs, H.C., and W.E.H. Stanner. 1974. *Council for Aboriginal Affairs – Program for Yuendumu and Hooker Creek*. Canberra: Australian Government Publishing Service.
Coughlan, F. 1991. 'Aboriginal Town Camps and Tangentyere Council: The Battle for Self-Determination in Alice Springs'. MA thesis, School of Humanities, La Trobe University, Bundoora, Victoria.
Coulehan, K.M. 1995. 'Sitting Down in Darwin: Yolngu Women from Northeast Arnhem Land and Family Life in the City'. PhD thesis, Charles Darwin University, Darwin.
———. 1996. '"Keeping Company" in Sickness and in Health: Yolngu from Northeast Arnhem and Medical Related Transience and Migration to Darwin', in G. Robinson (ed.), *Aboriginal Health: Social and Cultural Transitions*. Darwin: Northern Territory University Press, pp. 214–22.
Counts, D.A. 1992. 'Tamparonga: "The Big Women" of Kaliai (Papua New Guinea)', in V. Kerns and J.K. Brown (eds), *In Her Prime: New Views of Middle-aged Women*. Urbana, IL: University of Illinois Press, pp.61–74.
Cowling, M. 2002. 'Marx's Lumpenproletariat and Murray's Underclass: Concepts Best Abandoned?', in K. Marx, J. Martin and M. Cowling (eds), *Marx's Eighteenth Brumaire: (Post)modern Interpretations*. London: Pluto Press, pp. 228–42.
Cowlishaw, G., and L. Gibson. 2012. 'Locating an Australia-wide Anthropology', *Oceania* 82(1): 4–14.
Cummings, B. 1990. *Take This Child: From Kahlin Compound to the Retta Dixon Children's Home*. Canberra: Aboriginal Studies Press.
Curran, G. 2010. 'Contemporary Ritual Practice in an Aboriginal Settlement: The Warlpiri Kurdiji Ceremony'. PhD thesis, Australian National University.

———. 2011. 'The "Expanding Domain" of Warlpiri Initiation Rituals', in Y. Musharbash and M. Barber (eds), *Ethnography and the Production of Anthropological Knowledge: Essays in Honour of Nicholas Peterson*. Canberra: Australian National University E Press, pp. 39–50.

d'Abbs, P. 1987. *Dry Areas, Alcohol and Aboriginal Communities: A Review of the Northern Territory Restricted Areas Legislation*. Darwin: Northern Territory Department of Health and Community Services.

Day, B. 1994. *Bunji: A Story of the Gwalwa Daraniki Movement*. Canberra: Aboriginal Studies Press.

———. *A Bagot History*. drbilldayanthropologist.com, 2008 [cited 1 April 2015. Available from drbilldayanthropologist.com].

———. *Aboriginal People of Darwin: The Bagot Community*. drbilldayanthropologist.com, 2012 [cited 1 April 2015. Available from drbilldayanthropologist.com].

Delaney, N. 1996. 'Romantic Love and Loving Commitment', *American Philosophical Quarterly* 33(4): 339–56.

Department of Families, Housing, Community Services and Indigenous Affairs. 2008. *The Road Home: A National Approach to Reducing Homelessness*. Canberra: Commonwealth of Australia.

———. 2011. *Northern Territory Emergency Response Evaluation Report 2011*. Canberra: Australian Government.

di Leonardo, M. 1991. 'Introduction: Gender, Culture, and Political Economy: Feminist Anthropology in Historical Perspective', in M. di Leonardo (ed.), *Gender at the Crossroads of Knowledge: Feminist Anthropology in the Post Modern Era*. Berkeley, CA: University Of California Press, pp. 1–48.

Diaz, V.M. 2002. '"Fight Boys, 'til the Last…": Island Style Football as the Remasculinization of Indigeneity in the Militarized Pacific Islands', in P. Spickard, J.L. Rondilla and D.H. Wright (eds), *Pacific Diaspora: Island Peoples in the United States and Across the Pacific*. Honolulu, HI: University of Hawaii Press, pp. 169–94.

Doohan, K. 1992. *One Family, Different Country: The Development and Persistence of an Aboriginal Community at Finke, Northern Territory, Oceania Monographs 42*. Sydney: University of Sydney.

Dosman, E.J. 1972. *Indians: The Urban Dilemma*. Toronto: McClelland and Stewart.

Dussart, F. 1992. 'The Politics of Female Identity: Warlpiri Widows at Yuendumu', *Ethnology* 31(4): 337–50.

———. 2000. *The Politics of Ritual in an Aboriginal Settlement: Kinship, Gender, and the Currency of Knowledge*. Edited by W.L. Merrill and I. Karp, *Smithsonian Series in Ethnographic Inquiry*. Washington, DC: Smithsonian Institution Press.

———. 2004. 'Shown but not Shared, Presented but not Proffered: Redefining Ritual Identity among Warlpiri Ritual Performers, 1990–2000', *The Australian Journal of Anthropology* 15(3): 253–66.

Edmunds, M. 2010. *The Northern Territory Intervention and Human Rights: An Anthropological Perspective, Perspectives 3*. Sydney: The Whitlam Institute, University of Western Sydney.

Edwards, B. 2010. 'Adelaideala Nyinanytja – Living in Adelaide: A Report Prepared by Bill Edwards for the South Australian Social Inclusion Unit on Anangu Pitjantjatjara/ Yankunytjatjara People Now Residing in Adelaide'. Unpublished Report.

———. 2012. *Mission in the Musgraves: Ernabella Mission 1937-73, A Place of Relationships*. Adelaide: Uniting Church Historical Society (SA).

———. n.d. 'Adelaideala Nyinanytja – Living in Adelaide'. In *Unpublished Paper Delivered at the Perspectives on Urban Life Conference*.

Egan, J.N. 1983. 'The Yuendumu Aboriginal Cultural Pre-School', in F. Gale (ed.), *We Are Bosses Ourselves: The Status and Role of Aboriginal Women Today*. Canberra: Australian Institute of Australian Studies, pp. 122–23.

Elias, D. 1998. 'Looking for Kulpulurnu', in A. Wright (ed.), *Take Power, Like this Old Man Here: An Anthology of Writings Celebrating Twenty Years of Land Rights in Central Australia 1977-1997*. Alice Springs: Jukurrpa Books/IAD Press, pp. 200–204.

———. 2001. 'Golden Dreams: People, Place and Mining in the Tanami Desert'. Unpublished PhD thesis, School of Archaeology & Anthropology, Australian National University, Canberra.

Elkin, A.P. 1964. *The Australian Aborigines: How to Understand Them*. 4th edn. Sydney: Angus and Robertson.

———. 1977. *Aboriginal Men of High Degree*. 2nd edn. Brisbane: University of Queensland Press.

Ellis, L.M. 2016. *Pictures from My Memory: My Story As A Ngaatjatjarra Woman*. Canberra: Aboriginal Studies Press.

Etienne, M., and E. Leacock (eds). 1980. *Women and Colonisation: Anthropological Perspectives*. New York: Praeger.

Fabian, J. 1983. *Time and the Other: How Anthropology Makes its Object*. New York: Columbia University Press.

Fardon, R. 1990. 'General Introduction: Localising Strategies, The Regionalisation of Ethnographic Accounts', in R. Fardon (ed.), *Localising Strategies: Regional Traditions of Ethnographic Writing*. Edinburgh: Scottish Academic Press, pp. 1–37.

Fienup-Riordan, A. 2000. 'Yup'ik Community in the 1990s: A Worldwide Web', in *Hunting Tradition in a Changing World: Yup'Ik Lives in Alaska Today*. New Brunswick, NJ: Rutgers University Press, pp. 151–68.

Finlayson, J.D. 1991. 'Don't Depend on Me: Autonomy and Dependency and Aboriginal Community in Northern Queensland'. PhD thesis, Australian National University, Canberra.

Fisher, D. 2012. 'Running Amok or Just Sleeping Rough? Long-grass Camping and the Politics of Care in Northern Australia', *American Ethnologist* 39(1): 171–86.

———. 2013. 'Becoming the State in Northern Australia: Urbanisation, Intra-Indigenous Relatedness, and the State Effect', *Oceania* 83(3): 238–58.

Fixico, D.L. 2000. *The Urban Indian Experience in America*. Albuquerque, NM: University of New Mexico Press.

Fogel-Chance, N. 1993. 'Living in Both Worlds: "Modernity" and "Tradition" among the North Slope Inupiaq Women in Anchorage', *Arctic Anthropology* 30(1): 94–108.

Forster, C. 1991. 'Restructuring and Residential Differentiation: Has Adelaide Become a More Unequal City?', *South Australian Geographical Journal* 91: 46–60.

Frankenberg, R. 1993. *White Women, Race Matters: The Social Construction of Whiteness*. Minneapolis, MN: University of Minnesota Press.

Friedman, J. 2002. 'From Roots to Routes: Tropes for Trippers', *Anthropological Theory* 2(1): 21–36.

———. 2012. 'The Dialectic of Cosmopolitanization and Indigenization in the Contemporary World System: Contradictory Configurations of Class and Culture', in L. Dousset and S. Tcherkezoff (eds), *The Scope of Anthropology: Maurice Godelier's Work in Context*. New York: Berghahn Books, pp. 212–45.

Friedman, M. 2003. *Autonomy, Gender, Politics*. Oxford: Oxford University Press.

Gale, F. 1966. 'Patterns of Post-European Aboriginal Migration', *Royal Geographical Society of Australasia, South Australian Branch – Proceedings* 67: 21–37.

———. 1972. *Urban Aborigines*. Canberra: ANU Press.
Gale, F., and J. Wundersitz. 1982. *Adelaide Aborigines: A Case Study of Urban Life, 1966-1981, The Aboriginal Component in the Australian Economy*. Canberra: Development Studies Centre, Australian National University.
Gamaut, C. 2008. 'The Adelaide Parklands and the Endurance of the Green Belt Idea in South Australia', in M. Amati (ed.), *Urban Green Belts in the Twenty-first Century*. Aldershot: Ashgate, pp. 107–28.
Gans, H.J. 1995. *The War Against the Poor: The Underclass and Antipoverty Policy*. New York: Basic Books.
Gaykamangu, J. 2014. *Striving to Bridge the Chasm: My Cultural Learning Journey*. Darwin: Self-Published.
Giddens, A. 1991. *Modernity and Self-identity: Self and Society in the Late Modern Age*. Cambridge: Polity.
Giese, H. 1966. 'Discussion of Papers by Messrs. Smee, Felton and Busbridge', in I.G. Sharp and C.M. Tatz (eds), *Aborigines in the Economy: Employment, Wages and Training*. Melbourne: Jacaranda Press/Centre for Research into Aboriginal Affairs Monash University, pp. 127–29.
Gilroy, P. 1993. *The Black Atlantic: Modernity and Double Consciousness*. Cambridge, MA: Harvard University Press.
Glaskin, K. 2012. 'Anatomies of Relatedness: Considering Personhood in Aboriginal Australia', *American Anthropologist* 114(2): 297–308.
Glaskin, K., M. Tonkinson, Y. Musharbash and V. Burbank (eds). 2008. *Mortality, Mourning and Mortuary Practices in Indigenous Australia*. Farnham: Ashgate.
Glowczewski, B. 1991. *Du Rêve à la Loi Chez les Aborigènes – Mythes, Rites et Organisation Sociale en Australie*. Paris: PUF.
Granovetter, M.S. 1973. 'The Strength of Weak Ties', *American Journal of Sociology* 78(6): 1360–80.
———. 1983. 'The Strength of Weak Ties: A Network Theory Revisited', *Sociological Theory* 1: 201–33.
Haebich, A. 2000. *Broken Circles*. Fremantle: Fremantle Arts Centre Press.
Haebich, A., and D. Mellor (eds). 2002. *Many Voices: Reflections on Experiences of Indigenous Child Separation*. Canberra: National Library of Australia.
Hage, G. 2005. 'A Not So Multi-sited Ethnography of a Not So Imagined Community', *Anthropological Theory* 5(4): 463–75.
Hall, S. 1990. 'Cultural Identity and Diaspora', J. Rutherford (ed.), *Identity: Community, Culture, Difference*. London: Lawrence and Wishart, pp. 222–37.
Hamilton, A. 1986. 'Daughters of the Imaginary', *Canberra Anthropology* 9(2): 1–25.
Harris, S. 1990. *Two-Way Aboriginal Schooling: Education and Cultural Survival*. Canberra: Aboriginal Studies Press.
Hartigan, J. 2005. *Odd Tribes: Towards a Cultural Analysis of White People*. Durham, NC: Duke University Press.
Hartwig, M. 1960. 'The Coniston Killings'. BA Honours thesis, University of Adelaide.
Heatley, A. 1979. *The Government of the Northern Territory*. Brisbane: University of Queensland Press.
Heppell, M., and J. Wigley. 1981. *Black Out in Alice: A History of the Establishment and Development of Town Camps in Alice Springs*, Development Studies Centre Monograph No. 26. Canberra: Australian National University.

Hinkson, M. 1999. 'Warlpiri Connections: New Technology, New Enterprise and Emergent Social Forms at Yuendumu'. Unpublished PhD thesis, Department of Sociology, Anthropology and Politics, La Trobe University, Bundoora.

———. 2002. 'New Media Projects at Yuendumu: Intercultural Engagement and Self-Determination in an Era of Accelerated Globalisation', *Continuum* 16(2): 201–20.

———. 2005. 'New Media Projects at Yuendumu: Towards a History and Analysis of Intercultural Engagement', in L. Taylor, G.K. Ward, G. Henderson, R. Davis and L.A. Wallis (eds), *The Power of Knowledge, The Resonance of Tradition*. Canberra: Aboriginal Studies Press, pp. 157–68.

———. 2014. *Remembering the Future: Warlpiri Life through the Prism of Drawing*. Canberra: Aboriginal Studies Press.

Hoikkala, P. 1998. 'Feminists or Reformers? American Indian Women and Political Activism in Phoenix', *American Indian Culture and Research Journal* 22(4): 163–85.

Holcombe, S. 2004. 'The Sentimental Community: A Site of Belonging. A Case Study from Central Australia', *The Australian Journal of Anthropology* 15(2): 163–84.

House of Representatives Standing Committee on Aboriginal Affairs. 1982. 'Strategies to Help Overcome the Problems of Aboriginal Town Camps'. Canberra.

Human Rights and Equal Opportunity Commission. 1997. *Bringing Them Home: Report of the National Enquiry into the Separation of Aboriginal and Torres Strait Islander Children from Their Families*. Sydney: Human Rights and Equal Opportunity Commission.

Jagger, D. 2011. 'The Capacity for Community Development to Improve Conditions in Australian Aboriginal Communities: An Anthropological Analysis'. Unpublished Master of Philosophy thesis, School of Archaeology and Anthropology, Australian National University, Canberra.

Jamieson, K. 1978. *Indian Women and the Law in Canada: Citizens Minus*. Ottawa: Advisory Council on the Status of Women/Indian Rights for Indian Women.

Janovicek, N. 2003. '"Assisting our Own": Urban Migration, Self-Governance, and Native Women's Organising in Thunder Bay, Ontario, 1972-1989', *American Indian Quarterly* 27(3/4): 548–65.

Johnson, V. 1994. *Aboriginal Artists of the Western Desert: A Biographical Dictionary*. Sydney: Craftsman House.

Jordan, I. 2003. *Their Way: Towards an Indigenous Warlpiri Christianity*. Darwin: Charles Darwin University Press.

Kacha, S. 2009. 'The NT Intervention: Does the End Justify the Means?', retrieved 10 February 2015 from the Stop the Intervention website http://stoptheintervention.org/uploads/files_to_download/The-NT-Intervention-25-8-2009.pdf.

Kalra, V.S., R. Kaur and J. Hutnyk. 2005. *Diaspora & Hybridity*. London: SAGE Publications.

Keen, I. 1989. 'Aboriginal Governance', in J.C. Altman (ed.), *Emergent Inequalities in Aboriginal Australia*. Sydney: Oceania Monographs, University of Sydney, pp. 17–42.

———. 1997. 'A Continent of Foragers: Aboriginal Australia as a "Regional System"', in P. McConvell and N. Evans (eds), *Archaeology and Linguistics: Aboriginal Australia in Global Perspective*. Melbourne: Oxford University Press, pp. 261–73.

———. 2004. *Aboriginal Economy and Society: Australia at the Threshold of Colonisation*. Oxford: Oxford University Press.

———. 2006. 'Ancestors, Magic, and Exchange in Yolngu Doctrines: Extensions of the Person in Time and Space', *The Journal of the Royal Anthropological Institute* 12(3): 515–30.

Kerins, S. 2009. *The First-Ever Northern Territory Homelands/Outstation Policy, CAEPR Topical Issue No. 9/2009*. Canberra: Centre for Aboriginal Economic Policy Research, Australian National University.

Kerns, V., and J.K. Brown. 1992. *In Her Prime: New Views of Middle-Aged Women*. 2nd edn. Urbana, IL: University of Illinois Press.

Kesteven, S.L. 1978. 'A Sketch of Yuendumu and Its Outstations'. Unpublished Masters subthesis, Environmental Studies, Australian National University.

Keys, C.A. 1999. 'The Architectural Implications of the Warlpiri Jilimi'. PhD thesis, University of Queensland.

Khalidi, N.A. 1989. 'The Aboriginal Population of Alice Springs'. PhD thesis, Department of Geography, Australian National University, Canberra.

Killick, E., and A. Desai. 2010. 'Introduction: Valuing Friendship', in A. Desai and E. Killick (eds), *The Ways of Friendship: Anthropological Perspectives*. New York: Berghahn Books, pp. 1–19.

Kolig, E. 1981. *The Silent Revolution: The Effects of Modernisation on Australian Aboriginal Religion*. Philadelphia, PA: Institute for the Study of Human Issues.

Kowal, E. 2011. 'The Stigma of White Privilege: Australian Anti-racists and Indigenous Improvement', *Cultural Studies* 25(3): 313–33.

———. 2015. *Trapped in the Gap: Doing Good in Indigenous Australia*. New York: Berghahn Books.

Krouse, S.A. 2001. 'Traditional Iroquois Socials: Maintaining Identity in the City', *American Indian Quarterly* 25(3): 400–408.

Kuklick, H. 2006. '"Humanity in the Chrysalis Stage": Indigenous Australians in the Anthropological Imagination, 1899-1926', *The British Journal for the History of Science* 39(4): 535–68.

Lagrand, J.B. 2000. *Indian Metropolis: Native Americans in Chicago 1945-75*. Urbana, IL: University of Illinois Press.

Lahn, J. 2012. 'Aboriginal Professionals: Work, Class and Culture', in D. Howard-Wagner, D. Habibis and T. Petray (eds.), *Theorising Indigenous Sociology: Developing Australian and International Approaches*. Sydney: University of Sydney, pp. 1–11.

Laing, L. 2000. *Progress, Trends and Challenges in Australian Responses to Domestic Violence, Issues Paper 1*. Sydney: Australian Domestic and Family Violence Clearinghouse, University of New South Wales.

Laughren, M. 1981. 'Religious Movements Observed at Yuendumu 1975-81', in *Symposium on Aboriginal Religious Movements*. Canberra: Australian Institute of Aboriginal Studies (Unpublished).

Leacock, E. 1978. 'Women's Status in Egalitarian Society: Implications for Social Evolution', *Current Anthropology* 19(2): 247–75.

———. 1980. 'Montagnais Women and the Jesuit Program for Colonisation', in M. Etienne and E. Leacock (eds), *Women and Colonisation: Anthropological Perspectives*. New York: Praeger, pp.25–42.

———. 1983. 'The Origins of Gender Inequality: Conceptual and Historical Problems', *Dialectical Anthropology* 7(4): 263–84.

Leacock, E.B. 1981. *Myths of Male Dominance*. New York: Monthly Review Press.

Lee, R.B. 1992. 'Worker, Sexuality, and Ageing among !Kung Women', in V. Kerns and J.K. Brown (eds), *In Her Prime: New Views of Middle-Aged Women*. Urbana, IL: University of Illinois Press, pp. 35–46.

Lewandowski, J.D. 2000. 'Thematizing Embeddedness: Reflexive Sociology as Interpretation', *Philosophy of Social Sciences* 30 (One): 49–66.

Lobo, S., and K. Peters. 1998. 'Introduction to Special Issue on American Indians and the Urban Experience', *American Indian Culture and Research Journal* 22(4): 1–13.

——— (eds). 2001. *American Indians and the Urban Experience*. Walnut Creek, CA: Altamira Press.
Long, J. 1992. *The Go-Betweens: Patrol Officers in Aboriginal Affairs Administration in the Northern Territory 1936-74*. Darwin and Canberra: North Australian Research Unit of the Australian National University.
Long, J.P.M. 1970. *Aboriginal Settlements: A Survey of Institutional Communities in Eastern Australia*. Canberra: Australian National University Press.
Long, L., and E. Oxfeld. 2004. *Coming Home?: Refugees, Migrants, and Those Who Stayed Behind*. Philadelphia, PA: University of Pennsylvania Press.
Macdonald, G. 2000. 'Economies and Personhood: Demand Sharing among the Wiradjuri of New South Wales', in G.W. Wenzel, G. Hovelsrud-Broda and N. Kishigami (eds), *The Social Economy of Sharing: Resource Allocation and Modern Hunter-Gatherers*. Osaka: National Museum of Ethnology, pp. 87–111.
Macintyre, S., and A. Clark. 2003. *The History Wars*. Melbourne: Melbourne University Press.
Mackinnon, B.H. 2010. *The Liam Jarrah Story: From Yuendumu to the MCG*. Melbourne: Melbourne University Press.
Mackinolty, C. 2011. 'Memories of Yulyurlu', in M. West (ed.), *Yulyurlu Lorna Fencer Napurrurla*. Adelaide: Wakefield Press, pp. 21–26.
Maddock, K. 1981. 'Warlpiri Land Tenure: a Test Case in Legal Anthropology', *Oceania* 52(2): 85–102.
Mahood, K. 2008. 'Correspondence on Paul Toohey's Quarterly Essay "Last Drinks: The Impact of the Northern Territory Intervention"', *Quarterly Essay* 31: 98–105.
Manne, R. 2001. *In Denial: The Stolen Generations and the Right, Australian Quarterly Essay, No. 1*. Melbourne: Black Inc.
Marcus, G., and M.J. Fischer. 1986. *Anthropology as Cultural Critique: An Experimental Moment in the Human Sciences*. Chicago, IL: Chicago University Press.
Marcus, G.E. 1995. 'Ethnography in/of the World System: The Emergence of Multi-Sited Ethnography', *Annual Review of Anthropology* 24: 95–117.
Marcus, J. 2001. *The Indomitable Miss Pink: A Life in Anthropology*. Sydney: University of New South Wales Press.
Markowitz, F., and A.H. Stefansson (eds). 2004. *Homecomings: Unsettling Paths of Return*. Stanford, CA: Stanford University Press.
Martin, D. 1998. *The Supply of Alcohol in Remote Aboriginal Communities: Potential Policy Directions from Cape York, CAEPR Discussion Paper No. 162*. Canberra: Centre for Aboriginal Economic Policy Research, The Australian National University.
———. 2001. *Is Welfare Dependency 'Welfare Poison'? An Assessment of Noel Pearson's Proposals for Aboriginal Welfare Reform, CAEPR Discussion Paper No. 213*. Canberra: Centre for Aboriginal Economic Policy Research.
Maxwell, A.H. 1993. 'The Underclass, "Social Isolation" and "Concentration Effects": "The Culture of Poverty" Revisited', *Critique of Anthropology* 13(3): 231–45.
May, S. 2011. *Love: A History*. New Haven, CT: Yale University Press.
McCoy, B.F. 2008a. 'Death and Health: The Resilience of "Sorry Business" in the Kutjungka Region of Western Australia', in K. Glaskin, M. Tonkinson, Y. Musharbash and V. Burbank (eds), *Mortality, Mourning and Mortuary Practices in Indigenous Australia*. Farnham: Ashgate, pp. 55–68.
———. 2008b. *Holding Men: Kanyirninpa and the Health of Aboriginal Men*. Canberra: Aboriginal Studies Press.
McDonald, H. 2001. *Blood, Bones and Spirit: Aboriginal Christianity in an East Kimberley Town*. Melbourne: Melbourne University Press.

McKnight, D. 2002. *From Hunting to Drinking: The Devastating Effects of Alcohol on an Australian Aboriginal Community*. London: Routledge.

Mead, M. 1928. *Coming of Age in Samoa*. New York: Dell.

Meggitt, M.J. 1962. *Desert People: A Study of the Warlpiri Aborigines of Central Australia*. Sydney: Angus and Robertson.

———. 1966. 'Indigenous Forms of Government Among the Australian Aborigines', in I. Hogbin and L.R. Hiatt (eds), *Readings in Australian and Pacific Anthropology*. Melbourne: Melbourne University Press, pp. 57–74.

Merlan, F. 1986. 'Australian Aboriginal Conception Beliefs Revisited', *Man* 21(3): 474–93.

———. 1988. 'Gender in Aboriginal Social Life: A Review', in R.M. Berndt and R. Tonkinson (eds), *Social Anthropology and Australian Aboriginal Studies: A Contemporary Overview*. Canberra: Aboriginal Studies Press, pp. 17–76.

———. 1991. 'Women, Productive Roles, and Monetisation of the "Service Mode" in Aboriginal Australia: Perspectives from Katherine, Northern Territory', *The Australian Journal of Anthropology* 2(3): 259–92.

———. 1992. 'Male-Female Separation and Forms of Society in Aboriginal Australia', *Cultural Anthropology* 7(2): 169–93.

———. 1995. 'Vectoring Anthropology: A Critical Appreciation of Basil Sansom's Work', *Anthropological Forum* 7(2): 161–78.

———. 1997. 'The Mother-In-Law Taboo: Avoidance and Obligation in Aboriginal Australian Society', F. Merlan, J. Morton and A. Rumsey (eds), *Scholar and Sceptic: Australian Aboriginal Studies in Honour of L R Hiatt*. Canberra: Aboriginal Studies Press, pp. 95–122.

———. 1998. *Caging the Rainbow: Place, Politics, and Aborigines in a North Australian Town*. Honolulu, HI: University of Hawai'i Press.

———. 2005. 'Explorations Towards Intercultural Accounts of Socio-Cultural Reproduction and Change', *Oceania* 75(3): 167–82.

———. 2007. 'Indigeneity as Relational Identity: The Construction of Australian Land Rights', in M. De La Cadena and O. Starn (eds), *Indigenous Experience Today*. Oxford: Berg, pp.125–49.

———. 2009a. 'Book Review of Noel Pearson's "Up From the Mission" and Peter Sutton's "The Politics of Suffering"', *The Canberra Times Panorama Magazine* 15 August, p. 17.

———. 2009b. 'More Than Rights: The Northern Territory Intervention', retrieved 11 April 2016 from the *Inside Story* website http://insidestory.org.au/more-than-rights.

———. 2010a. 'Child Sexual Abuse: The Intervention Trigger', in J. Altman and M. Hinkson (eds), *Culture Crisis: Anthropology and Politics in Aboriginal Australia*. Sydney: University of New South Wales Press, pp. 116–35.

———. 2010b. 'Response to Lattas and Morris' "Blinkered Anthropology"', *Arena Magazine* 108(10/11): 15–16.

Meyers, D.T. 1997. *Feminists Rethink the Self, Feminist Theory and Politics*. Boulder, CO: Westview Press.

Michaels, E. 1986. *The Aboriginal Invention of Television in Central Australia 1982-1986*. Canberra: Australian Institute of Aboriginal Studies.

———. 1989. *For a Cultural Future: Francis Jupurrurla Makes TV at Yuendumu*. Melbourne: Art & Text Publications.

Michaels, E., and F.J. Kelly. 1984. 'The Social Organisation of an Aboriginal Video Workplace', *Australian Aboriginal Studies* 84: 26–34.

Miller, D.K. 2013. 'Willing Workers: Urban Relocation and American Indian Initiative, 1940s-1960s', *Ethnohistory* 60(1): 51–76.

Mitchell, J. 1959. 'The Mohawks in High Steel', in *Apologies to the Iroquois*. New York: Farrar, Straus & Cudahy, pp. 3–36.
Moore, H.L. 1988. *Feminism and Anthropology*. Cambridge: Polity Press.
——. 1999. 'Whatever Happened to Women and Men? Gender and Other Crises in Anthropology', in H.L. Moore (ed.), *Anthropological Theory Today*. Cambridge: Polity Press, pp. 151–71.
——. 2006. 'The Future of Gender or the End of a Brilliant Career?', in P.L. Geller and M.K. Stockett (eds), *Feminist Anthropology: Past, Present, and Future*. Philadelphia, PA: University of Pennsylvania Press, pp. 23–42.
——. 2010. 'Feminist Anthropology', in A. Barnard and J. Spencer (eds), *The Routledge Encyclopedia of Social and Cultural Anthropology*, 2nd edn. London: Routledge, pp. 284–87.
Moran, M. 2016. *Serious Whitefella Stuff: When Solutions Become the Problems in Indigenous Affairs*. Melbourne: Melbourne University Press.
Morgan, G. 2006. *Unsettled Places: Aboriginal People and Urbanisation in New South Wales*. Kent Town, SA: Wakefield Press.
Morris, B., and A. Lattas. 2010. 'Embedded Anthropology and the Intervention', *Arena Magazine* 107(8/9): 15–20.
Morton, J. 1987. 'Representing the Country, Disclosing the Self (A Review Article. F Myers Pintupi Country, Pintupi Self and N Munn Walbiri Iconography)', *Oceania* 57: 304–13.
——. 1998. 'Essentially Black, Essentially Australian, Essentially Opposed: Australian Anthropology and Its Uses of Aboriginal Identity', in J. Wassman (ed.), *Pacific Answers to Western Hegemony: Cultural Practices of Identity Construction*. Oxford: Berg, pp. 355–85.
Moss, R. 2010. *The Hard Light of Day: An Artist's Story of Friendships in Arrernte Country*. Brisbane: Queensland University Press.
Mountford, C.P. 1968. *Winbaraku and the Myth of Jarapiri*. Adelaide: Rigby Limited.
Mukhopadhyay, C.C., and P.J. Higgins. 1988. 'Anthropological Studies of Women's Status Revisited: 1977-1987', *Annual Review of Anthropology* 17: 461–95.
Munn, N.D. 1970. 'The Transformation of Subjects into Objects in Walbiri and Pitjantjatjara Myth', in R.M. Berndt (ed.), *Australian Aboriginal Anthropology*. Perth: University of Western Australia Press, pp. 141–63.
——. 1973. *Walbiri Iconography: Graphic Representation and Cultural Symbolism in Central Australian Society*. Ithaca, NY: Cornell University Press.
Museum of Contemporary Art. 2003. *Dancing Up Country: The Art of Dorothy Napangardi*. Sydney: Museum of Contemporary Art.
Musharbash, Y. 2000. 'The Yuendumu Community Case Study', in D.E. Smith (ed.), *Indigenous Families and The Welfare System: Two Community Case Studies*. Canberra: Centre for Aboriginal Economic Policy Research, Australian National University, pp. 53–84.
——. 2001. 'Yuendumu CDEP: The Warlpiri Work Ethic and Kardiya Staff Turnover', in F. Morphy and W.G. Sanders (eds), *The Indigenous Welfare Economy and the CDEP Scheme*. Canberra: Centre for Aboriginal Economic Policy Research, Australian National University, pp. 153–65.
——. 2003. 'Warlpiri Sociality: An Ethnography of the Spatial and Temporal Dimensions of Everyday Life in a Central Australian Aboriginal Settlement'. Unpublished PhD thesis, School of Archaeology and Anthropology, Australian National University, Canberra.
——. 2007. 'Boredom, Time, and Modernity: An Example from Aboriginal Australia', *American Anthropologist* 109(2): 307–17.
——. 2008a. '"Sorry Business is Yapa Way": Warlpiri Mortuary Rituals as Embodied Practice', in K. Glaskin, M. Tonkinson, Y. Musharbash and V. Burbank (eds), *Mortality, Mourning and Mortuary Practices in Indigenous Australia*. Farnham: Ashgate, pp. 21–36.

———. 2008b. *Yuendumu Everyday: Contemporary Life in Remote Aboriginal Australia*. Canberra: Aboriginal Studies Press.
———. 2010. 'Marriage, Love Magic, and Adultery: Warlpiri Relationships as Seen by Three Generations of Anthropologists', *Oceania* 80(3): 272.
———. 2011. 'Warungka: Becoming and Unbecoming a Warlpiri Person', in U. Eickelkamp (ed.), *Growing Up in Central Australia: New Anthropological Studies of Aboriginal Childhood and Adolescence*. New York: Berghahn Books, pp. 63–81.
Myers, F.R. 1980. 'A Broken Code: Pintupi Political Theory and Contemporary Social Life', *Mankind* 12: 311–26.
———. 1986. *Pintupi Country, Pintupi Self: Sentiment, Place, and Politics among Western Desert Aborigines*. Washington and Canberra: Smithsonian Institution Press and Australian Institute of Aboriginal Studies.
———. 2002. *Painting Culture: The Making of an Aboriginal High Art*. Durham, NC: Duke University Press.
Nagel, J. 1996. *American Indian Ethnic Renewal: Red Power and the Resurgence of Identity and Culture*. New York: Oxford University Press.
Napoleon, V. 2001. 'Extinction by Numbers: Colonialism Made Easy', *Canadian Journal of Law and Society* 16(1): 113–45.
Nash, D. 1986. 'Motor Vehicles in Central Australian Aboriginal Society: Some Preliminary Notes', in B.D. Foran and B.W. Walker (eds), *Science and Technology for Aboriginal Development*. Melbourne and Alice Springs: Commonwealth Scientific and Industrial Research Organisation (CSIRO) and Centre for Appropriate Technology, section 3.17 (unpaginated).
Neill, R. 2002. *White Out: How Politics Is Killing Black Australia*. Sydney: Allen and Unwin.
Neils, E.M. 1971. *Reservation to City: Indian Migration and Federal Relocation, Research paper no. 131*. Chicago: Department of Geography, University of Chicago.
Nelson, H.J. 1998. 'A Very Hard Battle', in A. Wright (ed.), *Take Power, Like this Old Man Here: An Anthology of Writings Celebrating Twenty Years of Land Rights in Central Australia 1977-1997*. Alice Springs: Jukurrpa Books and IAD Press, pp. 108–11.
Nicholls, C. 2003. 'Grounded Abstraction: The Work of Dorothy Napangardi', in *Dancing Up Country: The Art of Dorothy Napangardi*, edited by Museum of Contemporary Art. Sydney: Museum of Contemporary Art, pp. 60–67.
———. 2011. 'Painting Alone: Lorna Fencer Napurrurla', in M. West (ed.), *Yulyurlu Lorna Fencer Napurrurla*. Adelaide: Wakefield Press, pp. 29–64.
Northern Territory Emergency Response Review Board. 2008. *Report of the NTER Review Board*. Canberra: Australian Government.
O'Grady, F. 1977. *Francis of Central Australia*. Sydney: Wentworth Books.
O'Shannessy, C. 2005. 'Light Warlpiri: A New Language', *Australian Journal of Linguistics* 25(1): 31–57.
———. 2013. 'The Role of Multiple Sources in the Formation of an Innovative Auxiliary Category in Light Warlpiri, a New Australian Mixed Language', *Language* 89(2): 328–53.
Ono, A. 2007. 'Pentecostalism Among the Bundjalung Revisited: The Rejection of Culture by Aboriginal Christians in Northern New South Wales, Australia'. PhD thesis, School of Archaeology and Anthropology, Australian National University, Canberra.
Ottosson, Å. 2010. 'Aboriginal Music and Passion: Interculturality and Difference in Australian Desert Towns', *Ethnos* 75(3): 275–300.
———. 2014. 'To Know One's Place: Belonging and Differentiation in Alice Springs Town', *Anthropological Forum* 24(2): 115–35.
———. 2016. *Making Aboriginal Men and Music in Central Australia*. London: Bloomsbury.

Paine, R. 1974. 'Anthropological Approaches to Friendship', in E. Leyton (ed.), *The Compact: Selected Dimensions of Friendship*. Toronto: Institute of Social and Economic Research, Memorial University of Newfoundland, pp. 1–14.

Paradies, Y.C. 2006. 'Beyond Black and White: Essentialism, Hybridity and Indigeneity', *Journal of Sociology* 42(4): 355–67.

Patrick, S., and A. Box. 2008a. 'Milpirri: Performance as a Bridge that Joins the Ancient with the Modern', *Ngoonjook: A Journal of Australian Indigenous Issues* 33(53–60).

———. 2008b. *Ngurra-kurlu: A Way of Working with Warlpiri People*. Alice Springs: Desert Knowledge Cooperative Research Centre.

Pearson, N. 2000. *Our Right to Take Responsibility*. Cairns, Queensland: Noel Pearson and Associates.

———. 2005. *Welfare Reform and Economic Development for Indigenous Communities*. St. Leonards, NSW: Centre for Independent Studies.

———. 2009a. *Radical Hope: Education and Equality in Australia*, Quarterly Essay 35. Melbourne: Black Inc.

———. 2009b. *Up From the Mission: Selected Writings*. Melbourne: Black Inc.

Peel, M. 1995. *Good Times, Hard Times: the Past and the Future in Elizabeth*. Melbourne: Melbourne University Press.

Peterson, N. 1969. 'Secular and Ritual Links: Two Basic and Opposed Principles of Australian Social Organisation as Illustrated by Warlpiri Ethnography', *Mankind* 7: 27–35.

———. 1970. 'Buluwandi: A Central Australian Ceremony for the Resolution of Conflict', in R.M. Berndt (ed.), *Australian Aboriginal Anthropology*. Canberra: Australian Institute of Aboriginal Studies, pp. 200–15.

———. 1972. 'Totemism Yesterday: Sentiment and Local Organisation among the Australian Aborigines', *Man* 7(1): 12–32.

———. 1977. 'Aboriginal Involvement with the Australian Economy in the Central Reserve during the Winter of 1970', in R.M. Berndt (ed.), *Aborigines and Change: Australia in the '70s*. Canberra: Australian Institute of Aboriginal Studies, pp. 136–46.

———. 1993. 'Demand Sharing: Reciprocity and the Pressure for Generosity among Foragers', *American Anthropologist* 95(4): 869–74.

———. 2008. 'Just Humming: The Consequences of the Decline of Learning Contexts among the Warlpiri', in J. Kommers and E. Venbrux (eds), *Cultural Styles of Knowledge Transmission: Essays in Honour of Ad Borsboom*. Amsterdam: Aksant, pp. 114–18.

———. 2013. 'On the Persistence of Sharing: Personhood, Asymmetrical Reciprocity, and Demand Sharing in the Indigenous Australian Domestic Moral Economy', *The Australian Journal of Anthropology* 24(2): 166–76.

Peterson, N., and F.R. Myers (eds). 2016. *Experiments in Self-Determination: Histories of the Outstation Movement in Australia*. Canberra: Australian National University Press.

Peterson, N., and J. Taylor. 2003. 'The Modernising of the Indigenous Domestic Moral Economy', *The Asia Pacific Journal of Anthropology* 4(1): 105–22.

Petri, H., and G. Petri-Odermann. 1970. 'Stability and Change: Present-day Historic Aspects Among Australian Aborigines', in R.M. Berndt (ed.), *Australian Aboriginal Anthropology: Modern Studies in the Social Anthropology of Australian Aborigines*. Canberra and Perth: Australian Institute of Aboriginal Studies and University of Western Australia Press, pp. 248–76.

Pitt-Rivers, J. 1973. 'The Kith and the Kin', in J. Goody (ed.), *The Character of Kinship*. Cambridge: Cambridge University Press, pp. 89–105.

Poirier, S. 2005. *A World of Relationships: Itineraries, Dreams, and Events in the Australian Western Desert*. Toronto: University of Toronto Press.

Portes, A., P. Fernandez-Kelly and W. Haller. 2009. 'The Adaptation of Second Generation Immigrants in America: A Theoretical Overview and Recent Evidence', *Journal of Ethnic and Migration Studies* 35(7): 1077–104.
Povinelli, E.A. 2006. *The Empire of Love: Towards a Theory of Intimacy, Genealogy and Carnality*. Durham, NC: Duke University Press.
Preuss, K., and J.N. Brown. 2006. 'Stopping Petrol Sniffing in Remote Aboriginal Australia: Key Elements of the Mt Theo Program', *Drug and Alcohol Review* 25(3): 189–93.
Quinn, N. 1977. 'Anthropological Studies on Women's Status', *Annual Review of Anthropology* 6: 181–225.
Ramirez, R.K. 2007. *Native Hubs: Culture, Community, and Belonging in Silicon Valley and Beyond*. Durham, NC and London: Duke University Press.
Read, P. 1981. *The Stolen Generations: The Removal of Aboriginal Children in New South Wales 1883 to 1969*. Sydney: NSW Ministry for Aboriginal Affairs.
Reiter, R.R. (ed.). 1975. *Towards an Anthropology of Women*. New York: Monthly Review Press.
Reitman, E. 2006. 'An Argument for the Partial Abrogation of Federally Recognized Indian Tribes' Sovereign Power over Membership', *Virginia Law Review* 92(4): 793–866.
Reynolds, H. 2013. *Forgotten War*. Sydney: NewSouth Publishing.
Richards, J. 2008. *The Secret War: The True History of Queensland's Native Police*. Brisbane: University of Queensland Press.
Rintoul, S. 2012. 'Cry From The Heart: Bess Price Broke Free From Hardship and Violence, But the Fight for her People is Just Beginning', *The Weekend Australian Magazine*, 19–20 May, 12–16.
Robbins, J. 2004. 'The Globalization of Pentecostal and Charismatic Christianity', *Annual Review of Anthropology* 33: 117–43.
Rogers, S.C. 1978. 'Woman's Place: A Critical Review of Anthropological Theory', *Comparative Studies in Society and History* 20(1): 123–62.
Rosaldo, M.Z. 1974. 'Woman, Culture, and Society: A Theoretical Overview', in M.Z. Rosaldo and L. Lamphere (eds), *Woman, Culture, and Society*. Stanford, CA: Stanford University Press, pp. 17–42.
Rothwell, N. 2007. *Another Country*. Melbourne: Black Inc.
Rowley, C.D. 1970. *The Destruction of Aboriginal Society: Aboriginal Policy and Practice – Volume 1*. Canberra: Australian National University Press.
———. 1971. *The Remote Aborigines: Aboriginal Policy and Practice – Volume III*. Canberra: Australian National University Press.
Rowse, T. 1988. 'From Houses to Households? The Aboriginal Development Commission and the Economic Adaptation by Alice Springs Town Campers', *Social Analysis* 24: 50–65.
———. 1990. 'Enlisting the Warlpiri', *Continuum* 3(2): 174–200.
———. 1998. *White Flour, White Power: From Rations to Citizenship in Central Australia*. Cambridge: Cambridge University Press.
———. 2002. *Indigenous Futures: Choice and Development for Aboriginal and Islander Australia*. Sydney: University of New South Wales Press.
———. 2005a. 'The Indigenous Sector', in D. Austin-Broos and G. Macdonald (eds), *Culture, Economy and Governance in Aboriginal Australia*. Sydney: Sydney University Press, pp. 213–29.
———. 2005b. 'Review Article: Are Aborigines Rooted?', *Australian Aboriginal Studies* 1: 91–96.
———. 2012. *Rethinking Social Justice: From 'Peoples' to 'Populations'*. Canberra: Aboriginal Studies Press.
———. 2014. 'Indigenous Heterogeneity'. *Australian Historical Studies* 45(3): 297–310.

———. 2017. *Indigenous and other Australians since 1901*. Sydney: University of New South Wales Press.

Rubuntja, W., J. Green and T. Rowse. 2002. *The Town Grew up Dancing: the Life and Art of Wenten Rubuntja*. Alice Springs: Jukurrpa Books.

Russell, P.H. 2005. *Recognising Aboriginal Title: The Mabo Case and Indigenous Resistance to English-Settler Colonialism*. Toronto: University of Toronto Press.

Sackett, L. 1977. 'Liquor and the Law', in R.M. Berndt (ed.), *Aborigines and Change: Australia in the '70s*. Canberra: Australian Institute of Aboriginal Studies, pp. 90–99.

Saethre, E. 2013. *Illness Is A Weapon: Indigenous Identity and Everyday Afflictions*. Nashville, TN: Vanderbilt University Press.

Safran, W. 1991. 'Diasporas in Modern Societies: Myths of Homeland and Return', *Diaspora* 1(1): 83–99.

San Roque, C. 2011. 'The Yard', in U. Eickelkamp (ed.), *Growing Up in Central Australia: New Anthropological Studies of Aboriginal Childhood and Adolescence*. New York: Berghahn Books, pp. 156–79.

Sanday, P.R. 1981. *Female Power and Male Dominance: On the Origins of Sexual Inequality*. Cambridge: Cambridge University Press.

Sanders, W. 2008. 'In the Name of Failure: A Generational Revolution in Indigenous Affairs', in C. Aulich and R. Wettenhall (eds), *Howard's Fourth Government*. Sydney: UNSW Press, pp. 187–205.

Sansom, B. 1977. 'Aborigines and Alcohol: A Fringe Camp Example', *Australian Journal of Alcohol and Drug Dependence* 4(2): 58–62.

———. 1980. *The Camp at Wallaby Cross: Aboriginal Fringe Dwellers in Darwin*. Canberra: Australian Institute of Aboriginal Studies.

———. 1988. 'A Grammar of Exchange', in I. Keen (ed.), *Being Black: Aboriginal Cultures in 'Settled' Australia*. Canberra: Aboriginal Studies Press, pp. 159–77.

———. 2009. 'On Self and Licensed Solitude: "That Very Private Fella, Me"', *Oceania* 79(1): 65–84.

———. 2010. 'The Refusal of Holy Engagement: How Man-Making can Fail', *Oceania* 80: 24–57.

Scambary, B. 2007. '"No Vacancies at the Starlight Motel": Larrakia Identity and the Native Title Claim Process', in B.R. Smith and F. Morphy (eds), *The Social Effects of Native Title: Recognition, Translation, Coexistence*. Canberra: ANU E Press, pp. 117–34.

Sercombe, H. 2008. 'Living in Two Camps: The Strategies Goldfields Aboriginal People Used to Manage in the Customary Economy and the Mainstream Economy at the Same Time', *Australian Aboriginal Studies* (2): 16–31.

Sessional Committee on Use and Abuse of Alcohol by the Community. 1993. *Inquiry Into the Operation and Effect of Part VIII 'Restricted Areas' of the Liquor Act*. Darwin: Legislative Assembly of the Northern Territory and Northern Territory Government Printer.

Silman, J. 1987. *Enough Is Enough: Aboriginal Women Speak Out*. Toronto: The Women's Press.

Smee, R.A. 1966. 'Report on an Experiment Using Central Australian Aborigines As Seasonal Workers in New South Wales, January-April 1966', in I.G. Sharp and C.M. Tatz (eds), *Aborigines in the Economy: Employment, Wages and Training*. Melbourne: Jacaranda Press and Centre for Research into Aboriginal Affairs Monash University, pp. 69–72.

Smith, H.M., and E.H. Biddle. 1975. *Look Forward, Not Back: Aborigines in Metropolitan Brisbane 1965-1966, Aborigines in Australian Society 12*. Canberra: Australian National University Press and Academy of Social Sciences in Australia.

Smith, P.S. 2000. 'Into the Kimberley: The Invasion of the Sturt Creek Basin (Kimberley Region, Western Australia) and Evidence of Aboriginal Resistance', *Aboriginal History* 24: 62–75.
Smith, R.T. 1996. *The Matrifocal Family: Power, Pluralism, and Politics*. New York: Routledge.
———. 2001. 'Matrifocality', in N.J. Smelser and P.B. Baltes (eds), *International Encyclopedia of the Social and Behavioural Sciences*. Amsterdam: Elsevier, pp. 9416–18.
Sommerlad, E. 1976. *Kormilda, The Way to Tomorrow? A Study of Aboriginal Education*. Canberra: Australian National University Press.
Spencer, B., and F. Gillen. 1899. *The Native Tribes of Central Australia*. London: Macmillan.
Steer, P.J. 1996. *It Happened at Yuendumu*. Melbourne: Self published.
Stojanovski, A. 2010. *Dog Ear Cafe: How the Mt Theo Program Beat the Curse of Petrol Sniffing*. Melbourne: Hybrid Publishers.
Strathern, M. 1978. 'The Achievement of Sex: Paradoxes in Hagan Gender-Thinking', *Yearbook of Symbolic Anthropology* 1: 171–202.
Straus, T., and D. Valentino. 1998. 'Retribalisation in Urban Indian Communities', *American Indian Culture and Research Journal* 22(4): 103–15.
Strehlow, T.G.H. 1963. 'Men Without Leaders: Book Review of Meggitt's *Desert People*', *Nation*, 12 January, 22–23.
Sullivan, P. 2011. *Belonging Together: Dealing with the Politics of Disenchantment in Australian Indigenous Policy*. Canberra: Aboriginal Studies Press.
Sutton, P. 2001. 'The Politics of Suffering: Indigenous Policy in Australia Since the Seventies', *Anthropological Forum* 11(2): 125–73.
———. 2009. *The Politics of Suffering: Indigenous Australia and the End of the Liberal Consensus*. Melbourne: Melbourne University Press.
Tangentyere Council and Central Land Council. 2007. 'Ingerrehenhe Antirrkweme: Mobile Phone Use among Low Income Aboriginal People: A Central Australian Snapshot'. Alice Springs: Tangentyere Council and Central Land Council.
Tanner, N. 1974. 'Matrifocality in Indonesia and Africa and among Black Americans', in M.Z. Rosaldo and L. Lamphere (eds), *Woman, Culture, and Society*. Stanford, CA: Stanford University Press, pp. 129–56.
Tatz, C.M. 1964. 'Aboriginal Administration in the Northern Territory of Australia'. PhD thesis, Australian National University.
Taylor, J. 1988. 'Aboriginal Population Mobility and Urban Development in the Katherine Region', in D. Wade-Marshall and P. Loveday (eds), *Northern Australia: Progress and Prospects Volume 1 – Contemporary Issues in Development*. Darwin: North Australian Research Unit, Australian National University, pp. 201–23.
———. 1989. 'Public Policy and Aboriginal Population Mobility: Insights from the Katherine Region, Northern Territory', *Australian Geographer* 20(1): 47–53.
———. 2009. 'Social Engineering and Indigenous Settlement: Policy and Demography in Remote Australia', *Australian Aboriginal Studies* 1: 4–15.
Taylor, J., and M. Bell. 1996. 'Mobility among Indigenous Australians', in P.W. Newton and M. Bell (eds), *Population Shift: Mobility and Change in Australia*. Canberra: Australian Government Publishing Service, pp. 392–411.
———. 1999. *Changing Places: Indigenous Population Movements in the 1990s, CAEPR Discussion Paper No. 189*. Canberra: Centre for Aboriginal Economic Policy Research, Australian National University.
——— (eds). 2004. *Population Mobility and Indigenous Peoples in Australasia and North America*. London: Routledge.

Taylor, P. 1980. *An End to Silence: The Building of the Overland Telegraph Line from Adelaide to Darwin*. Sydney: Methuen.

Tilmouth, W. 2007. 'Saying No to $60 Million', in J. Altman and M. Hinkson (eds), *Coercive Reconciliation: Stabilise, Normalise, Exit Aboriginal Australia*. Melbourne: Arena Publications, pp. 231–38.

Tölölyan, K. 1996. 'Rethinking Diaspora(s): Stateless Power in the Transnational Moment', *Diaspora* 5: 3–36.

Tonkinson, R. 1974. *The Jigalong Mob: Aboriginal Victors of the Desert Crusade*. Menlo Park, CA: Cummings.

———. 1988. 'Reflections on a Failed Crusade', in T. Swain and D.B. Rose (eds), *Aboriginal Australians and Christian Missions: Ethnographic and Historical Studies*. Adelaide: Australian Association for the Study of Religions, pp. 60–73.

———. 1990. 'The Changing Status of Aboriginal Women: "Free Agents" at Jigalong', in R. Tonkinson and M. Howard (eds), *Going It Alone? Prospects for Aboriginal Autonomy: the Essays in Honour of Ronald and Catherine Berndt*. Canberra: Aboriginal Studies Press, pp. 125–47.

Toohey, P. 2008. *Last Drinks: The Impact of the Northern Territory Intervention*, Quarterly Essay Issue 30. Melbourne: Schwartz Media.

Trigger, D.S. 1986. 'Blackfellas and Whitefellas: The Concepts of Domain and Social Closure in Analysis of Race Relations', *Mankind* 16(2): 99–117.

Trudgen, R. 2000. *Why Warriors Lie Down and Die*. Darwin: Aboriginal Resources and Development Services.

Tsuda, T. 2009. *Diasporic Homecomings: Ethnic Return Migration in Comparative Perspective*. Stanford, CA: Stanford University Press.

Vaarzon-Morel, P. 2014. 'Pointing the Phone: Transforming Technologies and Social Relations among Warlpiri', *The Australian Journal of Anthropology* 25(2): 238–55.

Van Kirk, S. 2002. 'From "Marrying-In" to "Marrying-Out": Changing Patterns of Aboriginal/Non-Aboriginal Marriage in Colonial Canada', *Frontiers: A Journal of Women Studies* 23(3): 1–11.

Veracini, L. 2006. 'A Prehistory of Australia's History Wars: The Evolution of Aboriginal History during the 1970s and 1980s', *Australian Journal of Politics and History* 52(3): 439–54.

Vertovec, S. 1999. 'Three Meanings of "Diaspora", Exemplified by South Asian Religions', *Diaspora* 6(3): 277–300.

Vincent, J. 1993. 'Framing the Underclass', *Critique of Anthropology* 13(3): 215–30.

Vivian, A. 2010. 'Some Human Rights Are Worth More Than Others: The Northern Territory Intervention and the Alice Springs Town Camps', *Alternative Law Journal* 35(1): 13–17.

Wardlow, H. 2006. *Wayward Women: Sexuality and Agency in a New Guinea Society*. Berkeley, CA: University of California Press.

Wardlow, H., and J.S. Hirsh. 2006. 'Introduction', in H. Wardlow and J.S. Hirsh (eds), *Modern Loves: The Anthropology of Romantic Courtship and Companionate Marriage*. Ann Arbor, MI: University of Michigan Press, pp. 1–21.

Warner, L.W. 1937. *A Black Civilisation: a Social Study of an Australian Tribe*. New York: Harper and Brothers.

Watson, J., V. Lynn, H. Fink, H. Perkins and Baudoin Lebon (Gallery: Paris France). 1996. *Judy Watson*. Epernay, France: Moët & Chandon.

Watson, J., and L. Martin-Chew. 2009. *Judy Watson: Blood Language*, Contemporary Indigenous Art Series. Carlton, Victoria: Miegunyah Press.

Weibel-Orlando, J. 1998. 'And the Drum Beat Goes On: Urban Native American Institutional Survival in the 1990s', *American Indian Culture and Research Journal* 22(4): 135–62.
———. 1999. *Indian Country, L. A.: Maintaining Ethnic Community in Complex Society*. Revised edn. Urbana, IL: University of Illinois Press.
Wells, J. 1995. 'The Long March: Assimilation Policy and Practice in Darwin, the Northern Territory, 1939-1967'. PhD thesis, Department of History, University of Queensland.
Werbner, P. 2008. 'Introduction: Towards a New Cosmopolitan Anthropology', in P. Werbner (ed.), *Anthropology and the New Cosmopolitanism*. Oxford: Berg, pp. 1–29.
West, M. (ed.). 2011. *Yulyurlu Lorna Fencer Napurrurla*. Adelaide: Wakefield Press.
Wild, R., and P. Anderson. 2007. *Ampe Akelyernemane Meke Mekarle "Little Children are Sacred": Report of the Northern Territory Board of Inquiry Into the Protection of Aboriginal Children From Sexual Abuse*. Darwin: Office of Indigenous Policy, Department of the Chief Minister, Northern Territory Government.
Wild, S.A. 1975. 'Warlpiri Music and Dance in their Social and Cultural Nexus'. Unpublished PhD thesis, Anthropology, Indiana University.
———. 1977–1978. 'Man as Woman: Female Dance Symbolism in Walbiri Men's Rituals', *Dance Research Journal* 10(1): 14–22.
Wilkins, D. 2004. 'Exiling One's Kin: Banishment and Disenrollment in Indian Country', *Western Legal History* 17: 235–62.
Wilson, B., and J. O'Brien. 2003. '"To Infuse an Universal Terror": A Reappraisal of the Coniston Killings', *Aboriginal History* 27: 58–78.
Wolf, E.R. 1982. *Europe and the People Without History*. Berkeley, CA: University of California Press.
Wolfe, P. 1999. *Settler Colonialism and the Transformation of Anthropology: The Politics and Politics of an Ethnographic Event*, edited by P. Darby, M. Thornton and P. Wolfe. *Writing Past Colonialism Series*. London: Cassell.
Woodward, A.E. 1974. *Aboriginal Land Rights Commission Second Report, Parliamentary Paper No. 69 of 1974*. Canberra: The Government Printer of Australia.
Wright, A. 1997. *Grog War*. Broome: Magabala Books.
Yanagisako, S.J. 1979. 'Family and Household: The Analysis of Domestic Groups', *Annual Review of Anthropology* 8: 161–205.
Young, E., and K. Doohan. 1989. *Mobility for Survival: A Process Analysis of Aboriginal Population Movement in Central Australia*. Darwin: Australian National University, North Australia Research Unit.
Zelinsky, W. 1971. 'The Hypothesis of the Mobility Transition', *Geographical Review* 61(2): 219–49.

Index

A
Aboriginal art market, 30, 33, 95n15, 138, 151, 195
Aboriginal liaison officer, 48, 90, 98, 136
Aboriginal migration
    Adelaide bound, 95n14
    Alice Springs bound, 99–100
    Brisbane bound, 95n14
    Darwin bound, 35
    economic and legal impediments, 27
    Katherine bound, 35
    Melbourne bound, 35
Aboriginal NGOs, 35, 102, 109
Aboriginal people
    definition of, 3–4, 7n
    internal differentiation, 4–5
    See also Indigenous people (of Australia)
'Abraham', 87, 162–165
Adelaide, 10, 11, 29, 34, 35, 36, 51, 54, 56, 57, 66n50, 72, 76, 77, 78, 79, 80, 81, 82, 84, 85, 87, 88, 89, 90, 91, 95n14, 125–126, 129–53, 155, 167, 169, 171, 172, 173, 175, 178, 179, 181, 183, 187, 188, 191, 192, 193, 194, 197, 198, 199, 202, 203, 206, 207
    Elizabeth, satellite city of, 132–33
    geographic social stratification in, 132
    history of Warlpiri migration to, 130–31
    Hospital, 142, 149, 179
    parklands of, 132, 152n5
    Warlpiri diaspora locations, 132
    Warlpiri diaspora numbers, 131
agency, active and constructive, 41, 56, 67, 68, 130, 145

alcohol abuse, 6, 28, 76, 82, 94n2, 98, 104, 106, 128n9, 141, 146, 147, 152n5, 182, 189. *See also* drinker and non-drinker tensions, drinking household, drug dependency
alcohol rehabilitation centres, 11, 51, 85, 96n17, 100
alcohol restrictions, 6, 10–11, 35, 52, 71–73, 94n3, 114, 156, 177, 195
Alice Springs, 1, 2, 6, 10, 11, 26, 27, 29, 36, 43, 51, 54, 56, 57, 59 n10, 68, 69, 70, 71, 73, 76, 77, 79, 80–81, 83, 84, 85, 87, 88, 89, 90, 91, 92, 93, 96 n17, 97–128, 129, 130, 134, 135, 136, 137, 138, 139, 142, 144, 146, 148, 149, 150, 151, 154, 156, 157, 158, 159, 160, 162, 165, 166, 167, 171, 172, 175, 176, 177, 178, 181, 192, 183, 184, 187, 190, 191, 192, 194, 196, 199, 202, 203, 206, 207
    Aboriginal NGOs, 102
    attractions for young Warlpiri, 117–18
    Arrernte traditional ownership of, 99, 121–22
    location of Warlpiri residents, 101
    Warlpiri Camp (Ilperle-Tyathe), 100
    Warlpiri migration history, 99–100
    Warlpiri population of, 100–101
    Warlpiri sorority of, 80–81
Ali Curung, ix, 10, 19, 40, 51, 60 n14, 64 n38, 73, 76, 77, 78, 112, 127n5, 128, 131, 140–42
Anangu Pitjantjatjara Yankunytjatjara (APY) lands, 78, 148
Amoongana, 70, 100, 142

Anderson, Peggy Napurrula, 77, 95n12
Anmatjerr, 70, 84
'Annie', 70, 75, 80
Arrernte (language group), 19, 60, 70, 72, 97, 99, 100, 103, 111, 115, 121–22, 125, 122n3, 122n4, 128n16, 132, 135, 148, 174
artists. *See under* Warlpiri women
art wholesaler, 10, 48, 84, 130, 138, 151, 192, 197
Assemblies of God (Pentecostal church), 108, 111–13, 169, 191
  attitude to Warlpiri male initiation, 169
  denunciation of sorcery, 113
Austin-Broos, Diane, 26–27, 33, 61n19, 65, 126n1, 128n16, 141, 152n1
Australian rules football (AFL), 11, 33, 54, 66n48, 72, 83, 84, 95n16, 117
Ayers Rock. *See* Uluru

B

Baarda, Wendy, x, 61n21
Bagot camp (Darwin), 10, 69–71, 74, 85, 93n2
  history of, 93n2
Balgo, ix, 19, 51, 63n30, 66n50, 89
Baptist Church, ix, 22–23, 32, 55, 61n23, 70, 102–4, 106–8, 112, 113, 114, 121, 134, 139, 148, 191, 192
'Barbara', 10, 56, 129, 133, 134–37, 138, 146, 148, 150, 169, 176, 179, 180, 181, 193, 203
Barwick, Diane, 24, 35
Bauman, Toni, 73, 75, 93n2
'beats', 48, 72, 89
Beckett, Jeremy, 27, 35, 48, 72, 89, 155
Bell, Diane, 24, 25, 41–42, 43, 44, 62n25, 73, 77, 127n5, 168, 199
bi-cultural adept, 22, 23, 32–33, 40, 41, 43, 45, 47, 53, 55, 61n18, 68, 76, 88, 89, 105, 158, 159, 184n3, 191, 202
Billiluna, 19
'Boris', 134–35
Bourdieu, Pierre, 64n39
Brisbane, 83, 95n14
Broome, 19, 86, 87, 89
Bundaberg, 88, 169, 183
Bungalow, The, 70, 99, 100, 127n4

burial site, family politics of choosing a, 14, 29, 57, 120, 155, 165–67

C

'Camilla', 107, 108, 110, 127n6, 182, 198, 203
Canadian Indian Act definition of Indian, 95n13
Caribbean ethnography, 43, 135
Central Australia Aboriginal Congress, 109
Central Australian Aboriginal Legal Aid Service, 98
Central Australian Aboriginal Media Association, 83
Christianity, 10, 22, 23, 28, 32, 61nn22–23, 77, 98, 99, 106, 108, 109, 110, 111–114, 115, 123, 124, 130, 135, 140, 149, 150, 151, 162, 183, 184n6, 187, 191, 192, 194, 197, 199, 208. *See also* Baptist Church, Pentecostal churches
Christian *jilimi*, 106–11
'circular mobility', 89, 159
Clifford, James, 38
Cohen, Robin, 38
Collmann, Jeff, 27, 36, 43, 86, 100
colonisation of Australia, 2–3
'community' or 'settlement', preferred terminology, 28
Coniston massacre, 17, 59n11
contacts, 45, 55, 56, 94n7, 102, 104, 105, 111, 114, 124, 137, 138, 149, 179, 189, 190, 191, 193, 197
companionate marriage, 46, 47, 92, 198
Coober Pedy, 66n50, 72, 134, 191
cosmopolitanism, 16, 17, 38, 40, 202
Coulehan, Kerin, 35, 94n8, 130, 131, 153n10, 169, 183, 185n9
'Crocodile Dundee'. *See* Johnson, Cecil Japangardi
Curran, Georgia, 95n16

D

Darby, 174.
Darwin, 10, 11, 26, 35, 36, 51, 54, 56, 62 n27, 68, 93n2, 71, 72, 73, 74, 75, 76, 77, 78, 80, 81, 84, 85, 86, 87, 89, 90, 92, 93n2, 94n3, 94n8, 96n17, 98, 99, 111–13, 115, 118, 121, 125,

128n14, 130, 131, 136, 137, 146, 147,
153nn10–11, 154, 157, 159, 160, 161,
167, 169, 172, 174, 184n6, 185n6,
188, 189, 194, 197, 199, 202, 203,
206. *See also* Bagot, long-grassers
Delaney, Neil, 46
demand sharing, 16, 25, 26, 41, 90, 109,
113, 117, 128n16, 137, 143, 147, 151,
168, 178, 180, 190, 194, 199
dialysis patients, 11, 51, 85, 96n17, 111,
120, 121, 156
diaspora
  definition of, 38
  extension of the concept to indigenous
    peoples, 38–40
  feminised, 24, 37, 43, 85, 151, 156
  involuntary, 11, 51, 85 (*see also* dialysis
    patients)
  parallel, 143–145
  See also migration, Warlpiri diaspora
domestic moral economy, 26. *See also*
  demand sharing
Dosman, Edgar, 36–37, 64n37
Dreaming (*Jukurrpa*), 2, 5, 12, 14, 17, 19,
  59n8, 62n24, 63n29, 102, 142
Dreaming tracks, 2, 17, 58n8
drinker and non-drinker tensions, 77, 81,
  104, 114, 121, 141, 147, 157, 158
drinking household, 72, 82, 146, 147
drug dependency, 63n34, 106, 145, 181,
  182, 189, 191, 202
'dry areas'. *See* alcohol restrictions
'Dulcie', 1–2, 7, 10, 76, 99, 102–6, 114,
  115, 116, 119, 120, 123, 129, 138,
  151, 158, 169, 170, 190, 192, 197
Dussart, Françoise, 29, 44, 59n5, 61n16,
  61n22, 61n24, 104, 127n5, 161, 168,
  185n6, 196

E
Elizabeth (the location), 132–34, 135, 144,
  149
Ellis, Lizzie Marrkily, 116
'Emily', 133, 134–37, 150, 203
endosociality, 26, 33, 45, 117, 124, 191,
  204, 208
Enfield (suburb of Adelaide), 133

Engineer Jack, Japaljarri, 141
Ernabella, 78, 89

F
family feuding, 54, 66nn47–49, 107, 110,
  124, 125, 131, 158, 168, 173, 177,
  191, 192
feminist anthropology, 41–44, 64n41
feminist critique of romantic love, 151
feminist philosophers on personal autonomy, 44
feminist theorising, 42–44, 64n40, 194
fieldwork, 56, 66n50
Fitzroy Crossing, 19, 59n8, 87, 89
Fleming, Rev. Tom, 23, 32, 61n23, 77, 107
Fogel-Chance, Nancy, 37, 63n28, 64n35,
  95n14
Friedman, Marilyn, 37, 44, 151
friendship, 47–48
  and acquaintanceship, 48
  and 'weak ties', 48
  anthropology of, 47, 65n 42
  conferral of skin name, 103
  definition of, 47, 65n 42
  fringe camp studies, 35, 36, 58n3, 136. *See
    also* town camps

G
Gale, Fay, 35, 95n14, 131
gender relations
  critique of Bell, 24, 62n25
  effect of welfare payments on, 25–27
  gendered reception in the diaspora, 34
  See under Warlpiri (language group)
  See also Warlpiri women
'global pathways', 89
Gurindji, 30, 71, 94n6, 112

H
Haasts Bluff, 19
Halls Creek, 19, 66n50, 169, 185n10, 191
Hermannsburg, 19, 26, 91, 127n3
Hidden Valley town camp (Alice Springs),
  103–5, 128n10
home and away politics, 120, 155, 156–61,
  165–67, 184
homelands movement. *See* outstations movement. *See also* Warlpiri homeland

232 • Index

home settlements, 9, 10, 39, 41, 42, 53, 57, 58, 80, 85, 93, 97, 98, 102, 108, 113, 114, 119, 121, 123, 140, 148, 151, 156, 162, 170, 172, 173, 174, 175, 176, 178, 179, 187, 189, 193, 196, 202, 203, 204, 206. *See also* Ali Curung, Lajamanu, Nyirrpi, Willowra, Yuendumu
Hooker Creek. *See* Lajamanu
Hoppy's Camp (Alice Springs), 11
household management, 10, 37, 43, 44, 45, 76, 77, 99, 103, 104, 106, 107, 111, 112, 118, 129, 135, 142–43, 147, 153n11, 164, 177, 186, 189, 193, 194, 199, 203, 205, 206
humpy. *See yujuku*
Hutt Street soup kitchen, 133

I
Ilperle-Tyathe camp. *See* Warlpiri Camp
Indigenous diaspora, 12
  and 'fringe camps', 35
  and internal migration, 35
  assessment of the experiment, 206–8
  concept of, 37–40
  See also involuntary diaspora, Warlpiri diaspora
Indigenous people (of Australia)
  definition of, 3–4, 7n
  See also Aboriginal people
Institute for Aboriginal Development (Alice Springs), 102
intercultural anthropology, 5, 40, 41, 84, 189, 204, 207, 208n2
inter-group politics. *See* inter-tribal relations
intermediary positions. *See* bi-cultural adepts
inter-racial marriage, 45–47, 79–82
inter-tribal marriage, 69–70, 73, 75, 77–78, 86
inter-tribal relations
  Warlpiri and Arrernte in Alice Springs, 70, 121–25
  Warlpiri and locals in Adelaide, 149
  Warlpiri and locals in Darwin, 69–70,
  Warlpiri and locals in Katherine, 72–73
  Western Desert migrants and locals, 36
Intervention, the, 6, 52–54, 65n45, 66n46, 94n2, 98, 103, 105, 127n3, 160, 180, 200, 206; debate among anthropologists about, 65n45
involuntary diaspora, 11, 51, 85, 95n17, 100, 120, 207. *See also* dialysis patients

J
jilimi (widow's camp), 10, 71, 127n5, 199. *See also* Christian *jilimi*
Johnson, Cecil Japangardi, 60n15, 70
'Judith', 162–165
Jukurrpa Artists (Alice Springs), 102
Jukurrpa. See Dreaming, Dreaming tracks
Jurrah, Liam, 54, 66n49, 83, 84, 90, 180

K
Katherine, 11, 35, 36, 51, 57, 68, 69, 70, 71, 72–73, 75, 79, 83, 84, 85, 86, 89, 92, 93, 94n3, 98, 112, 126n3, 159, 172, 173, 174, 181, 188, 202, 207
Kaurna, 149
Kaytej, 73
'Kimberley', 176–78
Kintore (Walangurru), 89
Kolig, Erich, 16, 36, 59n8
Kormilda College, 24, 70, 75, 76, 77, 95n11
Kowal, Emma, 58n1, 145
Kununurra, 19, 52, 66n50, 79
kurruwalpa (spirit child), 12
kuruwarri (spirit essences), 12, 14, 188

L
Lajamanu, 6, 21, 51
Laughren, Mary, 23, 60n15, 94n5, 184n5
'Lesley', 162–165
Lhere Aretepe Aboriginal Corporation 121, 122, 128n12, 128n13
life-cycle. *See under* Warlpiri women
Light Warlpiri (language), 30–31
long-grassers, 75, 86, 112, 202
Luther, Maurice Jupurrula, 94n9

M
marriage
  companionate, 46, 47, 92, 190
  hypergamy, 47
  inter-racial, 45–47
  inter-tribal, 69–70, 73, 75, 77–78, 86

language group endogamy, 73, 92
romantic love, 46
social endogamy, 80
underclass 'marrying up', 189
Warlpiri endogamy, 16, 47
See also Warlpiri (language group): marriage
matriarchs. *See* Warlpiri matriarchs
matrifocal household, 37, 43, 57, 135, 186, 193–94. *See also* Warlpiri matriarchs
McCoy, Brian, 63n30
Meggitt, Mervyn J, 13–16, 17, 21, 24, 28, 58n5, 59n9, 59n11, 60nn15–16, 61n22, 127nn4–5, 162, 166, 168, 173, 185n8
Merlan, Francesca, 5, 13, 22, 24, 26, 27, 36, 42, 52, 57, 62n25, 72, 94n3, 105, 108, 110, 126n2, 156, 184nn3–4, 185, 188, 205
methodology, 54–56; methodological bias towards non-drinkers, 145
Meyers, Diana, 44
migration
　chain, 92
　internal, 35
　push-pull factors, 35
　reasons for, 67–93
　return, 65n43, 155, 175, 183, 184n1
　serial, 89–91, 100
　subcategories of, 65n43
　Western Desert Aboriginal migration, 36
　Yolngu migration to Darwin, 35
　See also reasons for Warlpiri migration, Warlpiri diaspora
mijilpa, 167
mining royalties, 30, 63n32, 63n33
missionisation, 23, 33, 61n23, 148
Mitchell, Joseph, 36
mobile phones, 134, 136, 159, 180
Morgan, George, 35
Mormon Church, 87
Mount Allen (Aboriginal settlement), 51
Mount Doreen Station, 18, 19, 108, 129
multi-sited ethnography, 54
Murray Bridge, 2, 11, 79–80, 87, 90, 91, 93, 146, 150, 176, 193, 206

Musharbash, Yasmine, 13, 28, 59, 62n26, 63nn30–31, 79, 96n18, 107, 117, 135, 153n12, 185n7, 208n2
Mussolini (a Warlpiri ancestor), 161–162
Myers, Fred R, 16, 25, 45, 47, 95n15
mythologising the diaspora, 161–65

N
nangkayi (traditional healer), 167
'Narelle', 181–82
Nash, David, 60n14, 65n44
'Natalie', 10, 42, 129, 133, 138–40, 147, 151, 195, 197
Nelson, Harry Jakamarra, 94n9, 99
Nelson, Topsy Napurrula, 141
Ngarrindjeri, 149
NGOs, 1, 28, 33, 35, 53, 80, 84, 89, 96n17, 97, 98, 100, 102, 109, 110, 121, 122, 124, 130, 144, 174, 175, 179, 185n12, 191, 195, 196, 199, 201, 203
Northern Territory Emergency Response. *See* Intervention
Northern Territory history
　Aboriginal legislation, 62n27
　Australian Army Aboriginal Corps, 70, 92, 99
　Second World War, 21, 70
Northern Territory Intervention. *See* Intervention
Northern Territory Register of Wards. *See* Wards
Northern Territory Social Welfare Ordinance 1964, 62n27
Nyirrpi, 6, 51, 73, 89, 153n8, 162, 179, 181

O
Old Timers camp (Alice Springs), 100
'orbiting', 53, 57, 58, 186, 200–5. *See also* Pearson, Noel
O'Shannessy, Carmel, 30–31
outstations movement, 1, 16, 19, 27, 28, 29, 63n29, 64n38, 77, 108, 123, 141, 158, 188, 198, 199

P

pan-Warlpiri solidarity in diaspora locations. *See under* Warlpiri diaspora
Papunya, 19, 60n12, 74, 89, 91, 195
parallel diaspora, 143–45; defined, 143–44; comparison with 'White anti-racists', 145
Pearson, Noel, 52, 53, 129n9, 141, 200–5, 208n1
Pentecostal churches, 10, 23, 32, 55, 85, 87, 99, 108, 111–14, 142, 150, 163, 185n10, 188, 191, 194, 197, 199, 203. *See also* Assemblies of God
personal autonomy, 7, 10, 21, 24, 43–44, 67, 74, 98, 102, 105, 114, 123, 130, 137, 145, 151, 164, 196, 199
   Diana Meyers on, 44
   dual aspects of, 44, 74
   Marilyn Friedman on, 44
   See also agency (active and constructive)
Peterson, Nicolas, 13, 14, 16, 23, 25, 26, 29, 58n5, 59n6, 63n29, 168
Phillip Creek, 19, 73
Pink, Olive, 99
Pitjantjatjara, 72, 78, 133, 143, 148, 149, 185n8
Port Adelaide, 131
Port Augusta, 72, 81, 134
Port Hedland, 87
Port Pirie, 51, 125, 131
Poulson, Neville Japangardi, 61n18, 152n2, 159
Price, Bess Nungarrayi, 116, 160, 192, 196, 197
private rental, 134–35
public housing, 29, 33, 34, 52, 88, 90, 94n2, 98, 100, 114, 125, 130, 132, 133, 135, 136, 146, 177, 192
purlapa (open ritual), Christian/Easter, 23, 61n22, 107, 168

R

Ramirez, Renya, 37
reasons for Warlpiri migration, 67–93
   adventure, 86
   army service, 99
   attractions of Alice Springs, 117–18
   balance of kin, 89–91
   boredom, 117–118
   careers (semi-professional), 83–84
   education, 76–79
   escape from alcohol restrictions, 71–72
   escape from drinking friends, 87–88
   escape from promised marriage, 73–76
   inter-racial marriage, 79–82, 95n14
   inter-tribal marriage, 69–70
   jobs, 88–89
   medical treatment, 85
   religious conversion, 87
return migration, 65n43, 155, 175, 183, 184n1
return to the home settlements, 174–80
   first-generation diaspora, 174–75
   pioneers of the Warlpiri diaspora, 174–75
   second-generation diaspora, 117–18, 175–78
   stolen generation, 178–79
   virtual return, 179–80. *See also* mobile phones
return visits to the home settlements, 167–75
   for initiation ceremonies, 168–70
   for mortuary rituals and funerals, 170–71
   for participation in the feud, 173
   for royalty meetings, 172–73
romantic love, 46, 79–82
'Rosie', 66n50, 76, 142–43, 147, 148, 151, 153n11, 191, 197, 203
Ross, Darby Jampijinpa. *See* Darby
Ross, Kim Jangala, 69–70, 74
Rowse, Tim, 4, 21, 25, 27, 28, 31, 36, 59 n10, 63n27, 95n9, 99, 102, 126n3, 127nn3–4, 156, 176, 200, 202, 208n2.
Royal Flying Doctor Service, 110

S

Safran, William, 38
Sansom, Basil, 26, 36, 75, 81, 94n3, 94n7, 125, 127n8, 136, 153n11, 157, 164, 165, 167, 184n3
'Sarah', 10, 106–111, 123, 183, 203, 217
second-generation diaspora. *See under* Warlpiri diaspora
Second World War, 21, 70, 92, 139
'settlement' or 'community', preferred terminology, 28

Snake Bay (Melville Island), 69
social embeddedness, 40–41, 64n39, 186–89
social networks
    'Dulcie's' personal social networks, 102–6
    expansion of personal social networks, 45–48
    expansion of Warlpiri networks, 32–33
    personal support, 143
    See also contacts, friendship
sorcery, 12, 16, 33, 34, 41, 66n48, 73, 86, 113, 123, 124, 155, 158, 165, 166–67, 170, 178, 187, 198, 205
sorry business, 28, 54, 36n30, 103, 115, 119–20, 126, 158, 168, 170, 173, 176, 178
    Alice Springs based, 119–20
    funerals distinguished, 28–29, 63n30
    traditional mortuary practices, 14–15, 28–29, 63n30
spirit child. *See kurruwalpa*
spirit essences. *See kuruwarri*
Stolen Generation, 175, 176, 178
Strehlow, T G H, 60n16
'Suzanne', 137–38, 192, 197
'Svetlana', 134

T

Tanami Desert, 3, 19, 40
Tanami gold rush, 17, 19
Tangentyere Council 109, 122, 126n2, 128n15, 153n8
'Tangier', 182
Taylor, John, 16, 26, 35, 89, 155, 159, 201
Tennant Creek, 11, 51, 59n10, 68, 69, 71, 73, 96n17, 141, 173
Ti-Tree (Aboriginal settlement), 51, 66n50
Tonkinson, Robert, 23, 61n23, 62n25, 79
Top Springs, 71, 72, 112
town camps
    defined, 58n3, 98
    of Alice Springs, 98
    See also Bagot camp (Darwin), long-grassers, Warlpiri camp (Alice Springs), 100
travelling circuits, 89. *See also* 'beats', 'circular mobility', 'global pathways'
'two laws talk', 22, 61n19
'two-way education', 22, 61n19

U

Uluru, 138
underclass, 33, 63n34
    predatory underclass men, 146
Uniting Church (in Adelaide), 148, 149

V

Vaarzon-Morel, Petronella, 73
'Valmae', 10, 76, 140–41, 148, 149, 198, 203

W

Wagga Wagga, 88
Walangurru. *See* Kintore
Wallaby Cross mob, 94n3, 94n7, 127n8, 157, 165, 167, 184n3
Wards (Northern Territory), Register of, 19, 60n13, 62n27
    Warlpiri, location of, 20
Warlpiri camp (Alice Springs), 99–100
Warlpiri camp (Katherine), 71, 72
Warlpiri camp (Port Adelaide), 131
Warlpiri diaspora
    Adelaide, 129–52
    Alice Springs, 97–125
    critical mass, 92
    Darwin, 69–70, 73–75, 111–14
    developmental stages, 92–93
    foundational couples, 69–70
    Katherine, 72–73
    life cycle and, 45, 68, 105, 182, 183
    locations, 11, 49–52, 101
    pan-Warlpiri solidarity in Adelaide, 148–49
    pan-Warlpiri solidarity in Alice Springs, 118–19
    pioneers, 67–70
    Queensland, 162–165
    second-generation, 117, 128n11, 170, 173, 175, 183, 188, 204
    Tennant Creek, 73
    visitors distinguished, 51
    See also burial site, diaspora, home and away politics, inter-tribal relations, reasons for Warlpiri migration, town camps, Warlpiri matriarchs, Warlpiri women
Warlpiri homeland, definition of, 40

Warlpiri (language group), 5–7
  anthropological literature, 58n5
  artists (*see under* Warlpiri women)
  autobiography, 55
  Baptist missionisation, 23, 61n23
  bi-cultural adapts, 22, 32–33, 45, 53, 55
  biography, 61nn17–18
  chauvinism, 111, 166
  culture, 12–17
  demographic changes, 29
  diaspora locations, 11, 49–52
  egalitarianism, 21, 60n16
  endosociality, 33
  family feuding, 54, 66nn47–49
  gendered reception in the diaspora, 34
  gender relations, 24,
  intermediary figures, 21–22
  kinship, 33–34, 41
  language change, 30–31
  life-cycle, 14, 45, 68, 105, 154, 182, 183, 206
  marriage, 24–25
  matriarchs, 9–10, 24, 41–45
  migration, 17–28
  mining royalties, 30, 63nn32–33
  mortuary practices, 14–15, 28–29, 63n30 (*see also* sorry business)
  outstations, 28, 63n29, 64n38
  painting, 30 (*see also* Aboriginal art market)
  personal autonomy, 7, 10, 21, 24, 43–44, 67, 74, 98, 102, 105, 114, 123, 130, 137, 145, 151, 164, 196, 199
  personhood, 11, 14
  social change, 28–34
  social embeddedness, 15–16
  social networks, expansion of, 32–33
  social problems, 28
  subsection system (skins), 103, 136, 139, 178
  traditional country (extent of), 13
  traditional land tenure system, 15
  wards, location of, 20
  welfare payments, effect of, 25–26
  See also inter-tribal relations, Warlpiri matriarchs, reasons for Warlpiri migration, sorcery

Warlpiri matriarchs, 7, 9–10, 12, 24, 26, 36, 40, 41–45, 47, 57, 95n15, 102, 109, 113–15, 119, 120, 123–25, 136, 137, 145, 147, 151, 154, 171, 181, 186, 187, 190–97, 203, 206.
  adventurousness, 10, 44, 102–6
  artists (*see under* Warlpiri women)
  befriending skills, 1, 55, 105, 124, 190
  functioning households, 43, 44, 112, 118, 193, 203
  Masterful, 136
  refashioning of tradition, 196–200
  ritual bosses (*see yamparru*)
  school for boldness, 24, 186, 196
  See also 'Barbara', 'Camilla', contacts, Bess Nungarrayi Price, 'Dulcie', 'Emily', friendship, household management, inter-racial marriage, 'Judith', matrifocal household, 'Natalie', personal autonomy, reasons for Warlpiri migration, 'Rosie', 'Sarah', 'Suzanne', 'Valmae', Warlpiri women.

Warlpiri women
  Adelaide based, 129–52
  Alice Springs based, 97–125
  artists, 10, 30, 34, 83, 102, 106, 126, 130, 137, 138, 142–143, 147, 148, 153n9, 162, 181, 192, 199, 202
  ceremonies. *See yawulyu*
  Darwin based, 69–70, 73–75, 111–14
  domestic violence, 74
  Katherine based, 72–73
  life-cycle, 45, 68, 105, 182, 183
  Queensland based, 162–165
  sorority of Alice Springs, 80–81
  Tennant Creek based, 73
  widows, 67, 71, 106, 195
  See also personal autonomy, reasons for Warlpiri migration, Warlpiri matriarchs

Warumungu, 73
welfare housing, 27, 85, 98, 103, 131, 140
welfare payments
  effect on gender relations, 25–27
  effect on kinship, 27
  effect on mobility, 25–27
'White anti-racists', 145
white friends, 105, 130, 143–45, 158. *See also* friendship, parallel diaspora

Whiteness, 58n1
Williams, Dennis Japanangka, 70
Willowra, 6, 19, 51, 54, 73, 75, 83, 86, 131, 137, 153n8, 179, 180

Y

yamparru, 44

yawulyu (women's ceremonies), 29, 127n5, 161
Yipirinya School (Alice Springs), 102
Yuendumu, 1, 6, 18, 19, 51, 54
yujuku (humpy), 29
Yulara, 138

www.ingramcontent.com/pod-product-compliance
Lightning Source LLC
Chambersburg PA
CBHW070920030426
42336CB00014BA/2475